The Theory and Practice

of

Life-Style Assessment

Fourth Edition

Daniel Eckstein, Ph.D., ABPP

Leroy Baruth, Ed.D.

KENDALL/HUNT PUBLISHING COMPANY
4050 Westmark Drive   Dubuque, Iowa 52002

CONTENTS

Contents

Contents

Foreword

Over the past 50 years, clinicians and mental health professionals have been employing the crown jewel intervention proposed by Alfred Adler. It is commonly referred to as "life-style assessment." However, with its heavy emphasis on individual creativity and therapeutic skill to conduct a life-style assessment, there has evolved numerous structured and unstructured life-style assessment tools created from his work. Hurrah for Dan and Lee to attempt to pull together these divergent views into some form of order in their text *The Theory and Practice of Life-Style Assessment!*

Be prepared as a reader to go on an out-of-consciousness journey at times when reading this adventure by the two scholar/clinicians. It reflects not only what others have done but integrates their own ideas, case studies, and "creative selves." I, as a clinician, professor, and researcher in the area of life-style assessment, plan to use this text in my graduate class to help students more fully understand "lifestyle" and its application to life.

Roy Kern, Ed.D.

Roy Kern is Professor, Department of Counseling and Psychological Services, Georgia State University, Atlanta, GA. He is author of numerous life-style articles and instruments which include the BASIS-A and The Kern Life-Style Scale. He and his colleagues have been researching the life-style construct for the past twenty years. From this focus, Georgia State University is now being considered the premiere institution for research on lifestyle.

Authors' Preface

Introduction

It has been twenty-one years since we originally published *Life Style: What It Is and How to Do It*. During that time many important new contributions have been made building on the strength of the original works of Alfred Adler and Rudolf Dreikurs.

In addition to several revisions of our original work, we also published *Life-Style: Theory, Practice and Research*. The present volume extends the original ideas initially presented in 1975 and 1978 and contains 25% new material.

Specific additions since our last revision in 1992 include new sections of multi-cultural implications, the five life tasks, the role of interpretation in life-style assessment, force-field analysis, plus a new section on change considerations for counselors. Other original contributions include Robert Willhite describing his early recollection technique, Daniel Eckstein and Roy Kern's "Early Recollection Role-reversal Process," Frank Walton's "Most Memorable Adolescent Moment," plus a new section on mistaken goals by Nancy Agan and Michael Popkin. We have also revised both the Life-Style Interview Guide as well as the suggested interpretation format.

At the suggestion of Bernard Shulman we also added a "second-born" birth-order category to our original list of first, middle, youngest, only and adopted primary birth-order typologies.

Also included is a "Top Card" chart devised by Jane Nelson and Lynn Lott to further illustrate the potential strengths and weaknesses of one's "#1 Priority."

Bernard Shulman and Harold Mosak helped develop the original "Life Style Form" which we have revised in this workbook. They are also acknowledged for such innovative life-style interpretive aids as the "Midas Technique," the "Headline Technique," the "Avis Complex," the "Teeter-Totter" principle, and the difference between a recollection and a report. Their *Manual for Life Style Assessment* continues to be a standard of excellence for Adlerian psychology

Robert Powers and Jane Griffith have also made significant strides in providing concrete interpretive life-style guidelines through their book, *Understanding Life-Style: The Psycho-clarity Process*. The authors agree in their belief that "a person does not have a life-style, in the sense of its being attached like a possession, a piece of clothing, or a shadow" (p. 7). And if one does not *have* a life-style, then perhaps it is similarly misleading to talk about *doing* one. Thus, it is our intention to provide an introduction to both the theory and practice of life-style assessment while simultaneously encouraging the reader to explore other resources for more advanced clinical training. We do not minimize the proficiency that is involved in a life-style analysis; however, we hope to encourage more people to develop their own skills at "life-styling."Rather than being spectators applauding the performance of experts we hope to get more people actively involved in the process of life-styling. We emphasize process, because we are still learning new interpretive clues and skills. As practicing counseling psychologists, we have found life-styles to be helpful in providing insights pertinent to an individual's subjective "private logic."

From a more academic and research perspective, Roy Kern, in the Department of Counseling and Psychological Services at Georgia State University, has not only contributed in the clinical area of life-style assessment with the Life-Style Questionnaire Inventory and the Kern Life-Style Scale, but he and his colleagues, Mary Wheeler and William Curlette, have developed the bonafide research instrument related to life-style assessment. The BASIS-A, Basic Adlerian Styles for Interpersonal Success—Adult Form has now provided the Adlerian community with a research tool which can be employed for research, as well as clinical interventions.

Research with this objective instrument is in many ways supporting these therapeutic interventions related to life-style assessment in our book with research findings validating the interplay of life-style dynamics, depression, stress, coping, diabetes, and leadership factors.

Perhaps an analogy will help clarify our intent in writing this workbook. Just as there are beginning, intermediate, and expert swimmers, so there are various levels of proficiency in conducting a life-style investigation. As intermediate swimmers, we are attempting to provide an introduction to the life-style process in hopes of obtaining new swimmers. Although completion of this workbook will not qualify you as an expert life-styler, it should provide basic interpretive skills.

Whenever possible, we have attempted to provide a reference for specific ideas or concepts. However, as Adler often noted, individual psychology stresses *use*, not possession. Thus, many of the thoughts contained within the workbook are widely espoused Adlerian concepts having multiple claims to personal ownership.

Samples of Interpretive Aids

In addition to summarizing the contributions of many individuals, we include the "Suggested Templates for Sibling Ratings and General Life-Style Themes" (Mosak) chart as well as the "Life-Style Summary Matrix" as examples of practical interpretive aids. Fourteen specific interview considerations and a Pre-interview checklist are also included. An introductory "Now & Then Life-Style Questionnaire" is provided, as is a specific section on general interviewing considerations checklist. A life-style form for adults and adolescents is also supplemented with a specific children's guide developed by Don Dinkmeyer, Sr. and Don Dinkmeyer, Jr. "Group" and "mini" life-style forms by Frank Walton are also included to provide a variety of different assessment possibilities. A specific section focuses on research, including a revised chart summarizing empirical birth order research studies.

An Outline of What's Ahead

The book is organized into seven chapters:
1. An overview of Adlerian theory
2. Life-style assessment theory and technique
3. Recommended life-style interview forms
4. Interpretive guidelines
5. Reorientation to Adlerian counseling techniques
6. A systematic case study, and recommended life-style interpretive summary interpretation form
7. Next Steps

Since this workbook has been used in many counseling preparatory courses, it is also valuable to remind prospective counselors and therapists that it is important to be in a "client" role prior to becoming the "counselor"

We feel it can and should increase your humility, compassion, and social interest.

For your convenience, the pages of the entire book are perforated to enable you to easily separate particular forms or pages for your ongoing use. You may freely duplicate any of these materials for educational purposes. *(When copying, if you enlarge the page by 121%, you will essentially have a new 8- 1/2 x 11 size worksheet.)*

We hope that you will find the material useful.

Acknowledgments

The authors would like to gratefully acknowledge the assistance of all who have allowed their work to be included in this book. Cheryl Booth helped typeset the manuscript in the initial stages. Diane Owens provided editing and typesetting in the final and most critical stage of the project. Whew, thanks Diane! The cover design, book layout and illustrations are by Barbara Kunze, Magical Creations. Our thanks to each of you for a job well done.

About the Authors

Daniel Eckstein, Ph.D., ABPP, is a counseling psychologist in Scottsdale, Arizona. He is an adjunct professor for Ottawa University, Northern Arizona University, and the Maricopa Community College system. He is also an adjunct associate professor for the Thunderbird American International Graduate School of Management in Glendale, Arizona.

Dr. Eckstein is co-author of seven books, including *The Encouragement Process in Life-span Development* and *Leadership By Encouragement*. He holds a diplomate in counseling psychology from the American Board of Professional Psychologists, and has twenty-four years of university teaching experience.

He was a participant in the 1968 Coaches' All-American Football Game and later played two years of professional football with the Green Bay Packers, the Hamilton (Ontario) Tiger-Cats, and the Miami Dolphins.

His current interests include international and transcultural awareness, team building, organizational development, Leadership By Encouragement, group dynamics, psychological factors affecting physical conditions, and sacred psychology.

Leroy G. Baruth, Ph.D., is a professor and chair of the Human Development and Psychological Counseling Department at Appalachian State University in Boone, North Carolina. Previous counseling and teaching experiences include the University of Arizona, the University of South Carolina, the Minnesota Department of Manpower Services and the Byron, Minnesota Public Schools.

Dr. Baruth has written numerous articles and more than twenty books. Some of his most recent books are *Multicultural Counseling and Psychotherapy* (Merrill), *Students At Risk* (Allyn and Bacon), *Multicultural Education of Children and Adolescents* (Allyn and Bacon), *An Introduction to the Counseling Profession* (Prentice-Hall), and *An Introduction to Marital Theory and Therapy* (Brooks/Cole). *Rational-Emotive Family Therapy* (Springer) was recently translated into Spanish for world-wide distribution.

Other Kendall/Hunt books
authored or co-authored
by Daniel Eckstein:

Leadership By Encouragement
The Encouragement Process in Life-Span Development

Chapter 1

AN OVERVIEW OF ADLERIAN THEORY

The study of human behavior is an ancient quest dating to the very origins of civilization's philosophers. Poets, spiritual teachers, political leaders, and others have spoken of their beliefs relative to the motivations and needs of the human condition. The specific discipline known as psychology is a modern twentieth century phenomenon.

Sigmund Freud, Carl Jung, and Alfred Adler are generally acknowledged to be three of the major formative personality theorists, cornerstones in the early development of psychological explanations of human behavior. Despite theoretical differences between them, they shared a common belief in the importance of early childhood experience in the formation of an individual's later personality. The purpose of this workbook is to provide the reader with a practical introduction and application of some of Alfred Adler's major contributions to the art and science of human behavior. The developmental sequence of the book involves an overview to Adlerian psychotheory in general and life-style assessment in particular. Subsequent chapters will include a sample life-style interview guide followed by suggested interpretative guidelines for an introductory "first-step" to Adlerian life-style personality assessment. Additional resources will be explored in a concluding "next-steps" chapter.

Alfred Adler: The Person

A brief biography of Adler the individual helps form a context for his theory. Alfred Adler was born February 7, 1870 in Penzing, a suburb of Vienna, Austria. He was the second of six children. His father was a middle-class Jewish merchant and his mother was a housewife. Adler's ill health as a child coupled with the death of his younger brother when Alfred was three profoundly effected him. His early recollections included memories of illness and pain, cemeteries, and death (Manaster & Corsini, 1982).

In his own autobiography, Adler (in Ansbacher & Ansbacher, 1964) writes that:

> When I was five I became ill with pneumonia and was given up by the physician. A second physician advised a treatment just the same, and in a few days I became well again. In the joy over my recovery, there was talk for a long time about the mortal danger in which I was supposed to have been. From that time on I recall always thinking of myself in the future as a physician. This means that I had set a goal from which I could expect an end to my childlike distress, my fear of death. Clearly I expected more from the occupation of my choice than it could accomplish: The overcoming of death and of the fear of death is something I should not have expected from human, but only from divine accomplishments. So I came to choose the occupation of physician in order to overcome death and the fear of death.

> On the basis of similar impressions a somewhat retarded boy decided to become a grave digger, in order, as he said, to bury the others and not to be buried himself. The rigid antithetical thinking of this boy who later became neurotic did not admit compromise solutions; his childish, saving fiction turned to the opposite, albeit in an unimportant detail (p. 199).

In Adler's grammar school years he continued to battle physical ailments as a means of developing his own strength for perfection. Orgler (1973) notes that Adler showed little confidence in his physical self and that he was often solitary. Because of his poor performance in mathematics, his teacher advised him to leave school and apprentice himself to a shoemaker. Fortunately his father disagreed with this suggestion; Adler subsequently became the best math student in the class.

Adler went on to the University of Vienna, from which he received his medical degree in 1895. Two years later he married Raissa Timofejewaa; they eventually had four children. Although his original specialization was in ophthalmology, later he became a psychiatrist.

After early formative associations with Freud and Jung, Adler formed his own group in 1911. It was originally called the "Society for Free Psychoanalytic Research" — one year later, the name was changed to "Individual Psychology."

During the first world war, Adler served in the Austrian army as a physician. Upon returning home in 1916, Adler was asked what he had learned. Instead of saying "We need new cannons, or a new government," he replied instead, "I think the only thing the world needs at the moment is a gemeinschaftsgefuehl (social interest)." (Bottome, 1967)

From there, Adler became more of an educator. He began to work within the school reform movement of the First Austrian Republic, establishing his first child guidance clinic in 1922. He first visited the United States in 1926. When Hitler came to power in 1936, all 32 Adlerian clinics in Austria and Germany were closed.

In 1935, Adler settled in America. His oldest daughter fled to Russia where, during a political and religious purge, she was jailed and later died. Adler died in 1937 in Aberdeen, Scotland, while on a lecture tour. His legacy includes more than 300 books and articles (Manaster & Corsini, 1982). His work was most notably continued by Rudolf Dreikurs, another immigrant to America escaping Nazi persecution. Dreikurs was the founder of the Alfred Adler Institute in Chicago. He started the Individual Psychology News, which later became the Journal of Individual Psychology and then simply Individual Psychology.

Currently the North American Society of Adlerian Psychology (NASAP) is Individual Psychology's central organization in the U.S. and Canada. Adlerian training centers are located in most major U.S. cities. There is also an International Association of Individual Psychology (IAIP) which has world-wide membership and training opportunities.

Albert Ellis (1970), Founder of Rational Emotive Therapy, identified Adler as "one of the first humanistic psychologists", a claim also made by Obuchowski. In addition, Phillip's Interference Therapy, Kelly's Psychology of Personal Constructs, Sartre's Existential Psychoanalysis, and Mowren's Integrity Therapy all appear to reveal Adler's influence (Allen, 1971).

Walter O'Connell (1976) referred to many modern theorists as having a "yes-but" acceptance of Adlerian principles. He says, that although such practitioners as Viktor Frankl, Colin Wilson, Ernest Becker, Ira Progoff, and Rollo May do not consider themselves as Adlerian, their belief in human development parallels Adler's. All of these "friends" acknowledge many of Adler's ideas in their own contributions to psychology, yet they qualify their similarities.

Ansbacher (1990) notes that all three leading co-founders of humanistic psychology—Abraham Maslow, Rollo May and Carl Rogers, actually studied with Adler in Vienna or New York early in their careers and increasingly appreciated what they had learned from him. Adler's direct approach, his holistic emphasis, and his concerns of social interest, guiding fiction and a pampered life-style were particularly noted by them.

When Maslow (1962) introduced his "third force," subsequently named "humanistic psychology," he listed Adlerians first among the groups included and the *Journal of Individual Psychology* among the five journals where these groups are most likely to publish (p. vi).

Shortly before his death, Carl Rogers paid tribute to Adler in the following manner:

> I had the privilege of meeting, listening to, and observing Dr. Alfred Adler. This was the winter of 1927–28, when I was an intern at the then new Institute for Child Guidance in New York City. Accustomed as I was to the rather rigid Freudian approach of the Institute — seventy-five page case histories, and exhaustive batteries of tests before even thinking of "treating" a child— I was shocked by Dr. Adler's very direct and deceptively simple manner of immediately relating to the child and the parent. It took me some time to realize how much I had learned from him. (personal communication, January 19, 1987) (In Ansbacher, 1990).

Adler was considered "perhaps the most important and certainly the most famous of Maslow's mentors" (Hoffman, 1988; p. 102). Hoffman concludes:

> Above all, Adler influenced Maslow in his optimistic and progressive outlook...Though never a disciple of Adler's—Maslow was always much too independent for that— he readily acknowledged the great intellectual debt he owed him. (p. 106).

Rollo May studied with Adler in Vienna during the summers of 1932 and 1933, while May was teaching at the American College in Salonika, Greece (Hall, 1967). Adler's influence on May is reflected especially in his first book, *The Art of Counseling* (1939/1989). In the original forward he acknowledged, "Particularly does this discussion owe a debt to the humble and penetrating wisdom of Alfred Adler." In an appendix note May wrote:

> It may be interesting to pass on some impressions of Dr. Adler the man, with whom I have had the prized privilege of studying, associating, and conversing intimately. Dr. Adler was the kind of person the French term "sympathique" — to talk with him was to have that rare privilege of a human relationship without barriers. One of his chief characteristics was his ability to remain relaxed, even in discussion; it was impossible to feel tense in his company...his system as a whole will go down in history as a lasting contribution to the endeavor of man to understand himself. (pp. 177-178)

In the last section of the book, *Counseling and the Infinite*, May writes:

> In the human situation, all is not right; there is disharmony within the self, and there is disharmony in this diseased world. Psychologically and religiously, illness follows from any attempt to escape this disharmony. It is the pampered child, Adler would say, who is willing to play only so long as the universe plays his or her way. The healthy individual, on the other hand, is willing to walk the knife-blade edge of insecurity and to affirm truth and goodness even though truth is on the scaffold and goodness is never perfectly achieved. (p. 171)

"SUPER" Adlerian Principles

A "SUPER" Theory

Fundamental Adlerian principles of human behavior can be illustrated by a "SUPER" acronym as developed by Eckstein. Each respective letter represents a major theoretical Adlerian belief.

Social Interest
U
P
E
R

"SUPER"— Social Interest

According to Ansbacher (1991), the most distinctive concept in Adler's individual psychology, but also the most difficult and the one that has the least recognition in general psychological literature, is Gemeinschaftsgefuehl, which is generally translated as "social interest" or "social feeling." There actually is no accurate English word which seems to communicate the German sense of community. Indeed, some early translations (Adler, 1924) used "community feeling" or "community sense" instead. O'Connell (1991) observes that the term "interest" appears too mild, volitional and intellectual. The word social is too narrow, compliant, and evolved by conventions and mores. He proposes the term "humanistic identification."

In essence, humanistic identification refers to a lifelong process characterized by a feeling of brotherly love or close kinship with other human beings in the present, as well as a strong affinity for the human race as a whole, past and future. Humanistic identification is demonstrated intellectually by "outsight," a commitment toward understanding the psychological needs of others and the tension generated by their lack of fulfillment; and by an active movement toward satisfying such needs and becoming a significant other.

But no matter what the precise English phrase is, the general concept of Adler (1927) is that social interest is a cardinal personality trait, with traits regarded as reflecting the relationship of an individual to his environment. Adler (in Ansbacher, 1991) stresses the core value of social interest as follows:

> It is almost impossible to exaggerate the value of an increase in social feeling. The mind improves, for intelligence is a communal function. The feeling of worth and value is heightened, giving courage and an optimistic view, and there is a sense of acquiescence in the common advantages and drawbacks of our lot. The individual feels at home in life and feels his existence to be worthwhile just so far as he is useful to others and is overcoming common, instead of private, feelings of inferiority. Not only the ethical nature, but the right attitude in aesthetics, the best understanding of the beautiful and the ugly, will always be founded upon the truest of social feeling. (pp. 28–29)

In more systematic fashion, Adler (1938, 1956) proposed Gemeinschaftsgefuehl as the measure of normality.

> This term, not quite adequately translated as social feeling or social interest, implies belongingness, cooperation, and responsibility towards society. It represents the socially integrated strivings towards adjustment to reality, which enhance cohesion and stability between the individual and his environment. There is much evidence that good adjustment depends upon and varies with the amount of social interest. Psychosis (for example), the severest of the mental illnesses, presents a picture of minimal social interest. Although at first seemingly superficial, the treatment, especially of the milder behavior disorders, for developing social interest, can have wider applicability than so-called deeper treatments. Such treatment is essentially a teaching for social living which can be applied early in life as a preventive measure. (pp. 80–81)

Ashley Montaqu (1991) paid tribute to Adler on the celebration of the 100th anniversary of his birth in 1870 by saying that Adler's notion of social interest was highly correlated to a reduction in the amounts and intensity of human aggression. Huber (1987) draws the following comparison between Adler and Judeo-Christian thought, as in the role of grace in salvation and the role of unconditional social interest in therapy.

Unconditional social interest and grace appear to be identical ... By accepting the client, the therapist encourages him or her to loosen the past and focus on the possibilities for the future. (p. 437)

Social interest is a "barometer" of effective mental health; conversely, mental illness is characterized as the absence of social interest. Nikelly (1971) advocates social interest as a "paradigm" for mental health or model for viewing the world educators:

Behavior anomalies are essentially characterized by an inability to deal with social reality, a lack of communal cooperation, and unpreparedness for social living. The issue becomes clear as one responds to the fundamental questions: "How much do others gain from my behavior? Do my actions enhance others?" By nature man is a social being, and it is social feeling that has to be cultivated. Religion has already made such an attempt.

Existentialist philosophers have used the term *Anomie* (lawlessness), to indicate the antipathy of social interest (Ansbacher, 1991). In contemporary sociology, MacIver (1950) observes that Anomie is a condition in which an individual's sense of social cohesion is broken or fatally weakened. Such a detachment from a feeling of "embeddedness" or a "connectedness" to others results in various anti-social behavior types. For example, immediate personal gratification, personal power through domination and destruction, insecurity, and dread as "displaced persons" who feel rejected and thus feel victims of a persecution complex are but some of the ways people who experience the ruthlessness of Anomie may react. It is as if such people have lost their "existential anchors" and thus drift aimlessly with no direction and are lost and tumbled by the "sea" of life that can bring turbulence and "rough" waters. Having no existential anchor often results in "drowning" (death) or severe damage (neurosis/psychosis) to such individuals.

There is a transcendent or extended meaning for social interest that goes beyond human-to-human "social" interactions. In 1908, Adler wrote that:

Gemeinschaftsgefuehl which is innate to man must be regarded as the most important regulator of the aggression drive. It is at the basis of any relationship of the child toward people, animals, plants and objects, and signifies the cohesion (die Verwachsenheit) with our life, the affirmation, the conciliation with it. Through Gemeinschaftsgefuehl in its rich differentiations (parental love, filial love, sexual love, love of one's country, love of nature, art, science, love of mankind) acting together with the aggression drive, there comes about the general attitude a person takes, which actually constitutes his psychological life. (p. 30)

Later Adler also said that:

The social feeling remains throughout life, changed, colored, circumscribed in some cases, enlarged and broadened in until it touches not only the members of the individual's own family, but also his clan, his nation, and finally, the whole of humanity. It is possible that it may extend beyond these boundaries and express itself toward animals, plants, lifeless objects, or finally towards the whole cosmos. (1954, p. 46)

The innate social feeling is actually a cosmic feeling, a reflection of the coherence of everything cosmic, which lives in us, which we cannot dismiss entirely, and which gives us the ability to empathize with things which lie outside our body. (1954, p. 60, new translation).

He concluded that:

Individual Psychology may claim as its contribution to have pointed out that empathy and understanding are facts of social feeling, of being in harmony with the universe. (in Ansbacher & Ansbacher, 1964, p. 43).

The fundamental relationship of social interest to empathy is stressed as well as contrasted with a more discovering form of sympathy in a statement by physician Lydia Sicher, one of Adler's early associates:

Empathy could not exist if we did not have any social interest. Empathy is only possible if we can place ourselves in the situation of the other person, otherwise it is sympathy. Sympathy means standing outside when something happens to someone else. One is very sympathetic and says, "Isn't it horrible that this is happening." Empathy is looking at the world from the standpoint of another person. It is an inner understanding of the other person, not just knowing something about the problem. Empathy is a large part of social interest. (in Davidson, 1991, p. 22).

Such a capacity for identification or empathy lies as potentiality within the human at birth (Edgar, 1985). Such a potentiality does not automatically spring forth full development but must be developed through training or education. Adler believed that one of the tasks of the counselor or therapist is to supplement the unfinished work of the parents, to develop the clients heightened sense of social interest. Through such an identification with humanity Adler links social interest and moral behavior. This connectedness by which Adler (1964) evaluates mental health with moral behavior refers to the identification with an evolving societal form which signifies the ideal community, the ultimate fulfillment of the human potential and societal evolution.

Adlerians are optimistic in their belief that human beings are born with the potential for cooperative, constructive behavior. Thus, they have the potentialities to develop into cooperative members of society.

Sicher (in Davidson, 1991) says that:

We assume, in general an inborn possibility to cooperate. Because of it, we assume that people from their beginnings would be willing to continue and move in this cooperative manner. Whenever we see difficulties arise, it is because something within this movement has been led astray, and therefore, everything that is noncooperative is more or less an artifact. The noncooperation is not something that is naturally or biologically possible. It has come about as a consequence of the different situations in which the child finds himself and with which he is unable to cope. (p.31)

The philosopher Nietzsche wrote that:

A man who has a 'why' for his life can withstand almost any 'how'. For Adlerians, social interest is that 'why'. As such, it is the cornerstone (*eckstein* in German) of Adler's theory.

"Rebellious" Social Interest

The notion of social interest is not to be confused with adaptation out of blind obedience or conformity to authority. The courage to confront systems and individuals who perpetuate nationalism, racism, and sexism are just a few of too often prevalent societal norms. Such rebellion characterizes aspirations of a better world for all people. For example, social interest paradoxically may take the form of civil disobedience, to preserve the environmen. Vedic philosopher Mafu observes that:

Wisdom is never born from understanding; it is born by rebelling against everything and everyone, and being different, and being a maverick, and loving that you live—that is power.

Thus, rebellion may paradoxically have much social interest. Again, the goals of such rebellion hopefully are motivated by a sense of social interest, a concern for the highest good of all life. That should be the yardstick by which an individual embarks in a *path of right action*.

Such legendary individuals as Ghandi and Martin Luther King, Jr., have been imprisoned and/or assassinated for their "insurrections" and "traitorous" behavior. Yet a higher commitment to such universal principles as non-violence and basic civil liberties are contemporary examples of "rebellious" social interest.

Abraham Maslow credited Adler's belief in social interest as a primary description of self-actualized individuals.

Maslow defined it as follows

This word (Gemeinschaftsgefuehl — Social Interest) invented by Alfred Adler is the only one available that described well the flavor of the feeling for mankind by self actualizing subjects. They have, for human beings in general, a deep feeling of identification, sympathy, and affection in spite of occasional anger impatience or disgust ... They have a genuine desire to help the human race. It is as if they were all members of a single family (in Ansbacher, 1991 b, p. 5).

Social Interest: Behaviors, Feelings, & Thoughts

Kaplan (1991) has described in very concrete ways specific behaviors, feelings and cognition (thoughts) associated with social interest.

Adapted from Howard Kaplan "A Guide For Explaining Social Interest Laypersons," *Individual Psychology*, V. 47, No. 1, 1991, 82–85. University of Texas Press, P.O. Box 7819, Austin, TX 78713.

A. Behaviors Associated with Social Interest

1. "Helping": A willingness to use one's abilities, knowledge, or talents to aid others.
2. "Sharing": Proving others with some of one's own possessions.
3. "Participating": Joining in group activities.
4. "Respectful": Showing others recognition of their human rights, knowledge, or experience.
5. "Cooperative": To work or play together with others to reach mutual benefits or goals.
6. "Compromising" (or Flexible): A willingness to give and take. Striving for mutually acceptable solutions to challenges.
7. "Empathic": Showing others their thoughts and feelings are understood and appreciated.
8. "Encouraging": Actions that helps motivate others.
9. "Reforming": Improving social conditions for the common good.

B. Feelings Associated with Social Interest

1. "Belonging": A secure feeling of being a member of a group or groups, family, peer group, friends.

2. "Feeling at home": At ease and comfortable when interacting with others.

3. "Commonality": Having characteristics in common with others and of being similar to others.

4. "Faith in others": Goodness, a realization and social interest in all people.

5. "The courage to be imperfect": Making mistakes is a natural part of being human, and that one does not have to be always "the first," or the "most" famous.

6. "Being Human": Being part of all humanity.

7. "Optimism": The world can be a better place to live.

C. Cognitions (Thoughts) Associated with Social Interest

1. "As a human being, my rights and obligations are equal to the rights and obligations of others."

2. "My personal goals can be attained in ways consistent with the welfare of the community."

3 "The prosperity and the survival of society are dependent on the willingness and the ability of its citizens to learn to live together in harmony."

4. "I believe in responding to others as I want them to respond to me."

5. "The ultimate measure of my character will be to what extent I promoted the welfare of the community."

Social Interest and Psychological Tolerance

Slavik and Croake (1995) suggest social interest (SI) is actually more understandable by Adler's concept of psychological tolerance (PT). There have been many attempts to convert SI into a construct and to create SI instruments of individuals; however, SI is an action or state, based on a decision or intention to behave in a manner designed to be beneficial to a community of which one is a member. SI is a movement and is not truly measurable; it can only be described as a property of *interactions* and relationships within a community.

Slavik and Croake believe Adler's concept of psychological tolerance (PT) better indicates a willingness to work toward common benefit — *Gemeinschaftsgefuhl* — than do measures of SI and is not likely to be confounded with altruism. Adler writes that PT is "the amount of threat a person can bear without losing courage...Psychological tolerance depends on the strength of social ties." (Adler, 1956, p. 243)

PT is the amount of threat a person can face without choosing anger and leaving a situation, "caving in" to despair or fear, renouncing one's ability to handle a situation or in general, withdrawing. PT is plainly related to habitual styles of safeguarding through distancing, to habitual styles of exclusion tendencies, to antithetical modes of apperception, and to limitations in courage (Adler, 1956). A measure of PT would be a measure of one's (un)willingness to stand out and display *Gemeinschaftsgefuhl*.

A measure of PT is a direct measure of willingness to stay with changes in life tasks as they present themselves, particularly difficult changes. Individuals with lower PT may have life-style convictions that encourage them to withdraw from situations. Beliefs that they are helpless, unable, and cannot cope, plus a perception that the world or others within it have more power than they and perhaps are malicious, often causes such people to withdraw from others. Other elements which affect PT are consistent objective factors: organ inferiorities, pampering, cruelty, hate or neglect, and exogenous factors. Many of these, however, are incorporated into life style through pessimistic convictions. (Slavik & Croake, 1995)

Self-Handicapping Strategies

Adler (1956) asserts that symptoms serve as strategies to preserve self-esteem by deflecting the threat of failure in the tasks. Symptoms can be utilized in the event of threat by providing reasons to oneself and to others for poor or absent performance.

Symptoms have been specified as a self-handicapping strategy (SHS), which Slavik and Croake (1995) define as "an impediment to performance in a threatening situation. Examples are anxiety or illness. It provides an individual with a reason not to perform and with a ready excuse for failure; in case of success it also provides an enhancement to esteem." (p. 11). A SHS can provide an additional reason besides incompetence for explaining failure; it is also a direct means to avoid performance and also functions as a means to secure material and psychological rewards.

Thus, social interest can also be conceptualized as psychological tolerance. Self-handicapping strategies cause a discouraged individual to withdraw or move away from meaningful contact with others.

There is a positive interactive effect involving social interest, self- confidence, and mental health. The more one behaves, feels, and thinks as charted above, the more others will respond positively to him or her. This enhances self-confidence which further expands social interest for both present reality and for building a better future. A balance of practicality and idealism also highly correlates with a high degree of mental health as well. Thus the cornerstone, the foundation of Adler's theory begins with an "S" for social interest.

Social Interest
Unity

P

E

R

"SUPER"—Unity

In contrast to Freudian theory which refers to such separate "parts" of the personality as "id," "ego" and "superego" or the transactional analysis "parent," "adult," and "child" ego states, Adler stressed the unity or wholeness of an individual. Manaster and Corsini (1982) stress that "individual psychology firmly takes the position that we are indivisible units. Like the flower which came from a single fertilized cell, we are a unity, we are not an assemblage of parts like a machine...The word individual in individual psychology does not mean the opposite of 'social' or 'group.' Individual psychology is not a psychology of individuals as opposed to groups of people. The term individual in German has the connotation and denotation of unity, an indivisible whole. It refers to the unique individuality of individuals." (pp. 2–3)

The unity of personality is what Adler called one's style of life. The concept of style includes the characteristic of cutting across ordinary boundaries and uniting what might otherwise be quite separate entities. Thus, in the case of Bach, Beethoven, and Mozart, if one knows their music at all, one can easily match the musical manuscripts with the composer. Adler used metaphor of the musical "notes" versus the total "melody" in the following way:

> The style of life commands all forms of expression; the whole commands the parts. In real life we always find a confirmation of the melody of the total self, of the personality, with its thousand fold ramifications... The foremost task of individual psychology is to prove this unity in each individual—in his thinking, feeling, acting in his so-called conscious and unconscious, in every expression of his personality... we are not satisfied with the Gestalt alone, or, as we prefer to say, with the whole, once all the notes are brought into reference with the melody. We are satisfied only when we have recognized in the melody the author and his attitudes as well, for example: Bach and Bach's style of life" (in Ansbacher & Ansbacher, 1964, p. 175).

The growing popularity of holistic health and holistic medicine are based on the mind/body/spirit interrelationships. An emerging discipline known as psychoneuroimmunology (PNI), explores such topics as the breakdown of the immune system as the total interrelated emotional and physical united self. For example, many researchers feel that self-hatred is correlated with the breakdown on the immune system in AIDS patients while unresolved anger often accompanies the onset of cancer. (More on the body/mind connection will be presented in Chapter 4.) Thus, the whole unified self is the focus of Adlerian psychology.

Social Interest
Unity
Private Logic
E
R

"SUPER" – Private Logic

We don't see things as they are, we see things as we are. — Anais Nin

Out of the countless events occurring in one's life, each individual personally decides what conclusions are to be drawn about life in general, others, and one's self. Such a "private" or "personal" decision relates to the philosophical field known as phenomenology. Although Adler never specifically used that term itself, he spoke of the need of counselor empathy in understanding the personal views of another by saying "we must be able to see with his eyes and listen with his ears" (in Ansbacher & Ansbacher, 1964). Phenomenology means that one does not experience reality directly/objectively; instead, it is subjectively "filtered" through our own personal "prescriptive" lens, our own "glasses" that uniquely focus the world.

Ten people viewing a fire will report ten different stories because of their own idiosyncratic personal "filter" which determines what is important to them. For example, one person may focus on the sight of the flames, another the attempts of the fire fighters to control the blaze, while another hears the crackling and crumbling walls.

An important consideration is that we do not experience reality objectively, but that external events are "filtered through" our own internal subjective frame of reference. In such a way we "distort" or "shape" objective reality to confirm our own internal attitudes. Myers & Myers (1973) describe private logic in using the following metaphor:

> Imagine you are given the task to find out the size of the fish in Lake Michigan. So you get yourself a net and go to the lake to gather a sample of the fish. Maybe your net has a 4-inch mesh. After you gather some fish you write a report in which you say, "the fish in Lake Michigan are 4 inches in diameter or bigger." Let's say a friend of yours is given the same assignment, but his net has 2-inch mesh. His report reads, "the fish in Lake Michigan are 2 inches in diameter or bigger." Now, which report is right? Both? What are you and your friend reporting on? The size of fish? No. Each of you is reporting on the size of the net you used. The size of the net you use determines the size of the fish you can collect. (p. 14)

Myers & Myers then conclude their "net" analogy in a manner which provides and excellent illustration of a private logic:

> We have nets in our heads. These nets are not made of threads, but of past learning, past experiences, motives, fears, desires, and interests: these nets act as a filter so the stimuli from our environment go through that filter to be perceived. Of course, each one of us has his own little net, his own little personal, individual filter. Even though we may be placed in the same environment we will not see it in the same way since we will filter different aspects. Most of us are not even aware that this filtering process is happening. Many of us have defective filters. Filters that are so clogged up that we see very little of what's going on. Some of us have filters that distort the stimuli that come to us from the environment. The important thing to remember, though, is that whenever we make a comment about something

we are not describing the something but rather our net, our filter. When I say that the painting is beautiful, I am not commenting on the painting as much as I am commenting on myself, my taste, my value system. (p.19)

Mozdzierz et al. (1986), note that while Adler appears to have been the first theorist to use the term "private logic" or "private intelligence," he associated the term with maladjustment and neurosis. Today the term "private logic" has taken a wider meaning to include the normal and abnormal. For example, Shulman (1973) calls it "the personal convictions and value systems of an individual by which he judges how to think, feel, and act about events." (p.7)

The ability to understand the private inner world of another person is a core component of empathy, the ability to "walk a mile in another person's moccasins." So, the "P" in the **SUPER** acronym refers to one's "private logic."

Social Interest
Unity
Private Logic
Equality
R

"SUPER"— Equality

According to Nikelly (1990), equal political, economic, and social rights are the essence of democratic ideology. Equality is also a pivotal principle of individual psychology as we find the authoritarian stance replaced by a dialogue between equals in an atmosphere of mutual respect, candor, and acceptance (Dreikurs, 1971). Bradshaw (1991) believes that although the trials of Nuremberg ended one form of patriarchy, parenting rules still tend to be patriarchal, stressing blind obedience without content.

Adler's term "masculine protest" was formulated as a precursor to the sexism upon which the woman's movement was founded. In a culture which inherently values what is "masculine" over what is "feminine," both men and women suffer negative consequences. Equality may be contrasted by describing the "vertical" versus the "horizontal" means of approaching people, a term which Dreikurs says was first introduced by Lydia Sicher (1955). The "horizontal" approach to life views all people as being equally worthy of respect and consideration, although people are obviously unequal in some other respects. Such equality does not mean sameness but rather a "no more or less than one" whole human being whose basic birthright is unconditional mutual respect and dignity. By contrast the "vertical" plane measures people in a "one up" or "one down" perspective. "Mirror, mirror, on the wall, who is the fairest one of all" the queen in Snow White implores. "Better than/less than" characterize the vertical plane while "different than" is the horizontal perspective. An orange is "different" (horizontal plane), not "better than" (vertical plane) an apple.

Inferiority" and "superiority" are two sides of the same coin for Adler. Both resulted in a feeling of separateness or disconnection from others. Manaster & Corsini (1982) observe that neurotics, by being filled with feelings of inferiority, see people vertically. Their world is constantly filled with people who are better or worse than they are. Allred (1974) discusses the horizontal view as leading to contentment and happiness, while the vertical view means one is "on a ladder" viewing others "up" and "down." Social interest is related to mental health based on equality and democratic living in contrast to striving for a personal superiority that is "above" others. Dreikurs (1967) writes that:

> Desire for self-elevation versus desire for usefulness may be understood to lead to movement on the "vertical plane" versus movement on the "horizontal plane" ...Although many beneficial contributions to mankind have resulted from vertical movement which also affords growth and accomplishment, its effect on the individual is fundamentally different from the effect of horizontal movement. The vertical movement of self-elevation, regardless of the height it leads to, both in status and accomplishments, can never bring lasting satisfaction and inner peace. There is a constant danger of falling and failing; the gnawing feeling of real or possible inferiority is never eradicated, regardless of success. There is no sense of security possible on the vertical plane; one remains highly vulnerable. The competitive individual can stand competition only when he wins. (p. 116)

Dreikurs contrasts the vertical and the horizontal planes in the following manner:

> Quite different is the function of horizontal movement. The desire to be useful can never be frustrated. Whatever life may have in store, something can be done about it. There may be no perfect solution to a predicament, but there is always a way to improve the situation. It becomes less important what one receives in return, because the satisfaction in doing is deeper than any reward can provide. Self-fulfillment no longer depends on what others

think or do, but on what one can contribute. Concern with status is unnecessary, since one can be sure of one's place in the group as an equal.

This basic distinction between self-elevation and usefulness has far-reaching consequences for the evaluation of other social values. Once the assumption that everybody is good enough as he is can be accepted without the fear of disastrous results, both for the individual and society, a new orientation in social living is possible and mandatory. (p. 117)

Personal superiority issues have a national correlate. Sociologists use the term **ethnocentricism** to refer to the personal preferences of one's own particular group or cultural norm. For example, an American was in Japan attending a funeral. When he observed food being placed on the casket, he said to his host "Why do you put food on the casket—the person surely can't eat it? His Japanese host replied, "Why do you Americans put flowers on your caskets—the person surely can't smell them?"

Ethnocentricism relates to regional, cultural, and national feelings of superiority or inferiority and is a major cause of strife between races. Thus, equality is a fundamental Adlerian principle. Just as kings and monarchies are giving way to democratic forms of government, so too interpersonal relationships ideally shift away from an inferior or superior vertical comparison to a more encouraging/connected "all life shares the same basic DNA molecules and God don't make no junk" orientation.

Social Interest
Unity
Private Logic
Equality
Reasons

"SUPER"— Reasons

Reasons or motivators include that all behavior is purposeful or goal-directed and that we are all striving for some type of significance or perfection. Adler disagreed with Freud's emphasis that people are driven by instincts or molded by heredity, experience, or environment. Rather it was goals or a "guiding self-ideal," as Adler called it, that motivated behavior.

He stressed that:

> The science of individual psychology developed out of the effort to understand that mysterious creative power of life—that power which expresses itself in the desire to develop, to strive, and to achieve—and even to compensate for defeats in one direction by striving for success in another. This power is teleological—it expresses itself in the striving after a goal (in Ansbacher, 1969, p. 1).

Sweeney (1989) defines "teleo" to denote the goal-striving nature of human beings. Behavior is positive even though an individual may not be consciously aware of the purpose or "payoff" for one's behavior. Dreikurs (1953) identified four classic "mistaken goals" of behavior which are formulated in early childhood as being *undue attention, power, revenge,* and *inadequacy.* Walton (1990) added a fifth mistaken goal of adolescence as being *excitement.*

Such goals are discouraged methods of striving for significance. Dinkmeyer, Dinkmeyer & Sperry (1987) believe that striving for significance is in essence a movement toward fulfillment of the goal to achieve unique identity as well as to belong. This movement toward a unique identity is the motivating force behind all human activity, what they call a type of "master motive." "Adlerians see this process too, from a teleological rather than casual perspective—as a *pull* by the goal rather than a push by the drive... A question counselors always ask themselves is: 'How is the person seeking to be known?' Most ways of behaving that are eventually accepted by the person reflect the current concept of the self." (p. 17)

Thus, teleology (from the Greek telos— goal) means "purposive, moving toward goals." Adler (1956) says "The most important question of the healthy and the diseased mental life is not coherent but, 'whence?' 'whither?' Only when we know the effective direction-giving goal of a person may we try to understand his movements" (p. 19). Manaster & Corsini (1982) add that basic life goals, while generally unknown to the person, give direction to all behavior. To the extent that goals are aligned with social interest, the direction of the person's life is useful, positive and healthy. Conversely, if goals lack social interest and are simply an expression for overcoming perceived inferiorities by achieving personal superiority, the direction of the person's life tends to be useless, negative and unhealthy.

Adler used such various terms as the need for completion, mastery, perfection, and the guiding fiction before finally settling on superiority as the master motive. What Manaster & Corsini call a "growth drive" is similar to

Maslow's "self-actualization." Carl Rogers (1951) similarly described the "up-wardly light" seeking tendency towards growth when he observed that "the organism has on basic tendency and striving — to actualize, maintain and enhance the experiencing organism." (p. 487)

Manaster & Corsini also point out a useful distinction between two different kinds of striving. Striving for perfection means to move in line with the common sense of communal living, while striving for superiority means to move in a vertical direction, toward personal superiority over others. "Movement in striving for perfection and movement in striving for superiority are both efforts to overcome the individual's feelings of inferiority. To the degree that one strives for perfection we can expect positive mental health, a greater sense of well-being, sense of connectedness with others and humanity. To the degree that one is striving for superiority we can expect dis-ease, a sense of separateness." (p. 75)

"Goals of Behavior"

Contributed by Nancy Agan, *Arizona Active Parenting Today* coordinator

Adler pointed out that behavior is goal-driven even though an individual may not be consciously aware of the purpose or "payoff" for one's behavior. Dreikurs (1953) identified four "mistaken goals" and Walton (1990) added the fifth mistaken goal of adolescence. Michael Popkin (1993) portrays the goals as a person's unconscious thinking which causes feelings to influence whether a child misbehaves or contributes in a positive way.

Active Parenting Today has the belief that there are no good or bad children, only those who choose to pursue these four basic goals in either positive or negative ways. Children with high self-esteem and courage will generally choose the positive approaches. Those with low self-esteem who are discouraged will more likely choose the negative approaches. (p. 60)

The **Goals of Behavior** chart outlines the different approaches a child might take. It is important for a parent (or teacher) to identify a child's goal so that they avoid "paying off" and therefore escalating misbehavior. We do this by identifying our own feeling during a conflict and becoming aware of the child's response to our correction. Following the chart are some sugges-tions of how the different goals may be dealt with successfully.

GOALS OF BEHAVIOR AND APPROACHES

POSITIVE APPROACH	GOAL	NEGATIVE APPROACH	PARENT'S FEELING	CHILD'S RESPONSE TO CORRECTION
Contributing, cooperating	Contact	Undue Attention-Seeking	Annoyed	Stops, but starts again very soon
Independence	Power	Rebellion	Angry	Escalates misbehavior or gives in but fights again later
Assertiveness, Forgiveness	Protection	Revenge	Hurt	Continues to hurt us or escalates misbehavior
Centering, Time Alone	Withdrawal	Undue Avoidance	Helpless	Becomes passive, refuses to try
Skill-Building, Reasonable Risk-Taking	Challenge	Thrill-Seeking	Fearful	Takes more reckless risks

Contact

If the child's goal is that of contact, the parent must be careful not to satisfy the negative approach by giving a lot of time and doing a lot of talking with the child. Ignore the behavior as much as possible. Taking a proactive approach, we can use the natural and logical consequences. Focus on providing opportunities for the child to have positive contact through cooperation and encouraging him to find ways to contribute to the good of the group.

Example

Mandy and Dawn were constantly arguing in the same room where their mother was trying to complete an assignment for work. They were supposed to be doing their Saturday house-cleaning chores but were spending more energy fighting with each other and attempting to get their mother involved. Mother was annoyed by this and asked them to leave her alone, but somehow their squabbles seemed to drift back within earshot every time.

At last mother decided to avoid paying off their undue attention-seeking. They made an agreement that mother would go to the library for one hour to complete her assignment. While she was gone, the girls had an opportunity to clean the house to the best of their ability. If they did the job well enough, they would have time to go to the park together before dinner.

As it turned out, the girls not only made an extra effort to clean the house to "surprise Mom" but Mandy and Dawn requested that they get to stay "home alone" each week while doing their chores. Mother was amazed at their pride in contributing positively to the family and their ability to cooperate when they knew they would receive future quality time (positive contact) with the family for their efforts.

Power

With the goal of power, it is best to initially remove yourself from the conflict rather than fighting or giving in. Parents can put their energies into exploring ways to empower her child to express his own independence and abilities by learning useful skills. Give the child choices you are comfortable with and encourage him to take more responsibility.

Example
When Johnny was in second grade he decided he did not like any of the lunches his mom was fixing for him. He complained every day about the ingredients she used and how she put the sandwich together. Mother felt very angry about this and when she tried to insist that he eat it anyway, Johnny refused and made a big show of making sure his mom knew he had thrown his lunch away.

Finally, Mom identified Johnny's goal of power and made a plan for teaching her son to make his own lunch. They worked together to create a shopping list and buy lunch items that mother and son could both be comfortable with. She educated her son on how to put together a nutritious meal and the specifics of the five food groups. With his new-found independence, Johnny spent less time in rebellion and more energies using his new skill creatively.

Protection

When a child is trying to protect his self-esteem with revenge, the parent needs to avoid being hurt and resist the temptation to hurt back. He may need to analyze why the child feels the need to lash out. Support or firm and calm discipline may be appropriate based on the situation. By showing unconditional love and acceptance as well as forgiveness for past misbehavior or mistakes, an adult can break the revenge cycle. He can model as well as teach assertiveness skills and how to stand up for yourself without putting others down.

Example

Eighth-grader Roberto had been giving his teachers trouble all year. Besides disobeying rules, back-talking and fighting with peers, he had been caught defacing school property. No matter how many times the adults yelled or sent him to detention, nothing seemed to work.

And then his dad took an Active Parenting class where he practiced speaking respectfully to children and teens. Dad taught his son how to create and use "I" messages effectively with peers and authority figures; being assertive but not aggressive. He also modeled forgiveness of past struggles, unconditional acceptance and the philosophy that "mistakes are for learning." When consequences were logically connected to Roberto's behavior, he began to take more responsibility for the choices he was making. Today, Roberto often decides to take a more positive approach to his goal of protection by standing up for his rights and privileges in a more acceptable way and accepting responsibility for negative consequences.

Withdrawal

A child engaging in undue avoidance needs to build his confidence with small successes before he can be expected to tackle large problems. Parents need to be careful of perfectionism (expecting too much) and overprotection (expecting too little). A parent's role may be that of listener and encourager while having positive, yet reasonable, expectations.

Example

April's mother is concerned because her thirteen-year-old daughter seems very stressed and depressed due to pressure from friends and a tremendous amount of school work. Lately, she has taken to hiding in her room for days and days at a time and has been making excuses to avoid going to school.

The mother feels helpless about her daughter's situation until she identifies the goal of withdrawal and works with April to develop a plan for dealing with stress and creating more positive time alone. Mother guides her on how to implement efficient study habits and helps her break down long-term projects into manageable pieces. Through consistent follow-through and support, her mother encourages April to build on small successes with school work and with expressing her individuality with friends. Mother also models and instructs on positive coping mechanisms to deal with stress such as journal writing, listening to soothing music, exercise, and reading worthwhile books.

Challenge

For the negative approach of thrill seeking, a parent must learn to identify what types of skill-building would provide an appropriate challenge for the child. The parent may discover that he will have to let go of power in some areas while there needs to be more specific limits on other areas of behavior.

Example

Six-year-old Christina enjoyed taking very dangerous physical risks. From the time she was a baby she had been a climber, managing to reach amazing heights on household furniture. When she decided to practice jumping off the roof, her dad decided that maybe supervised skill-building would help her meet the goal of challenge more appropriately. He enrolled her in a gymnastics class where she enjoyed the opportunity to test her physical limits, and her dad was much more comfortable with this reasonable risk-taking.

Conclusion

As the previous examples show, behavior is goal-driven. It may also escalate from small, almost unnoticeable annoyances to develop into a predictable downward spiral of lower and lower self-esteem. The negative approach may start out fairly mildly with undue attention-seeking, and then after a child is discouraged or punished he may move into rebellion, then revenge. The most extreme cases of undue avoidance and thrill-seeking could ultimately result in death.

Therefore, it is very important to avoid "paying off" someone's negative approach to a goal by responding with anger and other predictable responses. Each person must stop themselves long enough to become aware of their own feelings, recognize how the other person is responding, and identify their goal. Then we can create a proactive plan to change a downward spiral into an opportunity for learning, contributing and improving self-esteem. In this way we support others as they strive for some type of significance.

Jane Nelsen & Lynn Lott (1994) suggest the following:

Nine Steps for Changing from Mistaken Goals to Closeness and Trust

1. Look for the mistaken goal by recognizing patterns of behaviors for both you and your child and how the behavior makes you feel.

2. Acknowledge your part in creating the mistaken goal. (This may involve looking at issues based on your own mistaken beliefs.)

3. Decide to change your own behavior. (Awareness of your own issues, your own mistaken goals and your own ineffective behaviors is the impetus for changing your behavior.)

4. Acknowledge your mistakes to your child.

5. Show an attitude of faith in the basic goodness of your child. (When you have this faith, it will show.)

6. Let your child know specifically what you do appreciate about him or her.

7. Try to understand your child's reality by making some guesses about what it might be.

8. Really listen. Be curious. Keep inviting more information.

9. Be open to what comes next. It might be problem-solving, a hug, or simply the good feelings that come from understanding.

Thus, the final core Adlerian principle addresses core reasons or motivators for our behavior. The notion of teleology stresses our actions are consciously or unconsciously goal-directed. Strivings for vertical personal superiority is contrasted with a more social interest orientation for striving for perfection.

"SUPER"—Summary

The *SUPER* acronym has been used to typify Adlerian psychology as follows:

S — Social Interest

U — The unity of personality

P — Private logic is our unique personal "filter" (phenomenology) for perceiving humans.

E — Equality — the "horizontal" plane versus the "vertical" plane (one "up" or one "down").

R — Reasons or motivators for behavior are goal-directed ("teleology") coupled with striving for significance or perfection.

Multi-Cultural Counseling Implications

A Perspective for the Clinician

There are important multi-cultural perspectives to consider in Adlerian psychology.

Looff (1979) notes that:

Children do not grow up in a vacuum. They cannot be understood apart from the historical, geographical and socioeconomic characteristics of the area in which they develop. As evaluators, we are reminded, ever and again, the children we see are members not only of families but also of wider groups, whose training patterns affect them a good deal. To do our work well, we need to be aware of these cultural patterns; only then will we be able to understand the child's own functioning and that of his family in an adequate way.

In *Multi-Cultural Counseling and Psychotherapy*, Baruth and Manning (1991) introduce important counselor considerations. They believe that the following multi-cultural issues need to be addressed by counselors:

Multicultural counselors in the 1990s will need to (a) provide a rationale for multi-cultural counseling; (b) deal with the problems of labeling and stereotyping and their adverse effects on clients; (c) consider lifespan issues; (d) assess the effects of cultural diversity on counseling intervention; (e) deal with the issue of "sameness" ; (f) recognize the ethical and legal dimensions of counseling, and (g) respond to the need for research based on culture, counseling, and lifespan development.

Barriers to Effective Multicultural Counseling

The effective multicultural counselor must first understand the barriers that thwart counseling efforts, then strive to overcome socioeconomic class differences, value differences, lifespan difference and stereotypical beliefs.

Arredondo-Dowd and Gonsalves (1980) contrast the following frequent assumptions with the more frequent multicultural reality.

1. *"Americanization" or assimilation occurs quickly and naturally. Immigrants are grateful for being in the United States.* Although clients may be grateful, they may also experience grief, depression, and homesickness.

2. *Non-English speakers cannot learn or hold a job because they cannot communicate verbally.* People of all cultures possess common knowledge and life skills; although language is important, people also learn and communicate nonverbally.

3. *Attempting to learn in other than one's native language interferes with the learning process, and thus retards it.* Children pick up a second language easily; mastery of a second language promotes other learning.

4. *Everyone should "Americanize."* Language and culture are valued by culturally diverse people and American ethnic groups. Effective counselors can develop respect for other cultures.

5. *If someone is hurting and in need of counseling, that person only has to seek help.* Every culture has its unique way of handling personal and family issues. Some minorities are reluctant to seek counseling. The effective counselor is aware of individual differences.

Counselors Understanding Their Own Culture

Counselors need to understand their own culture in order to successfully understand the cultures of others. Ivey, Ivey, and Simek-Downing (1987) devised an exercise in cultural awareness for professionals preparing for counseling in multicultural situations. They suggested that counselors answer the following questions to start them thinking about how their cultural heritage may affect their counseling:

1. *Ethnic heritage.* With what ethnic background do you first identify? First identify your nationality— U.S. citizen, Canadian, Mexican, etc.

Beyond this first answer, you may find the words *white, red, black, Polish, Mormon, Jewish,* or others coming to mind. Record these words.

Then, where did your grandparents come from? Great-grandparents?Can you trace a family history, perhaps with different ethnic, religious, and racial backgrounds? Trace your heritage in list form or in a family tree. Do not forget your heritage from the country within which you live.

2. *Are you monocultural, bicultural, or more?* Review the list you developed and pick out the central cultural, ethnic, religious, or other types of groups that have been involved in your development.

3. *What messages do you receive from each cultural group you have listed?* List the values, behaviors, and expectations that people in your group have emphasized over time. How have you personally internalized these messages? If you are aware of the message, chances are you have made some deviation from the family, ethnic, or religious value. If you are unaware, you may have so internalized the values that you are a "culture-bearer" without knowing it. Becoming aware of obvious but unconscious culture-bearer messages may become the most difficult task of all.

4. *How might you cultural messages affect your counseling and therapeutic work?* This final question is the most important. If you believe in individuality as supreme, given your family history, you may tend to miss the relational family orientation of many Asians and African-Americans. As we all have cultural histories, it is easy to believe that our way of being in the world is "the way things are and should be."

According to the Education and Training Committee of the APA's Division 17 of Counseling, Psychology, the culturally competent counselor should have these qualities:

1. Awareness of his or her own cultural characteristics;

2. Awareness of how his or her cultural values and biases may affect minority clients;

3. Understanding of the American sociopolitical system in relation to minorities;

4. The ability to resolve differences of race and beliefs between the counselor and his or her client;

5. The ability to know when a culturally different client should be referred to a counselor of the client's own race or culture;

6. Knowledge and information about the particular group of clients with whom the counselor is working.

Avoiding Stereotypes and Generalizations

Stereotypes and generalizations have the potential for severely damaging counseling relationships and the outcome of intervention. It should be obvious that all minorities are not helpless. However, stereotypical thinking continues to persist, even in people who are well-educated and who pride themselves on their logic and reason.

In *Pathways to Multicultural Counseling Competence*, Bea Wehrly (1995) proposes the following developmental model for counselors:

1. Each counselor/helper and each counselee/helpee is unique.

2. Each individual has multiple identities. Some will be personal identities and some will be reference-group orientation identities.

3. Each counselor (or helper) and each counselee(or helpee) has an ethnic or racial identity. Conscious awareness of reference-group orientation identifications is on a continuum from very limited to highly developed. In addition, the salience of ethnicity or race as a reference group identity will vary from individual to individual.

4. Being born and socialized into an ethnic or racial group in and of itself does not quality an individual to be a culturally skilled counselor with other people of that ethnic or racial group.

5. Acquisition of the beliefs and attitudes, knowledge, and skills needed for multicultural competence is a learning process that extends for a lifetime.

6. A positive identification with one's own ethnic, cultural and racial heritage provides a firm base for understanding and respecting the world view of people with different ethnic, cultural and racial heritages.

7. Given the prevalence of violent ethnic and racial conflicts in the United States and in other countries, and given the reality that we now live in a global village and operate in a global economy, it is time to begin searching for a broader model of reference group orientation. A posi-

tive identification with one's ethnic and racial heritage is the starting point for this broader model, which includes stages leading to understand and accepting a global-reference group orientation.

Multicultural Assessment

Another perspective for learning about the impact of culture on the client is to do an assessment of ethnocultural identification. Comas-Diaz and Jacobsen (1987) define ethnocultural identification as "a process whereby patients attribute ethnocultural characteristics to their therapists..[and] a therapeutic process that fosters an identification in which the therapist reflects pieces of the patient's fragmented self". This type of assessment can be especially helpful in working with people who have moved from their original cultural setting, whether from inside or outside their home country.

Comas-Diaz and Jacobsen further describe five stages of counselor assessment of client ethnocultural identification:

1. Obtaining an ethnocultural history.

2. Focusing on circumstances of the translocation of the client and his or her family.

3. Assessing how the client perceives the family's ethnocultural identify since the translocation.

4. Assessing the client's personal perception of his or her ethnocultural adjustment.

5. Considering the counselor's own ethnocultural adjustment to see any areas that overlap those of the client to determine how this might affect transference and countertransference.

They also examine the process of transference and countertransference between client and counselor and possible problems of over-identification with the client by the counselor. Kleinman (1988) also addresses problems in counselor overidentification with clients; Kleinman calls this the "cultural blind spot." Ethnocultural identification is used "as an auxiliary therapeutic tool to facilitate coping with changing cultural values and transitional experiences" (Comas-Diaz & Jacobsen, p. 232).

Diagnostic Intakes

Diagnostic intakes with people who have been socialized outside the dominant White society may present special challenges to beginning counselors. The section "Ethical and Cultural Considerations" in the introduction to the *Diagnostic and Statistical Manual of Mental Disorders,* Fourth Edition (American Psychiatric Association, 1994) notes that the manual is used with people from culturally diverse populations in the United States and internationally. Clinicians are apprised of the challenge of using the DMS-IV criteria in evaluating persons whose ethnic or cultural heritage is different from the clinician's.

A clinician who is unfamiliar with the nuances of an individual's cultural frame of reference may incorrectly judge as psychopathology those normal variations in behavior, belief, or experience that are particular to the individual's culture. For example, certain religious practices or beliefs (e.g., hearing or seeing a deceased relative during bereavement) may be misdiagnosed as manifestations of a Psychotic Disorder. Applying Personality Disorder criteria across cultural settings may be especially difficult because of the wide cultural variation in concepts of self, styles of communication, and coping mechanisms. (American Psychiatric Association, 1994, p. xxiv).

In order to promote an international awareness and understanding, ICASSI (the International Committee for Adlerian Summer Schools and Institutes) was founded by Rudolf Dreikurs in 1962. Annual summer conferences are held in various places throughout the world. Additional information is available from Ms. Betty Haeussler, 9212 Morley Road, Lanham, MD 20706. Fax 301-345-1961.

SUMMARY

In this chapter an overview to the theory of Adlerian psychology has been presented. A specific focus has been on multi-cultural implications. In Chapter 2, the specific theory of life-style assessment will be addressed.

LIFE-STYLE THEORY AND INTERVIEWING CONSIDERATIONS

In this chapter general Adlerian theory will be applied to the specific issue of life-style assessment. Four developmental phases of Adlerian counseling will be defined and illustrated. Life-style assessment theory and techniques will then be presented.

Since a life-style assessment is one type of counselor interview technique, fourteen general interviewing considerations and a one-page checklist of core questions will be introduced. Life-style theory will then be related to the fourteen interview considerations. A "Now & Then" life-style questionnaire will assist the reader in discovering a personal "style preference." "Situational style" will also be introduced as well as applied to elementary school classrooms.

The Developmental Phases of Adlerian Counseling

Rudolf Dreikurs (1967) delineated the phases of an Adlerian counseling relationship in four developmental sequences: 1) the establishment of a **relationship**; 2) a **psychological investigation** (including a life-style assessment); 3) psychological disclosure (**interpretation**); and 4) **reorientation** and re-education. Mozdzierz, et al. (1986), point out that the phases of therapy are "neither linear nor sequential steps in a progression. The four component phases are ingredients that are constantly interacting and needing attention with one component having more focus at one time and the others more at another time." (pp. 155-156)

Specific therapist role functions in the four phases of Adlerian therapy as adopted from Mozdzierz et al., are outlined as follows:

A. Establishing a relationship

1. **Mutual friend** — caring, concern, involvement, and the capacity for empathic, humanistic identification.

2. **Partner/Collaborator** — working together while paradoxically recognizing that ultimately only the client alone can change his or her life.

3. **Confidante** — purveyor of respect, trust, confidence and good faith. Faith, hope, and love (Mosak, 1984) or Roger's (1957) "unconditional positive regard" apply here; also acts in accordance with established professional code of ethics.

4. **Model** — the therapist living a way of dealing with life's challenges through courageous trust in and openness to what life has to offer; also modeling effective skills of communication; also living with authenticity or congruence. (Rogers, 1957)

5. **Environmentalist** — nurturing the therapeutic climate just as the natural resources of the world need care and attention; have an office which nurtures; also respect the privacy and confidentiality of the client.

Most counselors will identify this phase through the important term "rapport," stressing the core conditions of helping that Carkhuff and Associates (1969) have so aptly demonstrated, such as: a) **Unconditional positive regard** — putting no strings on the relationship (i.e., "you would be an 'OK' person if you would only..."); b) **Genuineness** — being two real persons, not a "healthy" therapist and a "sick" patient; c) **Empathy** — accurate perception of the person's "world," including his/her emotional subjective "feeling tone" towards their environment; d) **Self-disclosure** — freely volunteering relevant personal information; and e) **Concreteness** — talking about specific concerns rather than vague abstractions (e.g., "you're hurt *because* your mom distrusts you" as opposed to "you're upset"). Carkhuff terms this phase "Facilitation," the foundation or cornerstone upon which the relationship is built. It is also during the relationship building phase that both the counselor and the client agree on future counseling procedures and goals. Clients experiencing interpersonal conflicts often have difficulty forming close relationships, making the counseling process an important first step toward social living. Therefore, counselors must continually "win" or "earn" the confidence of their clients, making the relationship phase on ongoing task.

B. Psychological Investigation

1. **Wide-Angle and Multifocus Observer** — Expanding the often narrow and restricted vision of the client; assisting in making connections between past, present, and future actions; understanding and appreciating cultural diversity and different life-style influences and backgrounds.

2. **Life-Style Interpreter** — Focusing on an individual's family constellation and early childhood history combined with a summary of early recollections or memories; helping the client understand his or her private logic.

3. **Explorer** — Assessing the three life tasks Adler (in Ansbacher & Ansbacher, 1956) identified as being the work task, the social or friendship task and the love task. To these Mosak (1984) added the task of self-esteem and the spiritual. The therapist also identifies the strengths and weaknesses of the client. "Adlerian explorers not only invite their clients on a journey through what has been and is, but also through the infinite possibilities of what can be. An exploration of options for growth and development, and an exploration of the road and choices/options that lead to a more productive and constructive future are two forms of exploration that facilitate client movement toward the future." (Mozdzierz, et al., 1986, p. 163)

C. Psychological Disclosure

1. **Interpreter** — giving the client "another set of glasses" with which to view the world; an explanation of the patient's behavior in relation to or in terms of his or her goals, intentions, purposes, private logic, or movement. (Dreikurs, 1967)

2. **Translator/Reframer** — Assisting the client to understand other people, life, and the issues involved with social living; "reframing" perceived negatives to strengths wherever possible.

3. **Creator of Meaning and Understanding** — Often created by suggestion, arrangement and rearrangement, connecting and disconnecting, focusing and clarifying, defining and redefining. (Mozdzierz, et al., 1976)

4. **Confronter** — Focusing on discrepancies between what a person is saying versus doing, feeling versus thinking, or between what another person says about the same situation.

In the interpretation phase, corresponding roughly to Carkhuff's action stage, basic "life-others-self" attitudes are shared with the individual. The constant emphasis is on goals or purposes rather than "why" people act the way they do. Here the individual's "private logic" is discussed, including important implications for present and future activities.

Confrontation concerning discrepancies between actions and words, or between ideal and real goals is also employed. Specific examples relating to one's current means of accomplishing desired goals are also obtained, and the person begins to experience greater personal insights relating to his or her goals and intentions.

D.   Reorientation and Re-education

1.   **Encourager** — O'Connell's (1975) model of encouragement includes stopping, looking, and listening through demonstrated interest, clarifying, being non-judgmental, giving feedback, looking for useless goals in behavior, and the development of a sense of humor. "Encouragement is the realization that every deficit can also be an asset: for every negative in life...there is also a positive, adaptive creative response that the individual makes. (Mozdzierz, et al., 1986, p. 168)

2.   **Dialectician** — understanding such paradoxes as, in human behavior, strength can be weakness and weakness can be strength; moving from "either-or" dualities and dichotomies to "both-and."

3.   Other roles include **resource person**, "fellow **pilgrim**," "**expert**" who puts clients in charge of their own lives, comforter (from the Latin word meaning "to make strong"), **educator** and **humorist**.

Henry Stein (1988) adapts the four developmental phases into the following twelve stages of creative psychotherapy, including: 1) empathy (relationship); 2) information; 3) clarification; 4) encouragement; 5) interpretation and recognition; 6) knowing; 7) group and marathon (if needed); 8) doing different; 9) reinforcement; 10) social interest; 11) goal re-direction; and 12) support and launching.

Life-Style Theory

The ability to understand as well as to predict human behavior is one of the major goals of psychology. A significant contribution to the achievement of the goal was Adler's (1930) unified concept of personal "life-style."

The Ansbachers (1967) note that when and how the term "life-style" originated has yet to be precisely determined. For example, the French naturalist and writer Georges-Louis de Buffon (1707-1788) stated "The style is the man himself" (*Le style est l'homme même*). More than 150 years earlier, the English philosopher and author, Robert Burton (1577-1640) observed (in Bartlett, 1951) "It is most true, *stylus verum arguit* - our style betrays us." Adler (1929) used the following analogy in presenting his definition of life-style:

> If we look at a pine tree growing in a valley we will notice that it grows differently from one on top of a mountain. It is the same kind of a tree, pine, but there are two distinct styles of life. Its style on top of the mountain is different from its style when growing in the valley. The style of life of a tree is the individuality of a tree expressing itself and molding itself in an environment. We recognize a style when we see it against a background of an environment different from what we expect, for then we realize that every tree has a life pattern and is not merely a mechanical reaction to the environment. (p. 98)

He then relates the pine tree analogy to the human experience as well as introducing the term life-style:

> It is much the same way with human beings. We see the style of life under certain conditions of environment and it is our task to analyze its exact relation to the existing circumstances, inasmuch as mind changes, with alteration of the environment. As long as a person is in a favorable situation, we cannot see his style of life clearly. In new situations, however, where he is confronted with difficulties, the style of life appears clearly and distinctly. A trained psychologist could perhaps understand a style of life of a human being even in a favorable situation, but it becomes apparent to everybody when the human subject is put into unfavorable or difficult situations...We have seen how human beings with weak organs, because they face difficulties and feel insecure, suffer from a feeling or complex of inferiority. But as human beings cannot endure this for long, the inferiority feeling stimulates them, as we have seen, to movement and action. This results in a person having a goal. Individual Psychology has long called the consistent movement toward the goal a plan of life. But because this name has sometimes led to mistakes among students, it is now called a style of life. (p. 98)

Adler's later writings equated the "style of life" with the self or ego, one's own personality, the unity of personality, individuality, individual form of creative activity, the method of facing problems, opinion about oneself and the problems of life, and the whole attitude to life. Rudolf Dreikurs (1953) followed Adler's "holistic" notion by noting that "the life style is comparable to a characteristic theme in a piece of music. It brings the rhythm of recurrence into our lives" (p. 44). Allen (1971) notes that Adler's basic notions of life-style overlap considerably with what Skinner (1969) has termed "rule-governed behavior," with what Galantier, Miller & Pribram (1960) call "plans," with Frank's (1961) "assumptive system," Kelly's (1955) "supraordinate constructs," and Rotter's (1966) "generalized expectancies of reinforcement."

Despite the vast diversity concerning different meanings for the term "life-style" itself, and despite related concepts by other psychologists employing slightly different terminology, the Ansbachers (1967) summarize the common "life-style" properties of all the various writers by systematizing the following similarities.

Unifying Aspect

The word "style" includes the characteristic of cutting across ordinary boundaries and uniting what might otherwise be quite separate entities. Thus, in the case of Bach, Beethoven and Mozart, if one knows their music at all, one can easily match the musical manuscripts with the composer.

Unique and Creative Aspects

One style is always different from others, although there are similarities between styles. For example, children learn to write following a standard cultural model; nevertheless, each person varies the model in a unique, idiomatic manner. Of course, spontaneous and unique behavior implies choices on the part of individuals. And such choices are based on a forward-oriented, purposive, value psychology rather than on a causalistic, reductionistic psychology.

Operational, Functional, and Constancy Aspects

Adler proclaimed life-style as a "psychology of use" as contrasted with a psychology of possession. Objective conditions or stimuli are focused on and used in accordance with a person's own unique life-style: the "inner" self is recognized as an active and creative center, rather than a passive reactor merely receiving stimulation from the external environment. In the introduction to their invaluable *Manual for Life Style Assessment*, two of the foremost post-Dreikurs clinicians, Bernard Shulman and Harold Mosak (1988) stress that while Adler often used the term in a collective sense (the life-style of a pampered child), he stressed that "the life style of any individual was a singular pattern of thinking, feeling, and acting that was unique to that individual and represented the context (*Zusammerhang*) in which all specific manifestations had to be considered" (p. 1). Shulman & Mosak further define the development of life-style as beginning at an early age when an infant uses elementary "trial and error" means to organize the world. Such early efforts are formed into beginning "rules" or **patterns** which serve as an integrator for the rules. Early patterns are continually reinforced as the child grows until what they call "the rule of thumb" is elevated to the status of a law, the unique law of movement. "Because it is a unique personal law, it receives all of the person's loyalties... Because it seems to permit better coping, it becomes as a private religion or personal myth" (p. 3). Mosak further writes that: "If it is recalled that the Life Style is a subjective bias which the individual embraces as if it were true, then the Life Style can be conceived as a personal mythology. This individual will behave as if the myths were true because for him, they are true" (as quoted in Lewis, 1983, p. 261).

Although individuals develop such a habitual pattern to organizing the world, Adlerian theory maintains that one can always change, modify, or "break" such patterns. Thus, insight and awareness of one's general "rules" of life is essential to the counseling process.

Dinkmeyer, Dinkmeyer & Sperry (1987) present an apt metaphor of the "theater of an ongoing drama" relative to the child's development of his or her personal life-style:

> The style of living is created in the course of an ongoing drama that takes place in the theater of the family, with parents and siblings all playing a part - a drama in which the child functions as his own director and whose last act he has already sketched out in broad outlines. The nuclear family is society to the small child, and the child's efforts to find a place in this society influence how he creates his life style. In elucidating an individual's life style, the counselor tries to get some idea of what it was like to be in that childhood drama, what roles were played by the different actors, and how the "director" interpreted the drama — that is, what the role he played and what conclusions he drew about himself and life. (p. 34)

A life-style investigation involves regression to formative childhood influences for the purpose of determining existential decisions regarding life, self, and others that affect present behavior and may affect future behavior. Although the time reference is the past, determination of implications for the present and future is the goal of a life-style assessment. An investigation of this type focuses on such familial concerns as birth order, interpersonal relationships between family members, the siblings' main competitors, family values, and the individual's early recollections of formative experiences. Adlerian theory, which represents a departure from orthodox, "stimulus-response" environmental behaviorism, is based on the assumption that one's phenomenological personal decisions and conclusions ("private logic") are the crucial determinants of behavior (Ansbacher & Ansbacher, 1956). Such a position is similar to Allport's "mode of being in the world" as well as Van Kaam's "mode of existence." The optimistic philosophies of all such theorists include the belief that an individual's past decisions and patterns can be continually reviewed, modified, and/or changed.

As the Ansbachers (1967) note, the concept of "life-style" is much more humanistic than that of a predestined "life plan." By exploring and assessing an individual's life-style, it is possible to develop an understanding of that person as a self-consistent and self-directed entity whose central theme is reflected in all personal actions as forward-oriented, purposive, and determined by individual values rather than by simple physiological responses to the environment.

Lombardi (1973) presented the following useful "rubber stamp" analogy as a means of further explaining the concept of life-style assessment:

> Each person is like a rubber stamp. The essence of personality is reflected in all that he does. If the rubber stamp has the imprint "John Doe" and is pressed on a surface, we see a reflection of the name John Doe. Some of the variables that determine the clearness and legibility of the imprint include the following: amount of ink on the rubber stamp, pressure on the stamp when making the imprint, texture and color of the surface upon which the imprint is made. For instance, a black imprint on a black rough surface will hardly be seen...But no matter where you press the rubber stamp...there is always a reflection of a part of the imprint John Doe. Each person is like a rubber stamp in that no matter what he does, his life style is reflected in his behavior, feelings, and thoughts. The life style is reflected in much, if not all, of what the person is and does. (p. 6)

According to Shulman & Mosak (1988), a child's formative decisions later become formulated into basic **convictions** about "'what is' — that is about the nature of our individual selves and the 'reality' we face; and those about the values and behaviors we will pursue in our efforts to master 'what is.'" (p. 5)

Convictions of life are further developed into what they call "I am..., Life is..., therefore..." **conclusions** about behavior. For example, to refer again to Adler's example in the previous chapter, consider two vastly different *therefores* or conclusions given a similar "fear of death" major life-style theme:

> A physician: "*I am* concerned about the disease, decay and ultimate death I see around me. *Life* is filled with much suffering but also contains the possibility of discovering cures for such discomfort; *therefore,* I will dedicate my life to conquering disease and extending life."

> A gravedigger: "*I am* afraid of death. *Life* is simply an inevitable progression toward death; *therefore,* I will celebrate my own superiority each time I bury another person who was conquered by death."

Note the similar motivating convictions but drastically differing decisions reflecting social interest or the lack thereof.

Mosak & Shulman call long-continued patterns of behavior the **methods** of obtaining a goal. The method for the physician involved enrolling in medical school, while the gravedigger symbolically triumphed in each burial. They summarize the major elements of an overall life-style as being:

A. *Convictions about "what is,"* including 1) Self-image (What am I?); 2) World-image – life in general (How does it work?); and 3) "Weltbild" — the social world (What is the relationship between myself and others?).

B. *Convictions about "what should be,"* including ethical value of 1) The ideal world (How should life be?); and 2) Moral judgments (What is good and proper behavior?).

C. *Instructions for behavior*, including 1) Dominant goal/self ideal (What shall I pursue? and What must I become?), and 2) Methods (How shall I do it?)

(adapted from Shulman & Mosak, 1988, p. 12).

Life Style: "The Story of Our Life"

A paradox of lifestyle is that while it is often constant and stable, each of us are continually growing and shaping our beliefs about ourselves, others and the world. According to Adler each of us as young children experienced inferiority feelings coupled with strivings for success. Although there is disagreement as to when an actual lifestyle begins or if it becomes experienced, there are early formulative patterns which form what Schulman called a "pre-formed working hypothesis" through which our later experiences are filtered. Jim Bitter (1995) calls a lifestyle the "story of our life." He also believes that the purpose of therapy is to help enlarge the client's story to make it fuller and richer.

In many ways, such a story of our life may in fact contain more core fiction than actual core truth. For example, some of our remembrances of previous stories are indeed made up, and many of us can't remember what is true and not true. For example, Adler relates an early formative childhood experience of being deathly afraid of having to cross a graveyard which he felt was between himself and his elementary school grounds. It was only many years later that he discovered that there was no actual graveyard that existed between those two places; however, the reality of such a graveyard in his own mind was as real to him as was the physical existence of that feared place. Thus one's lifestyle is a narrative in story form and is not necessarily "accurate" to the "objective" facts as we leave out certain incidences and re-emphasize others.

However, we act as if such conclusions are true, for we are living more in our own interpretations of our experiences than the actual events themselves. The process of understanding one's lifestyle consists of the ability to help to find meaning of what is being told to the counselor. As each of us journeys through life certain stories become what Bitter calls "dominant knowledge" with two primary functions of such events: 1) to reinforce itself and its own importance upon the self; and 2) to eliminate alternative ideas or stories which may be inconsistent with one's own self-perceived dominant knowledge.

For example, consider a person who has a dominant knowledge reflecting overall depression. Such an internal belief system will tend to accentuate experiences of sadness while concurrently diminishing moments of joy and happiness. One of the problems with one's "dominant story" is that it is often impossible for the individual to separate himself or herself from the story. For that very reason, one task of the skillful counselor is indeed to help create a separation, a proper boundary between one's own internal story, and one's own sense of Self.

An initial objective of lifestyle assessment is the process of attempting to understand a person's story. Although many counselors are adept at having a person relate such a story, the next issue becomes "Now what? What are the implications of knowing one's story?" Becoming aware of how one may "distort" experiences in order to perpetuate a fictional early-developed version of one's life is therefore the next step to which Adlerians refer to as reorientation. Reframing a "perceived minus" to a "perceived plus" is one of the most powerful therapist's interventions. It is based on the encouragement necessary to move from a "glass half-empty" approach to a "glass half-full" approach. For example, Bitter relates a client who was contemplating going back to school at age 46. Her comment was, "I am now 46 and in four years I will be 50. That's too old for a person to begin going back to school." Bitter reframed her statement to, "In four years you will be 50 years of age. At that time you will either be educated or you will not be educated."

Bitter also reframed a client's early recollection consisting of throwing an object which accidentally cut open the hand of a friend in which the client still had horrible memories of injuring someone else. Bitter encouragingly introjected that, "you're the kind of person I would want to go to for help because you're always carrying around a conscious memory of what can happen when you're not tuned into others around you."

One specific way counselors can help clients both become aware of their stories as well as to begin to help create new stories is to begin to ask questions to help separate the person from the problem. One of the unique problems of the behavioral sciences is that we use many labels to describe problems and challenges in our life; however, once having labeled the problem, we then become the label. Such a "psychological blend" is typified by the usual 12-step approach to alcoholism as indicated in the following introduction which people are asked to make: "My name is _____, and I am an alcoholic." Such a blending of a psychological label is a dysfunctional merger between one's symptom and one's Self. For example, no one goes to a doctor and says, "Hello Doctor, my name is _____, and I'm a headache."

An important child psychology principle is the ability to "separate the deed from the doer," meaning that effective parenting involves being able to distinguish a child's misbehavior from their sense of themselves. In a similar manner, one of the difficulties of one's own life story is the tendency to merge the self narrative with the problem. Thus the antidote is to begin speaking about the problem separate from the Self.

Another counseling technique to help "reframe" a challenging situation is to assist a person to notice when they're *not* doing the problem. For example, many people who have extreme anxiety might be helped to realize that it is almost impossible to be anxious 24 hours a day. The goal becomes to assist the client to observe the times when they are not anxious. Reframing is a practical skill to assist one to confront what works then to keep enlarging and expanding it. The life-style assessment is meant to be a creative process in which an individual is given an opportunity to explore "formative events and critical incidents from his or her previous experiences." Such stories have a formative beginning early in their life, have then been developed in the current or middle portion of their life and have a logical future projection to some type of anticipated end. The present book introduces some suggested specific structured formats which can assist a counselor in systematically examining formative events from another's life; however, it is the authors' encouragement that the life-style assessment is ultimately a creative process, which means to be allowed to "flow" in a spontaneous here and now journey between two individuals. After helping assist a person to tell and reflect upon his or her own story, counselors then need to ask the question, "what makes that story work for this individual?" Related questions to explore with the client include, "Is there anything you would like to experience being different in your life? If so, what would that be?" Thus, the life-style assessment is a creative way to help learn about "one's own personal story."

The American Indians often say, "if you want to understand my world, walk a mile in my moccasins." A life-style assessment is one way to learn about one's own inner world. Becoming aware of one's own inner world including potential fictional parts of that story can then help a person "rewrite," "recreate," or "expand" such a story to include new possibilities and new options.

Traditionally the interpretation process has included a counselor sitting down alone and writing his or her impressions based upon the life-style interview. However it's also suggested that it be done more in a collaborative egalitarian relationship with the client because ultimately it is that person himself or herself who is the ultimate determinor or the "truthfulness" of any interpretive guesses by counselors.

Therefore a suggested intervention may be, "Here are some of my ideas. How would you like to rewrite them to fit you?" Such a procedure helps to increase the psychological "ownership" of the investment and the involvement of the client himself or herself appreciating and valuing such a personal story.

"Cue sorting" or ranking items from most to least importance is one specific technique which Bitter recommends to begin the interpretation process. Another is to consider the issues in their life like a "room" in which ones that are at the "top" are important and need to be attended to right away versus issues that are in the "middle of the room" that are also important but can wait somewhat, while issues in the "bottom" part of the "room" are not necessarily to deal with in the immediate future.

Adapted from Bitter, J., Life-style assessment program presented at NASAP Annual Conference, Minneapolis, MN, May 27, 1995. (Additional interpretative guidelines and techniques will be presented in Chapter 4).

The Approach to a Life-Style Interview

The checklist on the following page was designed for use in General Interviewing Skills training workshops in counseling and business settings. Such preparatory contemplations help determine in advance the purpose and focus of the interview, whether it is to learn about an organization or an individual. Listed are 14 interview considerations; they are then summarized in a series of questions which can serve as a "final" checklist prior to conducting an interview. The 14 considerations are then specifically applied to the author's typical life-style pre-interview considerations.

Interviewing Considerations

by Daniel Eckstein

Effective interviewing is one of the most important skills for human relations workers. The following items are meant to serve as a pre-interview checklist to maximize the effectiveness of a proactive rather than reactive philosophy. They can also serve as a mid-session guide and debriefing evaluation at the conclusion of an interview.

General considerations include:

1. **What is the purpose of the interview?**

    A primary and fundamental consideration is an initial clear understanding of the reason for conducting an interview. Some representative purposes include: assessing, diagnosing, and/or counseling an individual, dyad, or group; conflict resolution via third-party negotiation; or teambuilding and/or assessment of a work unit.

2. **Who or what is my focus?**

    Having clarity relative to purpose helps establish an appropriate focus involving individual/group/ team/content parameters. The Gestalt concept of figure/ground helps determine the relevant focus and purpose issue. For example, if the session is designed to assess an organizational work team, the template that an interviewer applies is that the system itself is the figural focus, while individuals being interviewed/surveyed become the "ground." Thus, extended personal sharing would need to be redirected into an "individual as enmeshed within the organization" concept. A personal counseling session would appropriately reverse the individual/organizations figure/ground focus. Another approach involves a content topical interview where information gathering is needed. Thus, gathering facts involving sexual or racial discrimination gives a different "perceptual screen" relative to the session.

3. **Who gets the data?**

    An important ethical issue involves the parameters of confidentiality extending from the session itself. If a written or oral report is to be distributed or presented to others, clients need to be appropriately informed at the onset. Permission to take notes and/or tape also needs to be obtained. A frequent "limited confidentiality" agreement is made during teambuilding data gathering sessions such as "what you say here is anonymous in that it will not be attributed to you personally; however, everything you say is team business." Similarly, if you are mandated to report certain information obtained during a session (drug, sexual, or child abuse, etc.) clients should be so informed.

4. **What types of data are "admissible"?**
   Like an orchestra conductor, the "Gatekeeper" encourages and discourages pertinent client sharing. Thus, appropriate and inappropriate topics need to be determined. Prior to the actual interview it is helpful for the interviewer to consider what would be (a) *unacceptable* topics to discuss, (b) what would be *acceptable* areas of focus, and also (c) what would be especially *desirable* issues to be explored during the interview. Having an idea ahead of time helps make interventions that encourage more or less exploration in a particular direction. It also serves as a focusing guideline in critiquing the session at the conclusion. Such considerations help establish appropriate boundaries for the topics to be discussed.

5. **Skills of beginning the interview**
   Robert Carkhuff (1980) uses the SOFEL acronym to describe attending preparatory interview guidelines:

   S = sitting square

   O = open body posture

   F = leaning forward

   E = eye contact

   L = active listening skills

Allen Ivey (1971) describes the following opening and "minimal" interview encouragers: "could you tell me about …?"; "oh?"; "so?"; "then?"; "and?"; "tell me more"; "and how did you feel about that?"; "can you give me a specific example?"; "what does that mean to you?"; "umm-humm"; or the repetition of one or two key words.

Specific sensing interview content and process guidelines such as role goals, the job itself, organization, interpersonal relations, interpersonal perceptions, work team, desired changes, plus here and now feelings are synthesized by John Jones (1973). Additional information on assessment and interviewing is available in Cinnamon & Matulef (1979).

Other beginning considerations include a brief overview summarizing the preceding items. A related issue involves the degree of structure to be employed. For example, an advantage of highly structured sessions is the uniformity and comparability of different subjects; conversely, a disadvantage is that individual creativity may be stifled by a "filling in the dots" question and answer approach. An advantage of a more unstructured open-ended opening is the projective nature of the clients' initiations and responses; a disadvantage relates to a diffused lack of focus.

6. **Pacing and leading skills**

   The ability to match the client's tone of voice, body posture and "energy" level is defined as pacing by neurolinguistic programmers (NLP). Pacing communicates understanding and empathy through the ability to appropriately match the client's style through a reactive receptive approach. A related skill involves leading the person or group by a more pro-active directive interviewer manner. Thus, rather than matching the client, the intention is to provide a contrast. For example, a client speaking in a rapid, highly agitated manner may be calmed by a more slow, quiet interviewer style.

7. **Sharing vs. dumping**

   A frequent source of interviewer stress relates to clients who metaphorically "dump" all their "garbage" (complaints, criticisms, etc.). Although the experience may sometimes be cathartic for the client, it is a frequent cause of burnout for interviewers. Professional judgment is needed to distinguish between productive client sharing as contrasted to non-productive dumping.

One technique to minimize dumping involves "reframing" or "refocusing" the individual to another less "hot" topic. Another intervention could focus on the *motivation* behind the behavior (i.e., "I'm wondering what you hope to accomplish here now"). An unexpected emotional response is also possible (i.e., "augh — I'm really feeling dumped on"). *Termination* is always an option in extreme cases.

8. **The alone/together paradox**

   A paradox is an apparent contradiction which is nonetheless true (i.e., "to *gain* your life you must be willing to *lose* it"). The ability to be "connected" while concurrently maintaining a separateness helps prevent another source of burnout, that being the tendency to "catch" the client's "disease." Effective interviewers are both "with" the client and "apart from" the individual.

9. **Integration of the art of active listening with the science of effective interventions**

   Recent brain-integration research indicates the presence of two separate hemispheres with complimentary functions. The right "art" side is characterized by intuitiveness, feelings, and impressions. Conversely, the left "science" hemisphere includes verbalization, analyzation, and rationality. Effective interviewing combines receptivity to impressions and skill in formulating responses. Active listening involves attending to the congruence of verbalizations and nonverbal body language, and important self-references. Dinkmeyer, Dinkmeyer & Sperry (1987) list the following intervention skills: structuring, universalizing, linking, confronting, blocking, encouraging, paraphrasing, formulating tentative hypotheses, plus capping and summarizing.

10. **First and second order change**

    Watzlawick, et al. (1974), introduced the concept of first and second order change. First order change involves a change in behavior, whereas second order change is a paradigm shift relative to the underlying belief or attitude. For example, discrimination can be legislated through laws, whereas the root cause, prejudice, is more difficult to change.

    Consistent with the overall purpose of the interview, change may or may not be a function of the session. For example, Lippitt & Lippitt (1978) use the following non-directive to directive continuum relative to various consultant roles: observer/reflector, process observer, fact finder, resource linker, joint problem-solver, trainer/educator, information specialist, and advocate.

    The role of a change agent becomes more appropriate in the directive. Interviewers need to determine if behavior and/or attitude change is a desired outcome.

11. **Interviewer reactions**

    One of the most valuable sources of information relates to the *personal* impact of the session on the interviewer. Thus, at various times a private assessment of "how am *I* feeling... personally, interpersonally, and task-wise?" is suggested. For example, if the purpose is to assess the flavor of an organization's climate, the impact of non-obtrusive observations such as the bulletin boards and office arrangement upon the interviewer provides an excellent diagnostic component. Similar reactions to the individual being interviewed provide important diagnostic information.

12. **Encouragement and confrontation**

    Nikelly (1971) has coined the phrase "stroke and spit tactics" as an important interview skill. Stroking is synonymous with the crucial role of encouragement based on an optimistic building-on-str engths- not-weaknesses philosophy.

Alfred Adler describes confrontation as "spitting in the soup." If an individual is enjoying a bowl of soup and someone else spits in the soup, it can still be eaten but probably not near as pleasurably. The skill of confrontation is characterized by such discrepancies as: verbal and nonverbal body language (i.e., "I'm *not* mad" spoken through tight lips and a clenched jaw); what the client is saying compared to other's perceptions ("although you do not feel there is a problem in the shipping department, several other managers feel there is"); client vs. interviewer perceptions ("although you describe yourself as a 'cold unfeeling' manager, I see you as caring for your employees very much"); or what a person is saying contrasted to what (s)he is doing ("you said the report was going to be completed last week and I still do not have it"). A combination of encouragement and confrontation maximizes the potential for positive change.

13. **Closing the interview**

    As the session nears a conclusion it is often advisable to review the basic purpose and summarize the content. If notes have been kept, many interviewers suggest actually showing the client what has been written. A "next steps" focus upon what happens to the data, plus reviewing suggested behavioral or attitudinal changes, if relevant, are useful strategies. "Are there any questions you would like to ask me?" is also helpful.

14. **Follow-up and evaluation**

    When interviews are conducted as part of a total consulting develop-mental sequence (initial client contact, contracting, entry, assessment, diagnosis, intervention, and evaluation), it is important to provide follow-up information relative to the individual and/or organization. Summarized results plus problem-solving suggestions help clients see potential benefits. Written or verbal feedback should be provided if it is part of the client contract.

Interview Issues and Considerations: A Checklist Summary

The following chart provides a summary checklist of questions for designing, conducting, and critiquing interviews.

Issue	Considerations
1. Purpose	What do I hope to accomplish in this session?
2. Focus	Is my primary mission to highlight individual, group, team, or content-related issues?
3. Levels of confidentiality and/or anonymity	Who has access to the information? What are my ethical parameters?
4. Session content	What specific topics and behaviors are desirable? Acceptable? Unacceptable?
5. Initiating the interview	How will my verbal and nonverbal behavior help establish an atmosphere of trust and respect?
6. Pacing and leading skills	What is the appropriate balance of responsiveness and directiveness?
7. Sharing vs. dumping	How will I deal with inappropriate anger, cynicism, sarcasm, scapegoating, gossip, etc.?
8. The alone/together paradox	How can I be connected with the client while concurrently maintaining my own separateness?
9. Integrating left and right brain hemispheres	How can I be both an intuitive artist and a rational scientist in my listening and intervention skills?
10. First and second order change	Is client attitude and/or behavioral change part of my consultant role? If so, what strategies will facilitate such movement?
11. Interviewer reactions	How am I feeling in this interview and in this organization? How can I use my personal awareness as another assessment technique?
12. Encouragement and confrontation skills	How can I help the client identify strengths as well as appropriately confronting discrepancies?
13. Closing the interview	What needs to be done to have a sense of closure to the meeting?
14. Follow-up and evaluation	How can I assist in the proper organizational/individual feedback and implementation?

Interview — Considerations Applied

Although each particular life-style interview has its own unique aspects, the following general summary reflects the authors' most typical responses to Eckstein's 14 interview considerations.

1. *What is the purpose of a life-style interview?*

   A life-style interview is a systematic exploration of early formative childhood experiences. Although the focus is backward in time, current and future decisions become the purpose of exploring one's initial social experiences. Themes of life, hopes, dreams, and fears emerge from such a systematic examination.

2. *Who or what is my focus?*

   One's first family or social group, including brothers and sisters, mother and father as relevant is the focus. Although there is a structured interview available, the actual session may be spent on one or two key formative experiences. Family atmosphere and early recollections will be highlighted.

3. *Who gets the data?*

   Unless prior agreements are made with the interviewee relative to releasing the data to a particular agency or parent, ethical consideration of respecting the privacy and confidentiality of the individual needs to be followed.

4. *What types of data are "admissible"?*

   In keeping with the projective nature of a life-style interview, individual creative and spontaneous sharing is encouraged. When early recollections are explored, one specific memory is wanted in contrast to something someone else told the person. Basic respect dictates that the person may elect to "pass" on any question asked.

5. *Beginning skills of interviewing*

   These are accurately summarized previously - it is a challenge to take notes and maintain eye contact. Sometimes a co-therapist can assist; tape recorders are also possible.

6. *Pacing and leading*

   Listen for the language of your client and try to speak metaphorically and symbolically in that same manner initially. Later the "leading" takes place by means of the structured interview.

7. *Sharing vs. dumping*
   Since the interview itself is a "slice of life" for the person, expect the style to be present in the here and now. For example, in one interpretation it was stated "seems to me you have a tendency to be somewhat defensive." "No I'm not," the person immediately fired back.

8. *The alone/together paradox*
   It is very important to be both "with" the person and "separate" enough to respect that ultimately it is a very personal journey for the person.

9. *Integration of active listening and effective interventions*
   Open yourself up to allow your own creative intuitive problem-solver to cooperate with your own scientific exploration. Dreikurs used to call it "digging gold mines," that is, respecting and paying attention to a key word or phrase that impacts you. The more centered you can be, the more open to your own creative process you will be.

10. *First and second order change*
    Life-style interpretations focus both on behavior and attitudes or beliefs shifting. (More will be presented on this in Chapter 4.)

11. *Interviewer reactions*
    A valuable source of information, both as clues to your own possible counter-transference issues as well as how you personally feel being with the other person.

12. *Encouragement and confrontation*
    Core interpretive skills - more in Chapter 4.

13. *Closing the interview*
    After the initial data-gathering, set a follow-up appointment. Encourage the person to keep a journal for other thoughts that may emerge. Stress that the interpretation will be done collaboratively.

14. *Follow-up and evaluation*
    It is advisable to ask the person if he or she has any questions for you at the conclusion of the interview. Also solicit feedback on your own style.

Life-Style: An Assessment

In order to introduce the idea of personality differences as reflected in style, the following self-scoring questionnaire has been developed by Eckstein. It is based on Thorne's (1975) research-based personality typologies. An earlier version of this questionnaire by Driscoll & Eckstein appeared in the *1982 Annual for Facilitators, Trainers & Consultants.* (p. 105)

Life-Style: A Self-Assessment

A.   The first step is for you to consider the following five animals:

B.   Now answer the following questions:

   1. Which one of these animals is most like you?

      a) _____

   2. Why or how is it like you?

      _____

   3. How are the other four animals like or unlike you?

      b) _____
      c) _____
      d) _____
      e) _____

C.   Now take the "Now & Then" Life-Style Questionnaire (interpretation and scoring instructions will follow).

"Now & Then" Life-Style Questionnaire

by Daniel Eckstein

Instructions — Read each of the following statements and assign points according to these guidelines:

almost always true of me	5 points
usually true of me	4 points
sometimes true of me	3 points
seldom true of me	2 points
almost never true of me	1 point

A. Answer questions 1-30 based on your life **currently**:

____ 1. I persist at a task until it is finished.

____ 2. In a new job or class, I find out what is expected of me and then do it without a lot of fanfare.

____ 3. I am the kind of person who "sticks my neck out" to take a lot of chances.

____ 4. I am constantly seeking a better way of doing things.

____ 5. I have been fired or resigned from a job or failed a class because my boss or teacher thought I had a poor attitude.

____ 6. I am often recognized by others as an expert or an authority in one or more areas.

____ 7. Others can count on me to keep my agreements.

____ 8. I prefer to be alone or with just one or two friends than in a large group.

____ 9. I can anticipate problems before they arise.

____ 10. I protest causes of injustice, unfairness, or hypocrisy.

____ 11. I am interested in time management, planning the most efficient use of my day.

____ 12. I follow the rules.

____ 13. I think before I act.

____ 14. I like being my own boss.

____ 15. I mistrust authority.

____ 16. I set goals for myself and work hard to attain them.

_____ 17. I blend my feelings with those of others just to keep things harmonious.

_____ 18. I am "set" in my ways, my habits, and my opinions.

_____ 19. In a conflict, I am confident that I have the ability to "rise above it" and thereby gain a better perspective.

_____ 20. I believe most people compromise their true feelings just to conform to the status quo.

_____ 21. When I'm riding in a car, I'd prefer to be the driver.

_____ 22. I am seldom absent from school or work.

_____ 23. Compared with others, I feel I am more private and sensitive than them.

_____ 24. I will stick to my own opinion or beliefs even if others disagree with me.

_____ 25. Creating a better world will require destroying old habits, thoughts, and systems.

_____ 26. I go after what I want.

_____ 27. I focus so much on the feelings of others that expressing my own emotions makes me uncomfortable.

_____ 28. I am successful when people see that my way of doing things contributes to others.

_____ 29. I am confident as long as I am free to follow my dreams.

_____ 30. The truth is more important to me than social graces or what people think of me.

B.   A nswer questions 31-60 based on your **childhood** (up to age seven):

_____ 31. I would have been considered as a leader by my friends.

_____ 32. I went along with what was expected of me.

_____ 33. I spent a lot of time alone.

_____ 34. I was willing to speak my opinion.

_____ 35. I disagreed with my parents or teachers and I often got in trouble because of my strong beliefs.

_____ 36. I was competitive.

_____ 37. I was good at figuring out what was wanted or needed in a situation and then doing it.

____ 38. If someone yelled at me I would withdraw into myself.

____ 39. I wanted to have things go my way.

____ 40. I was aware of the amount of injustice and unfairness in the world.

____ 41. I could persuade my other friends to follow my ideas or wishes.

____ 42. I enjoyed helping around the house or at school.

____ 43. I had a private place in my house or neighborhood that was just mine.

____ 44. I sought new adventures.

____ 45. I didn't go along with the rules others made for me.

____ 46. I was very energetic, always on the go.

____ 47. I was interested in hearing other opinions of people.

____ 48. I often knew things were going to happen before they actually happened.

____ 49. I considered myself to be intelligent.

____ 50. I never understood why people didn't speak their own opinions.

____ 51. I was confident that ultimately I would succeed

____ 52. It was okay for others to have different opinions than me.

____ 53. I desired quietness, order, and safety.

____ 54. I considered myself to be a free-spirit.

____ 55. Early in my life

____ 56. I set high standards for myself.

____ 57. If the whole group was happy, then I was happy.

____ 58. To deal with my hurt, I developed a hard shell.

____ 59. I liked deciding things for myself.

____ 60. I stood up for the smaller kids or the outsiders if someone bullied them.

Theory Input

After reading the theory behind the "Now & Then" Questionnaire, you are invited to predict your results prior to actually scoring it. After scoring, you will be asked to reflect and compare these results to your own initial assessment of your personality or life-style.

According to Adler (1930) our characteristic reactions to life ("life-style") are formulated before the age of five. Once such a framework (or template) has been selected, all new experiences tend to be subjectively interpreted or "filtered" through that original framework (Shulman, 1973). Although each of us has our own unique and creative style, early formative experiences help establish a "pre-formed working hypothesis" through which later preferences, values, and beliefs are evaluated and formulated.

Through the use of factor-analysis research, Thorne (1975) identified the following five trait descriptive categories: **aggressive, conforming, defensive, individualistic,** or **resistive.** In order to identify possible negative stereotyping plus to identify the strengths of these more clinically- oriented personality descriptions, the five life-style categories are given five representative animal labels: **tiger, chameleon, turtle, eagle,** and **salmon.**

Tigers are generally considered to be *aggressive.* They enjoy exercising authority, like to be the center of attention, and may insist on having their own way. Tigers usually were childhood leaders and continue in this role as adults. They are also enterprising, vigorous, and ambitious.

Chameleons are generally seen as *conforming.* They are flexible, and more likely to face problems directly. Chameleons frequently move up rapidly in business as they are dependable, hard working, and honest. They are cooperative, sociable, warm, helpful, and practical and may be aesthetic.

Turtles are generally thought to be *defensive.* They are earnest and resourceful and lead self-controlled, stable lives. Turtles are frequently "loners" with one or two close relationships. They are intuitive and sensitive and have some trouble admitting fallibility. Others may consider turtles to be stubborn because they have no interest in changing the status quo.

Eagles tend to be seen as *individualistic.* They are not concerned with public opinion and may be egotistic and infringe on the rights of others to get their own way. Eagles are capable, industrious, assertive, and adventurous — idealizing "progress." They are found in any field that esteems independence and are frequently entrepreneurial.

Salmon usually are considered *resistive.* They prefer to "swim against the current" rather than support "establishment" values. Salmon may take up causes against oppression and demand that they be heard. They are vigorous, progressive, and rebellious and dislike what they consider to be false social niceties.

Predicting Your Score

First, circle the adjectives you feel are most characteristic of you now.

Tiger	Chameleon	Turtle	Eagle	Salmon
aggressive	cooperative	stable	capable	persuasive
confident	sociable	self-controlled	industrious	independent
persistent	warm	placid	strong	vigorous
persuasive	helpful	earnest	forceful	demanding
self-reliant	diligent	defensive	foresighted	rebellious
independent	persistent	stubborn	clear thinking	protecting
initiator	gentle	apologetic	independent	forceful
potential leader	sincere	resourceful	spontaneous	progressive
ambitious	honest	insecure	intelligent	competitive

Now based on the adjectives you have circled, and your answers in the Questionnaire, prioritize which animal you feel represents you:

1._____

2._____

3._____

4._____

5._____

Do you predict any significant difference between your 'now' versus 'then' ratings?

_____

_____

Now proceed to the next page, and find out how you scored. You will note that all five animal types are presented sequentially throughout the questionnaire. Simply transfer your scores horizontally across the answer sheet, then add the total column vertically for each animal type.

"Now & Then" Life-Style Questionnaire Scoring Sheet — Number One

Instructions:

- ✧ Transfer the points you assigned each item on the questionnaire into the appropriate box.
- ✧ Add the number of points in each column. This will give you your raw score for your a) 'Now' sub-total, and b) 'Then' sub-total.
- ✧ Record the total of the sub-scores in the large boxes at the bottom of the page for your Combined Raw Score.

	Column I	Column II	Column III	Column IV	Column V
	Item 1	Item 2	Item 3	Item 4	Item 5
	6	7	8	9	10
	11	12	13	14	15
	16	17	18	19	20
	21	22	23	24	25
	26	27	28	29	30
'Now' Raw Score Sub-totals					
	31	32	33	34	35
	36	37	38	39	40
	41	42	43	44	45
	46	47	48	49	50
	51	52	53	54	55
	56	57	58	59	60
'Then' Raw Score Sub-totals					
Combined Raw Score Sub-totals					
	Tiger	Chameleon	Turtle	Eagle	Salmon

"Now & Then" Life-Style Questionnaire Scoring Sheet — Number Two

Instructions: (you may want to use three different color pens)

✧ Mark your 'Now' Raw Score Sub-total scores from the previous page into the correlating columns below, and draw a connecting line.

✧ Mark your 'Then' Raw Score Sub-total scores from the previous page into the correlating columns below, and draw a connecting line.

✧ Using the scale in parentheses, mark your Combined Raw Score Totals from the previous page into the correlating columns below, and draw a connecting line.

	Column I	Column II	Column III	Column IV	Column V
30 (60)	□	□	□	□	□
29 (58)	□	□	□	□	□
28 (56)	□	□	□	□	□
27 (54)	□	□	□	□	□
26 (52)	□	□	□	□	□
25 (50)	□	□	□	□	□
24 (48)	□	□	□	□	□
23 (46)	□	□	□	□	□
22 (44)	□	□	□	□	□
21 (42)	□	□	□	□	□
20 (40)	□	□	□	□	□
19 (38)	□	□	□	□	□
18 (36)	□	□	□	□	□
17 (34)	□	□	□	□	□
16 (32)	□	□	□	□	□
15 (30)	□	□	□	□	□
14 (28)	□	□	□	□	□
13 (26)	□	□	□	□	□
12 (24)	□	□	□	□	□
11 (22)	□	□	□	□	□
10 (20)	□	□	□	□	□
9 (18)	□	□	□	□	□
8 (16)	□	□	□	□	□
7 (14)	□	□	□	□	□
6 (12)	□	□	□	□	□
	Tiger	Chameleon	Turtle	Eagle	Salmon

As a final summary, now respond to the following questions:
How did your predictions compare with your final scores, as well as with your original animal selection?

_____

_____

_____

Were there any surprises? If so, how?

_____

_____

_____

Now apply the results of this questionnaire to your own understanding of your personal style. Write one or two paragraphs summarizing your self assessment of the strengths and weaknesses of your style.

_____

_____

_____

_____

_____

_____

_____

_____

_____

Situational Style

In The Once and Future King, T.H. White (1965) vividly describes the efforts that led the young Arthur (named "The Wart" prior to being crowned king of England) to successfully pull the sword Excalibur from the stone. As a child he was trained by Merlin the magician, a wizard displaying the uncanny ability to temporarily transport Arthur out of his own body into various other animals. Upon his return back to his own body, Merlin would then ask Arthur what lessons he had learned.

Later, as a young adolescent Arthur was serving as a page to his half-brother Sir Kay in an annual jousting tournament. Kay broke his sword in one joust and much to Arthur's embarrassment, he realized he had not brought a back-up sword. Hurriedly, he ran into the town square where he spied a sword protruding from a stone. Twice he tried to remove the sword, but his efforts were in vain.

It was then the lessons learned from the other animals became invaluable to him. In poetic fashion, White described the epic triumph as follows:

> He tied his reins round a post of the lych gate, strode up the gravel path, and took hold of the sword.

> "Come, sword," he said. "I must cry your mercy and take you for a better cause."

> "This is extraordinary," said the Wart. "I feel strange when I have hold of this sword, and I notice everything much more clearly. Look at the beautiful gargoyles of the church, and of the monastery which it belongs to. See how splendidly all the famous banners in the aisle are waving...it is music that I hear?"

> It was music, whether of pan-pipes or of recorders, and the light in the churchyard was so clear, without being dazzling, that one could have picked a pin out twenty yards away...

> He took hold of the handles with both hands, and strained against the stone. There was a melodious consort of the recorders, but nothing moved.

> He took hold of it again and pulled with all his might. The music played more strongly, and the light all about the churchyard glowed like amethysts; but the sword still stuck.

> "Oh, Merlin," cried the Wart, "help me to get this weapon."

> There was a kind of rushing noise, and a long chord played along with it. All round the churchyard there were hundreds of old friends. They rose over the church wall all together, like the Punch and Judy ghosts of

remembered days...They loomed round the church wall, the lovers and helpers of the Wart, and they all spoke solemnly in turn. They had come to help on account of love. Wart felt his power grow.

"Put your back into it," said a Luce (or pike) off one of the heraldic banners, "as you once did when I was going to snap you up. Remember that power springs from the nape of the neck."

"What about those forearms," asked a Badger gravely, "that are held together by a chest? Come along, my dear embryo, and find your tool."

A Merlin sitting at the top of the yew tree cried out, "Now then, Captain Wart, what is the first law of the foot? I thought I once heard something about never letting go?"

"Don't work like a stalling woodpecker," urged a Tawny Owl affectionately. "Keep up a steady effort, my duck, and you will have it yet."

A white-front said, "Now, Wart, if you were once able to fly the great North Sea, surely you can co-ordinate a few little wing-muscles here and there? Fold your powers together, with the spirit of your mind, and it will come out like butter. Come along, Homo sapiens, for all we humble friends of yours are waiting here to cheer."

The Wart walked up to the great sword for the third time. He put out his right hand softly and drew it out as gently as from a scabbard. (pp. 207-208)

Situational style" is a concept which indicates that greatness lies in the ability to both appreciate and utilize the strengths of others who differ from ourselves. For example, the Tiger offers the strength of decisive leadership, while the Chameleon contributes flexibility and adaptability. The turtle has a strong protective shell with which to withstand severe external trauma. The Eagle's gift is to soar high above a problem in order to see the "big picture." Conversely, the Salmon continually strives for improvements by courageously confronting and resisting the "status quo."

Separately each animal also has vulnerabilities or blind spots. But social interest is the ability to integrate and harmonize the total community, making it possible for one's own "Excalibur" to be pulled from the stone.

Classroom Application

Henry Dunkerson is a fourth grade teacher at Lafe Nelson Elementary School in Safford, Arizona. After completing a graduate course in Adlerian psychology, he utilized the "Now and Then Questionnaire" (see pg. 57) in the following creative way with his elementary students. Here is his first-person account — a very creative adaptation which he utilizes with his students. (1996)

> In *The Mixed-Up Chameleon* (1984) by Eric Carle, there was a chameleon who found that his life was not very exciting. He ate flies and changed colors, like all chameleons, but he wished to be different. Upon arriving at the zoo, the chameleon began wishing to be like other animals. His wishes were granted and before long he was part flamingo, fox, fish, deer, giraffe, turtle, elephant, seal, and human. With each change he made a new chameleon was drawn, forming a unique looking creature. At the end of the story, the chameleon was feeling hungry but was unable to catch a fly because he was so mixed up about who he was. He decided the best thing to do was to wish to be back to his original self. Of course his wish was granted and he turned back into a chameleon. This story has great possibilities when working with children on being whom they are. When they attempt to be someone they're not, they become mixed up and are unsure about whom they truly are and how they fit in. With this book, children can identify with the animals and relate it to themselves, making it easier to make the choice of being whom they are inside.

Henry goes on to suggest ways to incorporate his ideas into the Life-Style Assessment:

> Here is an idea for a self-esteem building activity for the classroom. After reading *The Mixed-Up Chameleon,* generate a discussion with your class about why the chameleon may have wanted to change and be different from what he was.

> Introduce the five animals from the Life-Style Assessment. Lead your class into a discussion about describing these animals using human characteristics. For instance the turtle might be described as shy and would prefer to be alone, while the tiger might be strong and prefer to be the leader. Try to avoid descriptions like "it has legs, feet, eyes" but work for human behavior characteristics "shy, brave, clever, etc."

> For this next activity you may want to have a class set of coloring pictures of each of the five animals. Then have each student choose one of the five animals that most closely resembles his/her own characteristics. Lead the class into a discussion on what features of the other four animals they would like to add to the animal they chose. Let them cut and paste these features to their animal. Have them write a descriptive paragraph about this new animal. Have them name their new animals and color them.

> Following this activity generate and lead discussion into how each person is unique. Help them conclude that everyone has many different

characteristics that make each of us unique individuals. End the discussion by having a writing activity where each student fully describes him/herself. They may include a drawing of themselves and include what makes them different from other people.

Expanding Your Social Interest

One key ingredient that is lacking in the above five clinical scales is **social interest**, or what O'Connell has termed "humanistic identification." Altruism, nurturing, compassion, and empathy need to be healthy additions to each typology. One of Adler's frequent prescriptions to his clients was to "go out and help *someone else* — you are too preoccupied with yourself!"

One of our goals in writing this workbook is obviously for you to learn greater self-awareness. That then hopefully will translate to your helping others through the utilization of your own gifts for the betterment of humanity. Although this workbook is meant to be a self-guided experiential process, we encourage you to use a partner if possible. Let 'Person A' interview 'Person B' and then switch roles. Then let 'Person B' share a summary of 'Person A' and 'Person A' share the summary for 'Person B.' Because each of us has our own blind spots, it makes it difficult but not impossible, to conduct our own life-assessment — so we encourage you to share the experience with a partner. Of course, the forms in this book can (and hopefully will) be used in a dyadic partner in a college or university class, a family education center, etc.

Sheldon Kopp observes that:

> Along the way, on his pilgrimage, each man must have the chance to tell his tale. And, as each man tells his tale, there must be another there to listen. But the other need not be a guru. He need only rise to the needs of the moment. There is an old saying that whenever two Jews meet, if one has a problem, the other automatically becomes a rabbi. (pp. 21–22)

Chapter Summary

In this chapter, Adlerian life-style theory has been explored within the context of a developmental Adlerian counseling approach. Specific interviewing considerations were applied to life-style assessments. To introduce the concept of personal style, a self-assessment "Now & Then" Life-Style Questionnaire was included. The concept of "situational style" has also been introduced. Chapter 3 will contain several actual assessment interview forms as a suggested guideline for obtaining formative information.

SAMPLE LIFE-STYLE INTERVIEW GUIDES

In this chapter, several representative life-style interview guides will be presented. They will include the following: 1) A structured interview suggested for use with both adolescents and adults; 2) A modified version for children under the age of 10; 3) A sample group life-style interview; 4) A mini-life-style interview, and 5) a "most memorable adolescent observation."

Since Adler so often used musical metaphors, perhaps one might consider the following structured formats as important introductory musical "scales" that serve as a useful guideline for beginning the skill of learning life-style interviewing skills. However, as one masters those scales, creative and artistic "improvisations" are encouraged.

Historical Overview to the Development of Life-Style Formats

Despite encouraging a creative approach to life-style assessment, the authors agree with Powers and Griffith (1987), who state that "Structure reduces uncertainty; it strengthens the possibility of a useful process and beneficial results." (p. 18) They then provide a good overview to some of the historical precursors to the various structured interview formats. The Ansbacher's (1964) reference Adler's early children's and adolescent life-style forms (1929a, pp. 110–14; 1930a, pp. 251–258; 1933a, pp. 200–203; 1933b, pp. 299–304). Even then, he recommended the forms as an "informal act," not to be adhered to rigidly. His childhood assessment featured fifteen basic questions, using the following subheading: "Disorders, social relationships, interests, recollections and dreams, discouraged behavior, and positive assets." His adult form featured eighteen questions to which he noted that "by adhering to it the experienced therapist will gain an extensive insight into the style of life of the individual already within about half an hour."

Dreikurs (1967, pp. 88–90) created a longer questionnaire from which many of the questions in the present authors recommended format originated. Harold Mosak and Bernard Shulman (1988) revised their format into a Life-Style Inventory (LSI), published and copyrighted by Accelerated Development, Inc., of Muncie, Indiana.

Similar forms can be found in Manaster & Corsini (1982), Sweeney (1989), and Eckstein, Baruth, and Mahrer (1982). Raymond and Betty Lowe (appendices H & I, in Baruth & Eckstein, 1981), created two separate forms, an "Interview Guide for Establishing the Life-Style," and "Life-Style Interpretation." Dinkmeyer, Dinkmeyer & Sperry (1987) report on Roy Kern's "The Life-Style Scale" (available from CMTI Press in Coral Springs, Florida), as well as their format. Powers & Griffith (1987) describe their own "initial interview inquiry" (pp. 32-66) as well as a "Life-Style Assessment Inquiry" (pp. 67–97) as part of what they describe the "psycho-clarity" process.

In this edition Eckstein has created his own suggested "life-style interview" (LSI).

Part I explores the person's current "'Way of Being' in the World" by utilizing what Dreikurs (1967) calls the "subjective situation" in which all the client's concerns, complaints, illnesses, stressors, etc., are identified. The "objective situation" then focuses on one's own self-assessment of the five life tasks. Both sets of information are linked by what Dreikurs called "The Question"..."What would be different if you had all of these problems or concerns solved?" The answer to such a question helps explain the client's complaints and emotional stresses. It also indicates in what area the person is experiencing difficulty and where or on whom the problem is centered.

Next, in Part II, comes sibling descriptions, including sibling ratings. A description of one's parent(s) completes the family atmosphere. Of course, not all children grew up in a single family. In the case of an orphanage or a foster-home, one's first social group or family equivalent should be used. Also if one had no brothers or sisters, early childhood friends and/or cousins should be used as the basis for comparison. Cultural and ethnic heritage is also examined.

Part III consists of the early recollections (ER's) and recurring dreams. Recommended guidelines for early recollections recording include:

1. Introduce early recollection as follows: "Think back as far as you can and tell me the first thing you remember."

2. Distinguish between an early recollection and a report. An early recollection should be a specific event beginning with "one day I remember..."; Conversely, a report is more global typified by: "I (or we) used to..." or "Many times I..."

3. Also make sure the incident is personally remembered by the child as opposed to having been seen in a photograph or in home movies or

having been reported to the individual by someone else (i.e., a parent, sibling, or other significant person). While it is valuable to be aware of what others said to and about the interviewee, his or her own personal experience is the focus of early recollections.

4. Be certain to write down all the events exactly as stated word by word in the person's own memory, although some abbreviation maybe necessary in an extremely long language. The goal is to obtain first-person narratives using the clients own exact language.

5. After the person finishes speaking of the incident, encourage additional information by asking "and then what happened?" The memory itself is complete when the interviewee responds with "that's all I can remember."

6. After the report itself is recorded, ask (a) "what was most vivid about the incident?," and (b) "what were your feelings during this event?"

7. Obtain any similar re-occurring or formative dreams in a similar format as the early recollections.

8. A good guideline is getting three to five early recollections.

9. If a person says he or she can't remember any specific events, encourage the individual to "make one up." Projective theory will be just as valid for such a "fantasied" memory as a "real" one.

Life-Style Interview (LSI)

by Daniel Eckstein

Adapted from previous life-style instruments developed by Harold Mosak, Bernard Schulman, Robert Powers, Jane Griffin and Frank Walton

I. The Interviewee's Current "way of being in the world."
    A. The Subjective Situation:

    What are some of the things which bring you joy and happiness in your life now?

    _____

    _____

    What are your specific concerns physically and emotionally?

    _____

    _____

    What are your major stressors? Any major illness or sickness? School?

    _____

    _____

    B. The Objective Situation

    1. Rate yourself on a 1-10 scale, 1 being very low and 10 being very high, relative to your satisfaction with the following five tasks of living — (plot the numbers for each task on the following graph — ask for specific reasons why the person gave each numerical rating and fill in the response beneath the chart on the provided lines (2. Explanation of Ratings.)

	Work (or School)	Friendship	Love	Self-Esteem	Spiritual/ Existential
10	☐	☐	☐	☐	☐
9	☐	☐	☐	☐	☐
8	☐	☐	☐	☐	☐
7	☐	☐	☐	☐	☐
6	☐	☐	☐	☐	☐
5	☐	☐	☐	☐	☐
4	☐	☐	☐	☐	☐
3	☐	☐	☐	☐	☐
2	☐	☐	☐	☐	☐
1	☐	☐	☐	☐	☐

2. Explanation of Ratings

   a. Work: _____

   _____

   _____

   b. Friendship: _____

   _____

   _____

   c. Love: _____

   _____

   _____

   d. Self-Esteem: _____

   _____

   _____

   e. Spiritual/Existential: _____

   _____

   _____

C. The "question"

If you had all of these concerns resolved, how would your life be different?

_____

_____

_____

_____

_____

_____

_____

_____

_____

II.   Family Atmosphere

A.   Describe your awareness of how you came to be named.

1. For example, who decided your name?

_____

_____

_____

2. Were you named for someone or something special?

_____

_____

_____

_____

3. How do you feel about your name?

_____

_____

_____

_____

4. What nicknames have you had, and what are your personal reactions to them?

_____

_____

_____

_____

5. Have you ever wanted to (or actually) changed your name, e.g. last name through marriage? If not, what name do you wish to have and why? If you have actually changed your name, how do you feel about your new name(s)?

_____

_____

_____

_____

_____

B. Sibling Descriptions

Write the name and age of each sibling (including yourself) in descending order beginning with the oldest. Include any deceased siblings, siblings separated from the family, or living in institutions or elsewhere. Also note any other known pregnancies terminated by abortion, miscarriage or still-birth, entering the appropriate in the ordinal positions. Include any *step-siblings* and note when they entered the family. Using your age as a baseline, note the differences in years of age, plus or minus, between each other sibling and yourself.

When you have listed all the siblings, describe each sibling again including yourself. Circle the appropriate sex, male or female, for each sibling. (Attach another sheet if needed for more siblings.)

Sibling 1			Sibling 2			Sibling 3		
Name:		M F	Name:		M F	Name:		M F
Age:	+/-:		Age:	+/-:		Age:	+/-:	
Description:			Description:			Description:		

Sibling 4			Sibling 5			Sibling 6		
Name:		M F	Name:		M F	Name:		M F
Age:	+/-:		Age:	+/-:		Age:	+/-:	
Description:			Description:			Description:		

C. Further Sibling Descriptions

The following questions are to be answered as you would have responded when you were a young child of three to eight years of age.

1. Who was most different from you? How? If you are an only child, in your peer group who was the most different from you? How?

_____

_____

_____

2. Who was most like you? How?

_____

_____

3. Who fought and argued?

_____

4. Who played together?

_____

5. Who took care of whom?

_____

6. Who had a handicap or prolonged illness?

_____

D. Sibling Ratings

Following each adjective or description indicate which siblings demonstrated that characteristic most and least. If you are at neither extreme, show in which direction you were inclined by pointing an arrow. An example might be:

Characteristic	Most		Least
Idealistic	Sam	⟶	Rachel

This would indicate that regarding idealism, Sam was most idealistic, Rachel was least idealistic, and you tended to be on the least idealistic end of the continuum. If you are an only child, rate yourself in comparison to your peer group you associated with as a child or with "children in general." These ratings should focus on your personal opinion of your family situation during the first eight years of your life.

Now respond to each of the following characteristics:

Characteristic	Most	Least
1. Intelligence	_____	_____
2. Hardest Worker	_____	_____
3. Best Grades in School	_____	_____
4. Helping Around the House	_____	_____
5. Conforming	_____	_____
6. Rebellious	_____	_____
7. Trying to Please	_____	_____
8. Critical of Others	_____	_____
9. Considerateness	_____	_____
10. Selfishness	_____	_____
11. Having Own Way	_____	_____
12. Sensitive — Easily Hurt	_____	_____
13. Temper Tantrums	_____	_____
14. Sense of Humor	_____	_____
15. Idealistic	_____	_____
16. Materialistic	_____	_____
17. Standards of Accomplishment	_____	_____
18. Most Athletic	_____	_____
19. Strongest	_____	_____
20. Attractive	_____	_____
21. Spoiled	_____	_____
22. Punished	_____	_____
23. Spontaneous	_____	_____

E. Description of Parents *(ask the client to choose which parent he/she wishes to describe first)*

1. **Father**

   Current Age: _____ Occupation: _____

   Description of Father: _____

   _____

   _____

   Father's favorite child? Why? _____

   _____

   Ambitions for children? _____

   _____

   Relationship to children _____

   _____

   Sibling most like father? How? _____

   _____

2. **Mother**

   Current Age: _____ Occupation: _____

   Description of Mother: _____

   _____

   _____

   Mother's favorite child? Why? _____

   _____

   Ambitions for children? _____

   _____

   Relationship to children? _____

   _____

   Sibling most like mother? How? _____

   _____

3. Which of your parents (if any) was your personal favorite? Why?

   _____

   _____

4. Describe the nature of your parents' relationship.

_____

_____

_____

5. What was the "family motto" your parents had for their children?

_____

_____

6. What do you feel were some of the primary values that your parent(s) (or parent equivalents) had for the children?

_____

_____

7. To what extent did you accept, reject, or modify the family motto and other family values?

_____

_____

8. **Stepfather or stepmother** (if appropriate)

Current Age _____ Occupation: _____

Description: _____

_____

_____

Favorite child? Why? _____

_____

Ambitions for children?_____

_____

Relationship to children? _____

_____

Sibling most like him/her? How? _____

_____

9. If a stepfather or stepmother has been in your life, how has that affected you? _____

_____

_____

10. If there were other parental figures in your family, describe the effect they have had on your outlook on life.

_____

_____

11. Were there any other significant people in your life in childhood (aunts, uncles, cousins, teachers, priest, rabbi, minister, friend, etc.?) If so, describe their effect on your life:

_____

_____

_____

12. Describe your opinion of the impact of your own cultural heritage — what special holidays do you observe?

_____

_____

_____

F. Childhood and Adolescent Development Considerations

1. What were your favorite TV stories, movies, books, or fairy-tales that you remember as a child? What was it about them that you liked?

_____

_____

_____

2. What were some of your major childhood fears or traumas?

_____

_____

_____

_____

3. What were your major hopes and dreams as a child?

_____

_____

_____

_____

4. Were you ever physically or sexually abused? If so, by whom?

_____

_____

5. Were there any incidents of alchohol and/or drug abuse in your family? If so, describe its impact on you.

_____

_____

_____

6. Describe your bodily development (height, weight, speed, strength, etc.) as an adolescent in relationship to your peers. Were you more mature, average with others, or a "late bloomer"? Any specific difficulties (e.g., bedwetting, rocking back and forth)?

_____

_____

_____

_____

7. Describe a memorable or formulative adolescent experience:

_____

_____

_____

a. What were your feelings about the incident?

_____

_____

b. What conclusion do you feel you made about that incident?

_____

_____

III. Early Recollections

Think back as far as you can and describe the first specific incident that you remember. Describe what feeling you had at that time. Make sure it is a specific situation and not a generalization. When you have completed the information for the first incident, do the same with the second situation. Try to do this for at least three or four incidents. If you had a memorable or recurring dream when you were a child, describe the dream and discuss how you felt.

INTERVIEWER NOTE: Write the ER word for word in the person's own language. Keep asking "and then what happened?" until the memory fades from conscious awareness.

   A. First Incident

      Description:_____

      _____

      _____

      Most vivid moment:_____

      _____

      Your feeling: _____

      _____

   B. Second Incident

      Description:_____

      _____

      _____

      Most vivid moment:_____

      _____

      Your feeling: _____

      _____

   C. Third Incident

      Description:_____

      _____

      _____

Most vivid moment:_____

_____

Your feeling: _____

_____

D. Memorable or Recurring Dream

Description:_____

_____

_____

Most vivid moment:_____

_____

Your feeling: _____

_____

E. Global Reflections on all Memories and Dreams:

1. If you could change anything or anyone in these incidents, how would they be different?

_____

_____

_____

_____

2. Can you think of any connections these past events may have to your present life now?

_____

_____

_____

_____

3. What do you think some **future** indications, trends, or patterns might be indicated from these formulative experiences?

_____

_____

_____

_____

◆

4. Is there anything else you would like to add to this interview to assist me in learning more about formative events/experiences/people in your life?

_____

_____

_____

_____

_____

_____

_____

_____

_____

_____

5. Please conclude by sharing a "peak experience," an extra special moment in your life when you felt especially happy.

_____

_____

_____

_____

_____

_____

_____

_____

_____

_____

Thank you!

Children's Life-Style Guide (CLG)

Adopted from Dinkmeyer & Dinkmeyer. "Concise Counseling Assessment: The Children's Life-Style Guide." *Elementary School Guidance & Guidance & Counseling* 12, no. 2 (1977): 117–124.

Don Dinkmeyer, Sr., & Don Dinkmeyer, Jr., (1977) developed a children's life-style guide (CLG). The CLG has eight major sections, six of which are completed with information from the child, while two are summaries by the counselor. Additional information and a case study using the CLG is found in Baruth & Eckstein, 1981.

I.   Family Constellation

    A.   First list all members of the family from oldest to youngest.

_____

_____

_____

    B.   Then ask the following questions:

        1. Who is most different from you? How?

_____

_____

_____

        2. Who is most like you? How?

_____

_____

_____

        3. What was life like before you went to school?

_____

_____

_____

II.   Functioning at Life Tasks

    A.   Socially: How do you get along with adults? Children?

_____

_____

_____

    B.   Work: How do things go for you in school?

_____

_____

_____

    C.   What subject do you like best? Like least? Why

_____

_____

_____

    D.   What would you like to be when you grow up?

_____

_____

    E.   What do you fear the most?

_____

_____

_____

III. Family Atmosphere

    A. What kind of a person is your father?

_____

_____

_____

    B. What kind of a person is your mother?

_____

_____

_____

C. Which of the children is most like your father? In what ways?

_____

_____

_____

D. Which of the children is most like your mother? In what ways?

_____

_____

_____

IV. Sibling Characteristics

A series of questions (such as "who is most intelligent?") are asked until a child makes a response to each item with respect to other siblings or other children in general.

A. Intelligent _____

B. Hardest worker_____

C. Best grades in school _____

D. Conforming _____

E. Rebellious _____

F. Helps around the house _____

G. Critical _____

H. Considerate _____

I. Selfish _____

J. Tries to please_____

K. Sensitive — feelings easily hurt_____

L. Temper _____

M. Materialistic, likes to get things _____

N. Most friends _____

O. Most spoiled_____

P. High standards of achievement _____

Q. Athletic_____

R. Strongest _____

S. Attractive _____

T. Most punished _____

V.   Early Recollections

What can you remember that is a specific event (like a picture of one certain time) from when you were younger? What were you feeling at the time?

A.   Memory One _____

_____

_____

Feeling _____

_____

B.   Memory Two _____

_____

_____

Feeling _____

_____

C.   Memory Three _____

_____

_____

Feeling _____

_____

VI.   Three Wishes and Fantasy

A.   If you could have three wishes, what would they be?

1._____

2._____

3._____

B.   If you were going to pretend to be an animal, which would you choose? Why?

_____

_____

_____

_____

VII & VIII Summary Assets

Utilizing the information in Chapter 4 on interpretation skills, write a summary of the family constellation, including birth order and sibling ratings. Summarize general life-style themes, the "Number-one Priority," and early recollections.

_____

_____

_____

_____

_____

_____

_____

_____

_____

_____

_____

_____

_____

_____

_____

_____

_____

_____

_____

_____

_____

_____

_____

_____

Sharing Life-Styles Within a Group Context

Reproduced from Walton, Francis. "Group Workshop with Adolescents." *Individual Psychologist* 12, no.1 (1975): 26-28. Used by permission of the publisher and author.

Frank Walton (1975) adapted the following format originally developed by Robert Powers for use in adolescent and adult groups.

Part I: A Guide for Presenting Yourself to the Seminar

A. You have ten minutes, uninterrupted, in which to tell us who you are.

B. Stay, as much as possible, in the present tense. Later on you will have an opportunity to tell us about your childhood.

C. Life challenges each of us, and each person is now approaching its challenges in a way unique to himself. Tell us about your responses to these challenges.

    1. What kind of friends have you made? What kind of friend are you? How do you get along with strangers in chance meetings? How do people treat you generally? How do you feel about other people, most of the time?

    2. What kind of work do you do? What kind of worker are you? Do you enjoy what you are doing? Do those with whom or for whom you work appreciate your contributions?

    3. Whom do you love? What kinds of problems have you had over loving and being loved? Do sex, closeness, and intimacy have a comfortable place in your life or not? What does masculinity mean to you? What does femininity mean to you? How do you measure up to whatever you expect of yourself as a man or a woman?

Part II: A Guide for Sharing in Responses

A. Someone has just spent ten minutes presenting himself. How did you receive what he has presented?

B. Did you recognize things in yourself that were mentioned? Was it easy or difficult to understand him or her? Did he sound strange or familiar?

C. How do you feel toward one another? Did your feelings toward anyone change as a result of the sharing? How?

D. Do you feel invited to act in any particular way toward another? Did you welcome that invitation or resent it? What would you like to do for this person? What would you like to do with this person? What would you like to do to this person?

Part III: A Guide for Drawing Your Family Constellation

In childhood each of us learned how to define the place he had amongst others. Help the members of the seminar to see the kind of place you had as a pre-adolescent child in your family.

A. How many children were there in your family and where did you fit in amongst them? How were you different from the others, and how were you like them? Which of the others was most nearly like you, and which was most different? What were you good at? What was hard for you?

B. What was your father like? Who was his favorite?

C. What did he expect from you?

D. How did you feel about his expectations?

E. What was your mother like? Who was her favorite? What did she expect from you?

F. How did you feel about her expectations?

G. How did your parents get along with each other? What were their differences/arguments/fights about? To which parent did you feel closer? Why?

H. Were grandparents or other relatives important to you? How?

I. Did anything change at adolescence? How? What did puberty, physical development, and dating mean to you?

1. For boys: What did "being a man" mean to you? Did you think you would have been happier, luckier, better off if you had been born a girl?

2. For girls: What did "being a woman" mean to you? Did you think you would have been happier, luckier, better off if you had been born a boy?

89

Part IV: A Guide for Discussing a Family Constellation

    A. Can you share any feelings about yourself in your family with the person who just told you about his or her childhood?

    B. Can you understand this person better? How?

    C. Can you see something as a result of the sharing which initially didn't make sense to you?

    D. What more do you want to know about this person?

    E. Can you see a relationship between the role played as a child, in the family and among other children, and the way in which he or she has tried to find a place in this seminar?

    F. Each of us has the private goal of playing a certain kind of social role.

Parts I and II are repeated for each member of the group before the group moves on to Parts III and IV, which are also repeated for each member of the group. A fifth and sixth part can be added at the option of the leader. Part V would consist of obtaining two or three early memories, while Part VI would be devoted to the interpretation of the memories by the leader and participants. These additional segments are limited to ten minutes each in the fashion of Part I through IV.

A group may terminate at the conclusion of Part IV or Part VI, or it may continue to meet periodically in order to help group members work at relating the increased awareness of the purposes and patterns of their behavior to the challenges of social living.

Mini Life-Style Interview

Frank Walton has also developed the following five, what he calls, "Brief Life-Style Clues." These can be used as part of a general counseling session or part of a family or couples session, or in a group setting. It provides a brief "snapshot" or a "one-minute manager's life-style" from which the therapist can formulate some tentative hypotheses.

Brief Life-Style Formulation

My effort to be encouraging to clients (by being helpful to them quickly) stimulated me to be parsimonious in my questioning when gathering life-style clues. Clients can make substantial progress in understanding their approach to life (and its relationship to presenting problems) in the initial session + the practitioner can offer a holistic interpretation of the answers to five questions. Additional data can be gathered in subsequent sessions when desired.

— Francis X. Walton

1. I was the kid who always...

    _____

    _____

2. Which brother or sister was most different from you? How?

    _____

    _____

3. a) What was most positive about your mother?

    _____

    _____

    ... about your father?

    _____

    _____

    b) What did you reject or wish was different about your mother?

    _____

    _____

... about your father?

_____

_____

4. Do you remember making some conclusion or observation about life when you were a child or teenager that seemed very important? Perhaps a conclusion about how you wanted life to be different for you when you became an adult, or perhaps something you wanted to be exactly the same when you became an adult?

_____

_____

_____

_____

_____

_____

5. Describe two early memories (recollections).

_____

_____

_____

_____

_____

_____

_____

_____

Most Memorable Observation

—Francis X. Walton, Ph.D.

Adapted from a program presented at the North American Society of Adlerian Psychology, Minneapolis, MN, May 26, 1995 by permission of the author."

In recent years, it has occurred to me that when we are in our early teens, somewhere between the ages of 12-15, people often observe their family life and draw a conclusion about it. Sometimes the conclusion is positive, such as, *'This or that aspect of the atmosphere around here is really appealing to me. When I get to be an adult, I'm going to do everything I can to make it this way in my family.'*

Much more frequently the conclusion is framed in negative terms: *'This or that aspect of the atmosphere around here is really distasteful to me , or even, 'I hate the fact that... When I get to be an adult, I'm going to do everything I can do to avoid this sort of thing in my family.'*

Such a conclusion, whether positive or negative, reveals circumstances that the client regards as a state of inferiority. The technique reveals what psychiatrist Rudolf Dreikurs referred to as the 'hidden reason' for a client's behavior.

The compensation to avoid the imagined state of inferiority is frequently directly related to the manner in which the client contributes to the presenting problem.

In the introduction to his 1995 videotape, Walton notes:

My experience has been that interpretation of the observation allows counselors and therapists to understand and help parents understand why they may choose to offer the sort of parenting leadership they offer, and what it is they fear that makes it so difficult for some parents to part with the approaches they have been using.

He cites the following three key influences of one's most memorable adolescent experience:

1. An overemphasis on the **likelihood** of its occurrence.

2. An overemphasis on the **negative influence.**

3. A tendency to **underestimate** one's ability to effectively deal with similar situations.

Walton's videotape can be ordered for $30.00 plus $2.00 shipping and han- dling by writing to:

ADLERIAN CHILD CARE BOOKS
Box 210206
Columbia, SC 29221
or by calling:
(803) 798-0300
Fax: (803) 798-9005

A. My most memorable adolescent observation is:

_____

_____

_____

B. The way I see this, such an observation has "played itself out" in my
life by:

_____

_____

_____

C. Future implications for me are that:

_____

_____

_____

Chapter Summary

In this chapter we presented specific suggested life-style assessment forms
for adolescents and adults, for children, for use in a group setting, for a
formulative adolescent observation, and for a "one-minute manager's" mini
life-style interview. Chapter 4 will focus on beginning interpretive skills.

LIFE-STYLE INTERPRETIVE SKILLS

In Chapter 3, various formats for obtaining life-style information were presented. The purpose of this chapter is to provide beginning life-style interpretive guidelines. The chapter will begin with a general overview to the issues of counselor interpretation from several theoretical perspectives. Specifically, the developmental focus will be on life tasks, family atmosphere, sibling ratings, birth order, and early recollections. Additional life-style features to consider in the interpretation phase include the "#1 Priority," general life-style themes and a recommended systematic summary. A final section will focus on specific empirical research articles relative to life-styles.

The Role of Interpretation in Counseling

Portions of this section are abstracted from Clark, A. "An Examination of the Technique of Interpretation in Counseling." *Journal of Counseling Development* 73 (1995): 483-490. With permission of the publisher, The American Counseling Association.

An essential aspect of lifestyle assessment in an Adlerian counseling relationship consists of the following four developmental sequences: 1) A therapeutic relationship between counselor and client, 2) a psychological investigation (life-style); 3) psychological interpretation and 4) Re-orientation and re-education (Dreikurs, 1973). The present section begins with a summary of several major theoretical approaches. An actual case study by Eckstein involving "reframing" a "perceived minus into a plus" by a former seventh grade teacher will conclude the section.

Arthur Clark (1995) notes that interpretation as a counseling technique generates controversy among counselors and researchers in terms of both its therapeutic value and its strategic application. Proponents of interpretation believe that the technique therapeutically expands the frame of reference of clients (Brummer, Shostrum, & Abrego, 1989; Ivey, 1994) whereas critics assert that interpretation reduces the autonomy of clients while focusing on the past at the expense of the present. (Helner & Jessel, p. 174; Napier & Gershenfeld, 1988).

Definitions

Baruth & Huber (1985) define interpretation as explaining "Connections among seemingly isolated information (in the client's view) from the client. In doing so, the client is offered a different perspective on his or her concerns." (p. 160). Ivey (1994) writes that in interpretation "The counselor supplies the client with a new frame of reference and understanding. The words and meanings may be elicited from the client, but they are the counselor's impressions." (p. 244).

In Clark's (1995) synthesis, interpretation has the following two common themes: 1) The client is introduced to *a new frame of reference.* The meaning or frame of reference of a client's experience is reconceptualized when a counselor imparts an alternative perspective; and 2) Most definitions implicitly or explicitly are related to a *theory* of counseling and psychotherapy. However, interpretations may also be drawn from the counselor's personal observations, exclusive of counseling theory.

Frame of Reference and Interpretation

A component that consistently appears in the definitions and discussions of interpretation is that of the counselor explaining a new alternative perspective that goes beyond a client's awareness (Gelso & Fretz, 1992). With an interpretation, the intent of the counselor is to explain rather than merely describe a client's behavior and to change a client's frame of reference in a therapeutic direction. The counselor presents a point of view that is discrepant from the client's frame of reference and attempts to lead the client to experience a new perspective and coherent meaning. If the counselor's alternative and discrepant point of view is assimilated by a client through an interpretation, the individual begins to construe phenomena differently and, as a consequence, is positioned to act more adaptively (Strong & Claiborn, 1982).

Levy (1963) proposed a dual nature of interpretation based on *semantic* and propositional aspects. A semantic aspect of interpretation transposes the frame of reference of a client by altering the meaning of experiences through a *relabeling* procedure. A propositional aspect of interpretation transforms the frame of reference of a client by relating experiences that had not been previously connected, generally through a body of doctrine. For example, when a counselor reconceptualizes a client's self-proclaimed perception of being a "perfectionist" to one of being "highly organized" this involves a semantic aspect of interpretation. If a counselor associates a client's highly organized behavior with a need to please his or her parents, this relates to a propositional aspect of interpretation (Clark, 1995).

Some specific examples follow: A client's evaluation of his or her behavior is revised from "stubborn" to "determined." An individual's "patient" response to his or her spouse's alcoholism is reconstrued as "enabling." In a family system, perceptions of a daughter's acting out behavior is reframed from being "out of control" to being "scared or frightened." A propositional aspect of interpretation suggests causal ***relationships*** in a client's experience based on a counselor's theoretical orientation may be subdivided into two forms: generalizations and constructions (Levy, 1963). A generalization involves relationships or contingencies between events or classes of events such as when a client withdraws in challenging interpersonal situations. A construction attempts to account for causal relationships or to present a causal framework that is consistent with the client's behavior. For example, a counselor may propose that the submissive behavior of a client represents the defense mechanism of repression that the person developed in response to oppressive parental relationships.

Aspects of Interpretation and Attributions

Causal attributions establish relationships between referents that had not been previously connected. As an example, a client's lack of assertiveness may be related to a parental injunction, such as "Don't succeed," adopted from his or her childhood. In addition to causal attributions, dispositional attributions are used in counseling to ascribe behavioral qualities or characteristics of individuals to a client (Harvey & Weary, 1981). A client, for instance, may describe his or her teacher's behavior as intrusive and excessively demanding. When the counselor states, "It is also possible to view your teacher as being interested in you and believing that you can meet high standards." Dispositional attributions are inherent in semantic aspects of interpretations when a counselor recategorizes observed phenomena in a client's experience (Clark, 1995).

Although counselor attributions do not necessarily result in behavior change, they do provide a coherent framework that suggests a direction for change. Through a social influence model, the counselor presents discrepant information to the client, which provides a conceptual scheme related to a client's problem (Frank, 1973).

Why Should Interpretations be used in Counseling?

Clark (1995) observes that clear differences exist among practitioners and researchers on the value or even appropriateness of interpretation in counseling. Critics reject interpretation as a viable technique because it is perceived as undermining the counseling relationship, minimizing or subverting client responsibility, and restricting the counseling process to an intellectualized endeavor. In contrast, proponents of interpretation in counseling contend that the technique advances the counseling relationship, extends the assumption of client responsibility, and fosters client self-understanding gained through insight.

Interpretation and the Counseling Relationship

Carl Rogers consistently questioned the value of the counselor imposing his or her frame of reference on the client. Rogers (1942, p. 205) cautioned, "The more accurate the interpretation, the more likely it is to encounter defensive resistance. The counselor and his interpretations become something to be feared."

However, proponents of interpretations acknowledge such positive contributions of the technique to the counseling relationship as promoting client disclosure, enhancing counselor credibility and communicating therapeutic attitudes; increased client self-understanding and goal setting (Dyer & Vriend, 1975). Egan (1994) stated that interpretations provide an opportunity for counselors to demonstrate their caring, concern, and involvement with clients.

Interpretation and Client Responsibility

A potential disadvantage of interpretations is the temptation for counselors to impose their personal frame of reference on the client in an intrusive manner (Napier & Gershenfeld, 1988). The potential for a counselor's interpretations to provide excuses for a client's behavior is another criticism of the technique (i.e. "My counselor told me that I m a victim of circumstances.") Counselors who use interpretations may also assume responsibility for a client and fosters a dependent relationship in the elevated role of "grand interpreter"; it may limit the individual's self-exploration and self-discovery, as the counselor controls the process and content of the counseling experience during an interpretive sequence.

However, interpretations may actually increase a client's responsibility and control by generating considerations that ultimately enable the person to make choices from a broader range of alternatives (Weiner, 1975). As a client becomes aware of new perspectives through an interpretation, the individual may also make a responsible choice to accept, reject, or revise the interpretation. Brummer, Shostrum, and Abrego (1989) suggest that for some clients it is necessary to examine past issues and link them to current functioning to work toward resolving conflicts and unfinished business.

Interpretation and Client Insight

Rogers (1942) noted the limited relationship between client insight and behavior change by observing that, "It has come to be recognized that we do not change the client's behavior very effectively simply by giving him an intellectual picture of its patterning, no matter how accurate" (p.27). Many clients improve their behavior without the use of interpretation, and others gain insight through interpretations but continue to demonstrate dysfunctional actions. A related concern is that interpretations in counseling may produce a retreat into an intellectual examination of a client's problems (Gelso & Fretz, 1992; Troemel-Ploetz, 1980). Rather than dealing with conditions more directly, clients may over intellectualize conflicts as a means of avoiding expression of affect through abstract verbalizations. Spiegel and Hill (1989) identified client self-esteem, severity of disturbance, level of cognitive complexity, and psychological mindedness as moderating variable that need to be considered by the counselor when using interpretations.

Others view insight gained through interpretations as an intentional means to promote new and more rational perspectives. By gaining an in-depth understanding of the pattern of his or her functioning, the possibility for deliberate choice and behavior change is advanced. Furthermore, interpretations facilitate client emotional involvement (Brummer, Shostrum, & Abrego, 1989). Martin and Stelmaczonek (1988) reported that individuals found insight and understanding among the most significant factors and were able to recall the learnings up to 6 months after concluding counseling.

How Are Interpretations Used In Counseling?

To clarify how interpretations are used in counseling, content and explication issues are important considerations. The content of interpretation relates to the meaning and the words the counselor uses to express him- or herself and is largely based on the counselor's theoretical framework in treatment with a client (Claiborn, 1982). A counselor's explication of an interpretation will focus on the variables of timing, discrepancy, and form. Specific guidelines on timing, or when to deliver an interpretation, are usually derived from "theory, love and experience" (Spiegel & Hill, 1989, p. 126). Discrepancy involves the extent of the difference between a client's and a counselor's frame of reference in the context of an interpretation, and form relates to how interpretations are express by a counselor. (Clark, 1995)

Content of Interpretations

Possible topics for interpretation are wide-ranging and largely focus on deficiencies that inhibit the development or adaptive functioning of an individual (Baruth & Huber, 1985). Classical psychoanalytic defense mechanisms, dreams, and resistance (Auld & Hyman, 1991); and an expanded contemporary list includes conflicts, dynamics, impulses, personality traits, physical reactions, and gestures (Garduk & Haggard, 1972). Weiner (1975), suggested that the content of interpretations should focus on issues in a client's life that are "unusual, ineffective, inappropriate, contradictory, irrational, self-defeating, or anxiety arousing in actions, thoughts, and feelings" (p. 121).

Attempts have been made to develop interpretation content systems. Spiegel and Hill (1989) suggested the following as categories: obstacles to change, self-awareness, awareness of feelings, clarification of unconscious elements, and stressful life events. A categorical interpretation content framework may also be based on three increasingly comprehensive levels: situational, constructional, and thematical (Clark, 1993). At the situational level, content topics are broad in scope and reflect immediate and contextual conflicts in an individual's life. For example, a client may be expressing a conflict between accepting a new job or remaining in a current position, and the counselor offers a situational level interpretation, "Could it be that if you make a decision the excitement of a job search will be over for you?" Adlerians use such a statement to reflect the "payoff" or secondary gain from such behavior.

At the constructional content level, patterns of dysfunctional behaviors are conceptualized through various counseling and psychotherapy orientations. Examples of maladaptive patterns include Adler's basic mistakes

100

(Lundin, 1989), Ellis' irrational ideas (Ellis, 1962), Beck's cognitive distortions (Beck & Weisharr, 1989), Berne's games (Berne, 1972), transference (Auld & Hyman, 1991), and defense mechanisms (Clark, 1991). A client, for example, may repeatedly state the basic mistake. "Nothing that I do ever turns out right." The counselor might offer an interpretation, "Could it actually be that you think that almost everything you do has to be perfect?"

Thematical content levels involve broad and enduring personal convictions that affect a client's entire personality functioning. Adler's life style (Adler, 1931/1980) and Berne's scripts (Berne, 1972) are representative of thematic patterns of behavior established early in an individual's life. For example, a client may repeatedly be involved in fights and disputes, and the counselor offers and interpretation, "Is it possible that the conflicts that you get into with other people provide you with excitement in your life that is so important to you?" This interpretation may result from the counselor's knowledge of the client's life style: "Life must continually be exciting for me" (Clark, 1995).

Factors Influencing the Effectiveness of Interpretations.

The following three variables are significant issues regarding the timing of interpretations.

1. *Timing.* Baruth and Huber (1985) contend that establishing a counseling relationship that has a trusting and exploratory atmosphere sets conditions for interpretation accordingly in the counseling process. However, Ellis (1968) stated that he "does not wait for the patient to be ready for major interpretations" (p. 237). Instead, he immediately clarifies client issues and begins to challenge the individual's irrational ideas. Interpretations need to be repeated to a client to allow the individual to clarify and assimilate their meanings (Levy, 1984; Spiegel & Hill, 1989). They are also more effective when a client is experiencing pertinent issues in the here and now related to the interpretation (Brummer, Shostrum, & Abrego, 1989; Weiner, 1975).

2. *Discrepancy.* Discrepancy refers to the magnitude of the disparity between the frame of reference expressed by the counselor and the client's own frame of reference (Claiborn, 1982). Ellis (1995) stated that he usually makes direct, depth-centered interpretations beginning with the initial client interview; however, that it is the irrational ideas or cognitions that are attacked, not the personhood of the client.

3. *Form.* Interpretations may be phrased by the counselor in absolute or certain terms ("You worry about many things because...") or in a tentative or approximate way ("Could it be possible that...") Absolute interpretations convey a decisive and emphatic tone whereas tentative interpretations are presented in the form of a hypothesis, often phrased as a question. For example, the Adlerian approach of A) "Do you wonder why you _____?" B) "Would you mind if I tell you what I think?" "Could it be that _____?" For example, a child constantly sharpening his pencil would be told that, "Could it be that you want your teacher's attention?" (Goal disclosure) The counselor then looks for a spontaneous "recognition reflex" to see if that observation "fits" for the child. It is important to note that it is ultimately the client who decides the "correctness" of the interpretation.

Nelsen (1996) utilizes the following reflective questions to facilitate client self-understanding: a) What happened? b) What caused it to happen? c) What did you learn from it? d) What can you do to solve the problem?

Case Study:
Reframing a Perceived "Minus" into a Perceived "Plus"
— A Personal Example

In *The Encouragement Process in Life-Span Development* (1995), Eckstein presents the following case study involving reframing as demonstrated by a seventh grade teacher named Mr. King. A practical use of encouragement involves helping a person discover a strength that has been previously defined in a discouraging manner. This redefining of a minus into a plus creates what is known as second order change.

Content changes can be identified as a first order change. This is a change that leaves unaltered the fundamental organization of the system. Thus a family with a "problem" child can be said to undergo first order change whenever it adapts to the child's "problem" but does not stop its symptomatic functioning and continues to relate to the child as the "problem." Second order change redefines the problem so that a fundamental change within the system's organization structure is created. For example, a family undergoes second order change when a therapeutic intervention creates a disruption in the pattern of symptomatic interaction so that the problem ceases (Torrance, 1979; Foley and Everett, 1982).

Reframing is a therapeutic intervention that helps facilitate second order change. Reframing is to change the conceptual or emotional setting or viewpoint in relation to which a situation is experienced, and places it in another frame of reference which fits the facts of the same concrete situation equally well if not better. Consequently there is a shift in how the situation is perceived, in the meaning given to the situation, or how one behaves towards the situation. For example, a salesman's nervous stuttering could be viewed as a problem or reframed as a way to get customers to listen to him (Watzlawick, Weakland and Fisch, 1974).

Reframing can be used as an encouragement technique. It is a way to redefine one's negative interpretation of a situation into a positive interpretation. Parents, teachers, coaches, clergy and other professionals could positively influence children by learning how to reframe a child's behavior.

In *The Encouragement Process in Life-Span Development,* Eckstein (1995) presents seventeen articles relative to specific applications of encouragement. The following is an example illustrating a teacher's use of reframing. Parents also have the potential to encourage their children by reframing a specific behavior or personality trait into a positive attribute. For instance, a child's laziness could be reframed as a child who is selective in what he/she chooses to do.

The following vignette was written at midnight one Thanksgiving Day, a time in which the author was reflecting on those who had positively influenced his personal and professional life.

A Tribute to Many Uncrowned Kings and Queens

by Daniel Eckstein

It was the spring of 1962. I was in the seventh grade at Johnnycake Junior High School in Baltimore, Maryland, section "7B" to be precise. In earlier years the distinction between classes had been the "redbirds" and the "bluebirds," in a vain attempt to avoid labeling one class the smart one and the other class (mine) the "dummy" group. But we all knew who was who relative to the hierarchy of redbirds and bluebirds. So in seventh grade the pretense was dropped in favor of "7A" and "7B." All my neighborhood friends were in the coveted "A" class — as for me, I was majoring in playground. I was also an "honor" student ... as in "yes, your honor, no your honor, I won't do that anymore your honor."

I was a classic left-handed, dyslexic, hyperactive boy who consistently received "unsatisfactory" conduct scores under the category vaguely defined as "self-control." D's masqueraded as B's, P's as Q's, and M's and N's were indistinguishable to me. Classes were much too long, the desks far too small, and the outdoor activities way too short. Like a prisoner about to be granted a three-month furlough prior to returning to the cell I called a classroom desk, I was counting down the days until June.

The teacher for both "7A" and "7B" was like a great redwood tree to me, a colossal giant who, at 6 feet 2 inches tall, seemed twice as awesome from my diminished vantage point. "Mr. King" was the well-named title of our teacher — he was kind, knowledgeable, and much revered by both sections "A" and "B," a rare feat in and of itself for any teacher.

One day quite unexpectedly, Mr. King approached my "7A" friends and observed that ..."There is someone in "7B" who is just as smart as any of you — trouble is, he just doesn't know it yet. I won't tell you his name, but I'll give you a hint — he's the kid who out-runs all of you and knocks that ball over the right field fence."

Word of Mr. King's declaration reached me that afternoon as we boarded the school bus. I remember a dazed, numb, shocked feeling of disbelief. "Yeah sure, you've got to be kidding," I nonchalantly replied to my friends; but on a deeper, more subtle level, I remember the warm glow that came from the tiny flicker of a candle that had been ignited within my soul.

Two weeks later, it was time for the dreaded book reports in front of the class. It was bad enough to turn in papers that only Mr. King read and graded. Alas, there was no place to hide when it came to oral book reports!

When my turn came, I solemnly stood before my classmates. I began slowly and awkwardly to speak about James Fennimore Cooper's epic book The Pathfinder. As I spoke, the images of canoes on the western frontier of 18th century America collided with lush descriptions of the forest and native Americans who glided noiselessly over lakes and streams. No Fourth of July fireworks has ever surpassed the explosion that took place inside my head that day — it was electrifying!

Excitedly, I began trying to share my experience with my classmates. But just as I began a sentence to tell about the canoes, another scene of the land collided with the native Americans. I was only midway through one sentence before I jumped to another.

I was becoming "hyper" in my joy, and my incomplete sentences made no sense at all. The laughter of my classmates at my "craziness" quickly shattered my inner fireworks. I felt embarrassed and humiliated. I wanted so badly to either beat up my tormentors or run home and cry in my mother's arms ...but long ago I had learned how to mask those feelings ...so, trying my best to become invisible and disappear, I started to return to my desk.

The laughter ceased at the sound of Mr. King's deep, compassionate voice ..."You know, Danny," he reigned forth ..."you have a unique gift — that being the ability to speak outwardly and to think inwardly at the same time. But sometimes your mind is filled with so much joy that your words just can't keep up with it. Your excitement is contagious — it's a wonderful gift that I hope you can put to good use someday."

There was a pause that seemed to linger forever as I stood stunned by Mr. King's words once more ...and then it began ...clapping and congratulatory cheers from my classmates as a miracle of transformation occurred within me on that great day.

Thirty years later, I take my turn to say, "thank you" to all the nameless Mr. and Ms. Kings who are the teachers of our young people. I now have fancy sounding names like "encouragement," or "turning a perceived 'minus' into a 'plus' " to describe how Mr. King helped me to reframe my life forever.

It's been said that "the greatest use of a life is to spend it in a cause that will ultimately outlive it." Though often underpaid and faced with far too many students and far too few resources, I salute you, our teachers — and hope you and your community will take a moment to acknowledge that in many subtle ways, you **do** make a difference."

Eckstein, D. *The Encouragement Process in Life-Span Development.* Dubuque, IA: Kendall Hunt Publishing Co., 1995, pp. 37-39.

Thus, the examination of interpretations presents wide variations in how they are defined, perceived, and practiced among counselors and researchers. Considering the relationship of interpretation to counseling theories, propositional and semantic aspects and attributional theory assist counseling professionals in understanding interpretation (Clark, 1995). From an Adlerian perspective, interpretation is considered to be an essential aspect of client's increased self-awareness. However, the Adlerian philosophy is one of equals, not of a "superior" therapist. In the final analysis, then, it is the client who is the ultimate interpreter."

NEEDS

A first step in the interpretation process is to consider major client wants, needs, or values. Henry Murray (1963) developed the following checklist:

TWENTY HUMAN NEEDS

Adapted from Murray, Henry, A. Explorations in Personality. New York: Oxford University Press, 1963. Used by permission of the publisher.

Need	Description
Abasement	To submit passively to external force. To accept injury, blame, criticism, punishment. To become resigned to fate. To admit inferiority, error, wrongdoing, or defeat.
Achievement	To accomplish something difficult. To master, manipulate, or organize physical objects, human beings, or ideas. To do this as rapidly and as independently as possible. To overcome obstacles and attain a high standard.

Affiliation	To draw near and enjoyably cooperate or reciprocate with an allied other (an other who resembles the subject or who likes the subject). To please and win affection of a cathected object. To adhere and remain loyal to a friend.
Aggression	To overcome opposition forcefully. To fight. To revenge an injury. To attach, injure, or kill another. To oppose forcefully or punish another.
Autonomy	To get free, shake off restraint, break out of confinement. To resist coercion and restriction. To avoid or quit activities prescribed by domineering authorities. To be independent and to act according to impulse.
Counteraction	To master or make up for a failure by restriving. To obliterate a humiliation by resumed action. To overcome weaknesses, to repress fear. To search for obstacles and difficulties to overcome. To maintain self-respect and pride on a high level.
Defendance	To defend the self against assault, criticism, and blame. To conceal or justify a misdeed, failure or humiliation. To vindicate the ego.
Deference	To admire and support a superior. To praise, honor, or eulogize. To yield eagerly to the influence of an allied other. To conform to custom.
Dominance	To control one's human environment. To influence or direct the behavior of others by suggestion, seduction, persuasion, or command. To dissuade, restrain, or prohibit.
Exhibition	To make an impression. To be seen and heard. To excite, amaze, fascinate, shock, intrigue, amuse, or entice others.
Harmavoidance	To avoid pain, physical injury, illness and death. To escape from a dangerous situation. To take precautionary measures.
Infavoidance	To avoid humiliation. To quit embarrassing situations or to avoid conditions which may lead to belittlement; the scorn, derision, or indifference of others. To refrain from action because of the fear of failure.

Nurturance	To give sympathy and gratify the needs of a helpless object; an infant or any object that is weak, disabled, tired, inexperienced, infirm, defeated, humiliated, lonely, dejected, sick, mentally confused.
Order	To put things in order. To achieve cleanliness, arrangement, organization, balance, neatness, tidiness, and precision.
Rejection	To separate oneself from a negatively cathected object. To exclude, abandon, expel, or remain indifferent to an inferior object. To snub or jilt an object.
Sentience	To seek and enjoy sensuous impressions.
Sex	To form and further an erotic relationship. To have sexual intercourse.
Succorance	To have one's needs gratified by the sympathetic aid of an allied object. To be nursed, supported, sustained, surrounded, protected, loved, advised, guided, indulged, forgiven, consoled. To always have a supporter.
Understanding	To ask or answer general questions. To be interested in theory. To speculate, formulate, analyze, and generalize.

Encouraging Social Interest to Different Life-Styles

Life-Style & "The Guiding Line"

According to Adler (Ansbacher & Ansbacher, 1964), a style of life comes about through the exclusion of forms of expression unsuited to a guiding line. To create a life-style, one organizes activity and feelings around a guiding line, or goal, regulating emotional and behavioral response according to criteria expressed in life-style convictions (Shulman and Mosak, 1988).

A guiding line is an overriding, coherent strategy for attaining success or safety in life. This strategy governs judgments about possibilities and constraints of situations and directly influences feelings and behavior in a given situation. One can conceptualize life-style as movement toward or attraction to certain situations taken to constitute success, or as avoidance or elimination of certain situations take to constitute danger. The individual may have become sensitive to, or oversensitive to, and hence overvalues, certain situations and behaviors (Ansbacher & Ansbacher, 1964).

The life-style allows an individual to cope in known and familiar fashions in many life events, and to operate within a relatively or distinctly narrow range of interpersonal activity. One maintains feelings of security by behaving in known ways, in selected environments, rather than by taking risks and feeling insecure (Losoncy, 1977). In times of stress, rather than try new behaviors, a person typically does "more of the same." Chronic or acute influences that tend to move one into unfamiliar territory may result in new behaviors, but may also promote counter-movements designed to preserve security and self-esteem. On one hand, a life-style offers accustomed ways to behave in most situations; on the other, an individual can be caught in inflexible activity and in fear of moving outside an accustomed range (Slavik, 1995).

Slavik (1995) believes that social interest is the antidote to worry, suffering, and temptation, or lack of inner freedom. High social interest implies a flexible ability to operate with others (Adler, 1979). It means, at least in part, that one knows when a task is completed and when one can simply quit thinking about it. One is neither driven to do a "better" job for the sake of self-enhancement nor driven to excuse oneself from a task. Dreikurs (1971) relates higher levels of social interest to inner freedom and confidence in oneself: "We can respect others only if we respect ourselves and trust life only if we trust ourselves"(p. 4)

Greater social interest and inner freedom can become a goal in the therapeutic process. Social interest is a guiding therapeutic principle that is related to inner freedom through the assumption that inner freedom enables one to contribute to the welfare of others. Any therapeutic strategy which helps increase one's inner freedom contributes to one's social interest. A guiding line increasing inner freedom, decreasing worry, temptation, or suffering, enables one to become task-oriented. Conversely, a guiding line oriented to the welfare of others increases inner freedom and reduces one's suffering and temptation. (Slavik, 1995)

Typologies of Life-Styles

In interpreting a life-style, it is often useful to utilize "typologies" or broadly-based general categories. No one is any pure "type" and such categories merely help provide a "template" to begin the initial steps in understanding a particular unique individual. It has been humorously noted that "there are two types of people in the world—those that believe there are two types and those that don't."

The strength of typologies is in assisting a counselor to have a way of exploring a person. The weakness is that they can over generalize and "lump" individuals into broadly defined and more clinically-oriented categories.

Such typologies are used as an expedient aid to thinking and should not substitute in practice for ascertaining the convictions of an individual (Adler, 1929). Neither does the use of a typology assume that any set of categories is a complete presentation of human styles or themes (Mosak, 1977), nor that any individuals are actually "types."

Kern (1986) defines five types: the controller, the perfectionist, the pleaser the victim, and the martyr. These types are discussed by Slavik (1995) in terms of guiding line, attraction and avoidance, implicit temptation or suffering, and stress created. The idea of social interest that will make the most sense to that position and that is inherently attractive to the type is also described. Although each scale has a more clinical or self-defeating aspect of itself, specific ways to increase social interest in each typology will be noted.

1. The Controller

The guiding line of the controller is to be in control of situations, to take charge, and to solve difficulties (Kern & White, 1989); to be God (Mosak, 1977). They preserve security and self-esteem by movement toward situations where they can have influence, and by avoidance of those in which they can have little influence. The controller emphasizes cognitive abilities at the expense of feelings. They seldom feel sufficiently in control and are oversensitive to actual or possible ridicule by others. The assumption used by a controller to justify the position is that others are scornful, hostile, and lying in wait to ridicule (Kefir, 1981).

In increasing social interest, controllers will use their abilities in the service of a community where they can organize and manage events to aid others and be regulated by needs of community tasks. This will increase inner freedom and being to free thinking from excessive demands to prove self-worth in the face of a hostile world.

In order to effect this goal in therapy, the controller is challenged with the idea of "keeping as much control as possible in a situation, feeling whatever fear can be tolerated, and letting go of what can't be controlled." The controller is confronted with this idea at appropriate times, and therapy is guided by this idea. Social interest is thereby presented in an immediately and obviously understandable form. (Slavik, 1995).

2. The Perfectionist

The guiding line and striving of the perfectionist is to avoid mistakes and be correct at all times (Kern and White, 1989) Perfectionists seek to preserve security and self-esteem in situations and with people where they can be right or correct, and in avoidance of situations in which they are "wrong." The perfectionist is oversensitive to criticism and overvalues appropriateness. The possibility of being criticized, of appearing foolish, will always be present in this person's thinking (Kefir, 1981). This assumption creates constant stress and justifies driven attempts to "do better," which in turn increases felt stress.

The perfectionist can be a nit-picker, obsessional, and critical of others. However, on the useful side of life, with focus on task rather than on oneself or others, the perfectionist can be a helpful teacher, mentor, or auditor wherever expert. Most people prefer an operation by a "perfectionist doctor" who is less likely to forget to remove a sponge prior to sewing up an incision. Slavik (1995) suggests that to encourage movement to a more useful side of life, a therapist might present social interest through the idea that "to be more perfectly human, one sometimes muddles along without all the i's dotted or all the t's crossed, frequently helping one another along the way." (p. 17). This appeals to both the temptation to be less demanding of oneself and others and to the perfectionism simultaneously.

3. The Pleaser

The pleaser attains significance through pleasing others (Kern & White, 1989). Pleasers will move toward situations and people where they can make others happy, and will move away from those in which this is not possible. Security comes with the "good housekeeping seal of approval." Insecurity comes from a lack of approval or lack of feedback about the opinions of others. Such individuals have a difficult time when not liked or approved, and seek feedback for reassurance rather than for task-correction.

The possibility of doing the wrong thing and of thereby being disliked or unpopular will be foremost in this person's thinking. The pleaser's challenge is to find sufficient inner freedom to be able to take an interest in others not motivated by self-enhancement. Their risk will be to find sufficient self-confidence to do as one pleases without denigrating or withdrawing from others — that is, pleasing oneself and simultaneously being interested in others.

Slavik (1995) notes that social interest is represented to the pleaser by confirming the temptation that "one can live without everyone's approval. Many people just please themselves and find that they please others and have an interest in others without making special efforts to do so." Pleasing oneself is usually not contrary to pleasing others. Such an intervention appeals to the temptation to please oneself, without changing the style of pleasing others. Pleasing oneself enables one to work cooperatively and constructively on the useful side of life without letting others covertly direct one's behavior. Maslow (1990) describes self-actualized people as getting twice as many inner self-oriented positives as from others. Pleasers usually have the opposite ratio.

4. The Victim

The victim tries hard in life but seldom succeeds; lack of success is usually someone else's fault (Kern & White, 1989). One will always be thinking about how others prevent the attainment of the success one could have, if only... Victims move toward situations in which they can "try hard" yet fail without blame. They will move away from situations where there is a clear allocation or expectation of self-responsibility. In such movement, the victim seeks to avoid anonymity. The guiding line is both a way to keep others involved and a way to avoid addressing the tasks of life. The victim cannot tolerate being alone, unknown, unimportant, or unnoticed. A victim both overvalues and is sensitive to "looking good."

A victim acting with social interest can be a barometer for difficult living conditions and can realistically strive to correct them. One gains inner freedom through this focus.

Slavik (1995) observes that when successfully encouraged "to be in the world without feeling abused, to be ordinary, to go about one's business without thought of success or failure," (p. 172) the victim can notice stress due to difficult conditions and work to correct those conditions. One can accept some stress as necessary in life and accept the daily notoriety one gains by doing so. Such a suggestion appeals simultaneously to the victim's goal of noticing and responding to difficulties, and thereby avoiding anonymity, and to the temptation to actually accomplish something.

5. The Martyr

The martyr struggles for a cause against all odds. His or her guiding line is to be an overt hero seeking out unjust conditions to correct (Kern & White, 1989). A martyr is oversensitive to and overvalues justice and/or fairness. According to Covey (1989), martyrs do not distinguish a Circle of Influence from a Circle of Concern; they also cannot distinguish what they can influence from what they would like to influence. The assumption which justifies this position is that one is indispensable and that no one else can do the job.

A martyr living on the useless side of life is full of complaints and has a life of indiscriminately fought battles. The martyr working on the useful side of life may see and correct certain selected injustices without heroic drama. "It's an important job to be done," rather than "This is a job for Superman/Superwoman," expresses a useful attitude.

To present social interest to this person a therapist can say, "It's okay to let others help you, it's okay not to take on more than you're able just now. It's okay to live for yourself, and to catch up on your reading. You can live with yourself as your own cause." Such a presentation appeals to the goal of correcting injustice and to the temptation to become ordinary. (Slavik, 1995)

Our Creative Life-Style

Albrecht Schottky (1987) notes that although all of us have a somewhat faulty, erroneous life-style, simultaneously the life-style is a creative achievement of a small child:

> Often it is a remarkable achievement, frequently it contains a very useful philosophy developed in order to understand and interpret the world. Of course, a life-style may be formulated as the sum of mistaken ideas, basic errors, or faulty perceptions, or it may be formulated in a more positive way. Both formulations are lopsided and of doubtful therapeutic value. How could a patient feel accepted and encouraged if his or her personality is represented as a bundle of basic mistakes? How should the therapist proceed? Should one take out the basic mistakes in the life-style and put in social interest? That sounds like some magic potion or powder. That would be similar to advertising: "Detergent X takes the dirt out and forces cleanness into the laundry." That does not work. It is important to understand the life-style in an accepting way, its weaknesses and its strengths.

The initial approach to beginning a life-style summary needs to be conducted with *compassion* and a type of *reverence* or genuine *respect* for the person who shared his or her intimate world with you, the counselor. Despite mistaken ideas and faulty evaluations in some instances, the data shared represents that individual's own creative ways of coping with his or her formative childhood.

Counselors who find disgust rather than a sense of respect need to confront their own needs for self-elevation — if a sense of appreciation and compassion cannot be felt, then the relationship should proceed no further. Such basic respect needs to be present in all phases of a counseling relationship. As such, it forms a cornerstone as an essential element of social interest.

The usual life-style developmental therapeutic process generally involves explaining the purpose of the interview and gathering data in the initial one or two sessions. Sometimes the interpretation occurs spontaneously in the moment —simply focusing one's awareness back to core childhood issues sometimes results in spontaneous "a-ha's," thus flexibility and the ability to be "in the moment" with the client should always be a counselor's response.

Most often the counselor collects the basic information and then spends some time alone organizing the data. This chapter presents some guidelines to assist that organization. Remember to trust your own intuitive guesses or hunches. Perhaps for no apparent (linear) reason a word or a phrase may suddenly "pop" into your head. The authors have had some dramatic results by having the courage to trust that spontaneous inner creative wisdom. For example, recently Eckstein was completing an initial interview. The name "Shirley" just kept "flashing" in his mind. But no where did her name appear in the siblings, ER's, etc. So, towards the end of the session, he simply acknowledged the name "Shirley" was haunting him, and asked the client if the name had significance.

Her immediate "recognition reflex" was a look of shock and disbelief. "How did you know about her?" she exclaimed. "She is my best friend — we share our most intimate secrets together — but she, like me, is an alcoholic and we often get drunk together. I just left her before I came to see you. She acknowledged my courage in coming to see you and said she should come too," she continued.

One needs the courage to trust one's own inner creativity and to realize that counselors, in essence, "step into" the other person's private world during an interview. In the above example, alcohol dependence was identified in a direct manner by taking a risk.

Dreikurs continually encouraged his trainees to make guesses, or as he called it, to "dig gold mines" early in the interview. They may simply appear in the margin as hypotheses to be further explored. Even when a guess is "wrong," that too helps the person further refine the issue, even if it's reacting *against* or *clarifying* the hypothesis.

The initial approach should be one of compassion and respect to the client, plus appreciation for one's own personal intuitive creative problem-solver that may identify key themes, phrases, feelings, formative incidents, etc.

Although the following sections will explore the various components of the interview (i.e., life tasks, family constellation, early recollections), Powers & Griffith (1987) wisely note that a life-style assessment is not a "systematic collection of a heap of tiles; it is the imaginative reconstruction of a pattern which allow each tile of information to be fitted into the context of the whole. This context, furthermore, is a pattern of movement in line with what Adler recognized as the 'great line of action' of the 'whole of human life...from below to above, from minus to plus, from defeat to victory.'" (pp. 21-22)

Powers & Griffith focus their overall interpretation on the following seven key features of the child's environment:

1. **Masculine & Feminine Guiding Lines and Role Models** — "This is the way men are, and the way women are...therefore, this is what is going to unfold for me as a man or as a woman."

2. **Family Atmosphere** — "This is what I have to expect and prepare for in my dealings with others."

3. **Family Values** — "These are the issues of central importance, on which I must be prepared to take a stand."

4. **Other Particularities** (including the ethnic, religious, social, and economic situation) —"It is possible for me to make a place in the broader community on these terms and to this extent."

5. **Birth Order Position** — "This is where I stand and must stand amongst others in order to maintain my bearings."

6. **Genetic Possibility/Self-Assessment** — "These are my personal limits and possibilities for making a place amongst the others."

7. **Environmental Opportunity/Openings for Advancement** —"This is what is open to me in life, and this is what stands in my way." Such a global overview can be of assistance as we now explore the various components of the Life-Style Interview (LSI).

Life Tasks

The tasks of living provide a useful overview as to how the client is *currently* functioning in the core issues confronting everyone. The rating scale provides a self-assessment and can identify strong and challenging areas. Look for the range of scores — the gap between between the highest and lowest provides a measure of **stress**. It also can help utilize strengths from one area and how they might be generalized into the low scored task.

Their personal explanation also provides insight into the client's own subjective "private logic." It is a good indication of hopes and dreams, as well as fears and disappointments. The answer to what Dreikurs called "the question" provides the payoff for the client's stressors. For example, "If I weren't so depressed and had my problems solved, I wouldn't be alcoholic" shows that depression is "useful" in providing a motive (excuse) for alcoholism.

Another reason for the *current* here and now focus of the person's world is that after the formative "there and then" childhood experiences have been explored, the interpretation should then integrate the *past* with the *present* and focus toward *future* changes/improvements/goals.

Five Life Tasks

Portions of this section are abstracted by permission of the American Counseling Association from: Witmer, J.M. & Sweeney, T. "A Holistic Model for Wellness and Prevention Over the Life Span." *Journal of Counseling & Development* 71 (1992): 140–147.

Witmer and Sweeney (1992) relate their own five life tasks in exploring "A Holistic Model for Wellness and Prevention Over the Life Span." They note that:

> With the primary attention being given to "sickness" and "dysfunction," resources are almost exclusively committed to remediating problems. For example, the United States Public Health Service (USPHS, 1979) reported that at least 53% of the deaths in the United States are caused by life-style and self-destructive and negligent behavior.

The Healthy People 2000 report established the nation's health promotion and disease prevention goals for the next decade (U.S. Department of Health and Human Services, 1990). The federal government currently spends more than 75% of its health care dollars caring for people with chronic diseases, such as heart disease, strokes, and cancer. At the same time, less than one-half of 1% is spent to prevent these same diseases from occurring.

Witmer and Sweeney believe the characteristics of the healthy person over the life span are described under the five life tasks they define as:

1. Spirituality
2. Self-regulation
3. Work
4. Love
5. Friendship

These life tasks dynamically interact with the life forces of family community, religion, education, government, media, and business/industry. Global events, both natural and human, have an impact on and are affected by the life forces and life tasks. As a member of the human community, we engage in these life tasks as identified and suggested by Adler in our striving for well-being (Dreikurs, 1953; Mosak & Dreikurs, 1967).

At the center of wholeness is *spirituality* (i.e., oneness, purposiveness, optimism, and values). *Self-regulation* is the second life task, which includes such characteristics as sense of worth; sense of control; realistic beliefs; spontaneous and emotional responsiveness; intellectual stimulation, problem solving, and creativity; sense of humor; and physical fitness and nutrition. *Work* as a third life tasks not only affords economic sustenance but also serves psychological and social functions. The fourth life task of *friendship* enables us to connect with the human community. Wellness is enhanced by the fifth life tasks of *love*, in which our health is nurtured in marriage or intimate relationships through trust, caring and companionship. (Witmer & Sweeney, 1992). They define the specific tasks as follows:

LIFE TASK 1: Spirituality

All cultures have expressed and practiced religious beliefs that represent values that reflect what is considered sacred and essential for the sustenance of life.

These spiritual beliefs are translated into ethical, moral, and legal codes, all of which in part are intended to protect and sustain the sacredness of life. Individual character and life-style are developed in a way that is thought to nurture the soul while at the same time be acceptable or harmonious with the supreme being-force of the universe.

Specific characteristics of spirituality include:

a) Oneness and the Inner Life

Through nature and the world of thought the individual is in awe of the universe and desires to experience the universe as a single significant whole (Einstein, 1954/1984; Harman, 1988). Both Eastern and Western religions tend to recognize the oneness of the person and the desire to attain an inner peace and sense of wholeness, free from inner conflict and fragmentation. Sources of spirituality probably come from within as well as outside the person. Inner voices, inner wisdom, higher consciousness, or the Spirit of God are all forms of the spiritual side of wholeness. Traditionally religion and spirituality have sought peace, guidance, and contact with the universal force through meditation, prayer, worship, contemplation or introspection.

b) Purposiveness, Optimism, and Values

Other dimensions of spirituality to be mentioned are purposiveness or meaning in life, hope or optimism in anticipation of future events, and values for guiding us in human relationships and decision making. Longevity and stress research support the importance of meaningfulness for coping with stress and for enhancing one's own health and wellness. In stress research, Kobasa (1979) found that psychological hardiness could decrease chances of becoming ill by as much as 50%. Contributing to this was the commitment factor of hardiness described by Kobasa as the tendency to involve oneself in whatever one is, does, or encounters.

Optimism is another dimension of spirituality. Seligman's (1992) Learned Optimism demonstrated significant personality differences between a "glass half-full" philosophy (optimism) and a "glass half-empty" philosophy (pessimism). Tiger (1979) developed a strong argument that optimism is a biological phenomenon and that religion is deeply intertwined with optimism. Values important to the spiritual self are those that are moral in nature. Moral values are those that guide our behavior in acting for our own well-being and demonstrating respect and compassion for the good of others (Young & Witmer, 1985). Maslow (1968) emphasized, "The human being needs a framework of values, a philosophy of life, a religion or religion-surrogate to

118

live by and understand by in about the same sense that he needs sunlight, calcium or love: (p. 206). Valuelessness is the ultimate disease of our time and leads to value illnesses, illustrated by Maslow (1959, 1968) as apathy, alienation, hopelessness, and cynicism. Such conditions can become physical illnesses as well as lead to psychological and social ills. Healthy (self-actualized) people in Maslow's (1968) research were strongly ethical with definite moral standards. Their values tended to be universal in nature, transcending time and culture, with the ability to distinguish between means and ends. (Witmer & Sweeney, 1992).

And literally "out of the mouths of babes..." comes the following story.

God

An essay by Danny Dutton, age 8, of Chula Vista, California via the Rhode Island Episcopal News

 One of God's main jobs is making people. He makes these to put in place of the ones that die so there will be enough people to take care of things here on earth. He doesn't make grown-ups. Just babies. I think because they are smaller and easier to make. That way He doesn't have to take up His valuable time teaching them to talk and walk. He can just leave that up to the mothers and fathers. I think it works out pretty good.

God's second most important job is listening to prayers. An awful lot of this goes on, as some people, like preachers and things, pray other times besides bedtime. God doesn't have time to listen to the radio or TV on account of this. As He hears everything, not only prayers, there must be a terrible lot of noise going into His ears unless He has thought of a way to turn it off.

God sees everything and hears everything and is everywhere, which keeps Him pretty busy. So you shouldn't go wasting His time by going over your parents' head and ask for something they said you couldn't have.

Atheists are people who don't believe in God. I don't think there are any in Chula Vista. At least there aren't any who come to the Episcopal Church.

Jesus is God's Son. He used to do all the hard work like walking on water and doing miracles and trying to teach people about God who didn't want to learn. They finally got tired of Him preaching to them and they crucified Him. But He was good and kind like His Father and He told His Father that they didn't know what they were doing, to forgive them and God said OK. His Dad (God) appreciated everything He had done and all His hard work on earth, so He told Him He didn't have to go out on the road any more. He could stay in Heaven. So He did. And now He helps His Dad out by listening to prayers and seeing which things are important for God to take care of and which ones He can take care of Himself without having to bother God with. Like a secretary, only more important, of course. You can pray anytime

119

you want and they are sure to hear you because they've got it worked out so one of them is on duty all the time.

You should always go to Sunday School because it makes God happy, and if there's anybody you want to make happy, it's God. Don't skip Sunday School to do something you think will be more fun, like going to the beach. That is wrong. And besides, the sun doesn't come out at the beach until noon anyway.

If you don't believe in God, besides being an atheist, you will be very lonely because your parents can't go everywhere with you, like to camp, but God can. It's good to know He's around when you're scared of the dark or when you can't swim very good and you get thrown in real deep water by big kids. But you shouldn't just always think of what God can do for you. I figure God put me here and He can take me back any time He pleases.

LIFE TASK 2: Self Regulation

Self-regulation includes sense of worth; sense of control; realistic beliefs; spontaneity and emotional responsiveness; intellectual stimulation, problem solving, and creativity; sense of humor; and physical fitness and health. Self-regulation is the process involved in how an individual coordinates relatively long-term patterns of goal-directed behavior (Bandura, 1986; Heppner & Krauskopf, 1987; Mischel, 1981). Through this life task, the individual is able to direct, control, and manage the self in ways that are self-enhancing, but within norms as prescribed by the larger society.

What are the healthy traits that enable the individual to regulate the self successfully on the pathways to wholeness? In this section, we briefly sketch each characteristic and cite support from the health and wellness literature. The following traits define self-regulation according to Witmer & Sweeney:

a) **Sense of Worth**

Self-esteem is the greatest single factor that affects individual growth and behavior (Frey & Carlock , 1989; Witmer, 1985). Adler (1954) referred to this as striving for superiority or significance. The healthy individuals of Maslow's (1970) research had a strong acceptance of themselves and their own nature. They accepted their own weaknesses and imperfections without being upset or disturbed.

Self-esteem was significantly related to physical and mental health in a large survey conducted by the California Department of Mental Health (1979). Those who had high self-esteem reported having better mental and physical health. Low self-esteem also went along with more self-reported physical illness and with disturbances such as insomnia, anxiety and depression. Low self-esteem was also related to higher frequencies of marital problems, financial problems, emotional problems about illness, and problems with self. Persons who sensed that they had a high degree of control over their lives were more likely to feel good about themselves mentally and physically, and reported fewer ailments. The California State Legislature (1990) revealed that self-esteem is the likeliest candidate for a social vaccine to empower us to live responsibility and inoculate us against the personal and social ills plaguing our society.

b) **Sense of Control**

Beliefs about personal control have to do with feelings about mastery and confidence as well as issues of competence, locus of control, or self-efficacy.

Control is sometimes defined as a sense of competence as in the research by Witmer et al. (1983). One factor that described the good copers was competence, which included items on optimism, control, and perceived overall ability to cope with stress. Those who had perceived life as manageable had less anxiety and fewer physical symptoms.

Control along with challenge and commitment made up the three dimensions that Kobasa (1979) found to characterize hardiness in her study of several hundred telephone company executives. Control was defined as the opposite of powerlessness - more in control of events; expressed as a tendency to feel and act as if one is influential (rather than helpless) in the face of varied contingencies of life; and perception of oneself as having a definite influence through the exercise of imagination, knowledge, skill, and choice.

Those with internal locus of control believe that events are contingent upon their own actions and as such yield more effort and persistence in achievement situations (Lazarus & Folkman, 1984). An external locus of control refers to the belief that events are contingent on luck, chance, fate, or powers beyond their control. Persons with a sense of inner control are more likely to collect information about disease and health maintenance, take action to improve their health habits, and engage in preventive care (Strickland, 1978).

c) **Realistic Beliefs**

Healthy people have a keen perception of reality, seeing reality more as it is, not as one might want or desire it to be. The superiority in the perception of reality leads to a superior ability to perceive the truth, come to conclusions, and be logical and cognitively efficient (Maslow, 1968).

Private logic is the Adlerian conceptualization of personal beliefs that guide the feelings and behavior of individuals (Sweeney, 1989). Unhealthy persons who have mood disturbances are not emotionally sick, but cognitively wrong. That is, they are thinking irrational thoughts, doing faulty reasoning, or living by maladaptive rules made up of unrealistic or inappropriate "shoulds" and "oughts" or "do's" and "don'ts." (Beck, 1976, 1984; Ellis, 1962).

Witmer et al. (1983) indicated that those persons with a more positive outlook and those who scored lowest on five of Ellis' irrational beliefs were less anxious and had fewer physical symptoms. The five irrational beliefs contributing to stress were the following: 1) The past continues to influence me so much that it is hard for me to change or prevent bad things from happening; b) I can't help getting down on myself when I fail at something or when something goes wrong; c) it is very important for me to be liked and loved by almost everyone I meet; d) I must be perfectly competent, adequate, and achieving in all that I do to consider myself worthwhile; and e) I have little control over my moods, which are caused mostly by events outside myself.

d) Spontaneity and Emotional Responsiveness

Maslow (1970) described "self-actualizing" people as relatively spontaneous in behavior and far more spontaneous than others in their inner life, thoughts impulses, emotions, desires, and opinions. Montagu's (1981) list includes a sense of wonder, playfulness, joyfulness, laughter and tears, and dance and song.

Behavioral medicine, psychosomatic medicine, and psycho- neuroimmunology have established a relationship between thoughts, feelings, and illness (Benson with Proctor, 1984; Borysenko, 1987; Locke & Colligan, 1986; Rossi, 1986; Siegel, 1986). When negative emotions become chronic or are suppressed, they can become destructive to our well-being.

Ornstein and Sobel (1987) found that hostility seems to be the most likely characteristic that contributes to high blood pressure, coronary artery disease, and death among those who have the competitive, hard-driving Type A personality. Researchers have gathered a wealth of data suggesting that chronic anger is so damaging to the body that it ranks with cigarette smoking, obesity, and a high-fat diet as a powerful risk factor for early death (Williams, 1990). He reported that people who scored high on a hostility scales as teenagers were much more likely than were their more cheerful peers to have elevated cholesterol levels as adults.

Julius (1990) found that women who had obvious signs of long-term suppressed anger were three times more likely to have died during the study than were women who did not harbor such hostile feelings. Research findings also suggest that anxiety, loneliness, and depression are associated with suppressing the immune system, thus increasing the chance for illness to occur (Locke et al., 1984).

By contrast, relaxation and positive emotional states seem to strengthen immune function (Dillon, Minchoff, & Baker, 1985; Kiecolt-Glaser et al, 1984; McClelland, Ross, & Patel, 1985). Indeed, responses to daily events influence internal bodily functions. Not only does a negative mood result in lower antibody response but a positive mood is associated with a higher antibody response (Stone, Cox, Valdimarsdottir, Jandorf, & Neale, 1987).

In his best-seller *Ageless Body, Timeless Mind,* Deepak Chopra (1993) uses the mind/body connection to demonstrate important physical and mental health implications. He says the following new assumptions give us the ability to create a new paradigm by rewriting the program of aging that directs our cells.

1. The physical world, including our bodies, is a response of the observer. We create our bodies as we create the experience of our world.

2. In their essential state, our bodies are composed of energy and information, not solid matter.

3. The mind and body are inseparably one. The unity that is "me" separates into two streams of experience. I experience the subjective stream as thoughts, feelings, and desires. I experience the objective stream as my body.

4. The biochemistry of the body is a product of awareness. Beliefs, thoughts, and emotions create the chemical reactions that uphold life in every cell. An aging cell is the end product of awareness that has forgotten how to remain new.

5. Although perception appears to be automatic, it is in fact a learned phenomenon. If you change your perception, you change the experience of your body and your world.

6. Although each person seems separate and independent, all of us are connected to patterns of intelligence that govern the whole cosmos. Our bodies arc part of a universal body, our minds an aspect of a universal mind.

7. Time does not exist as an absolute, but only eternity. What we call linear time is a reflection of how we perceive change. If we could perceive the changeless, time would cease to exist as we know it and we would be ready to create the physiology of immortality.

8. Deep inside us, unknown to the five senses, is an innermost core of being, a field of non-change that creates personality, ego, and body. This being is our essential state — it is who we really are.

9. We are not victims of aging, sickness, and death. These are part of the scenery, not the seer, who is immune to any form of change. This seer is the spirit, the expression of eternal being.

Chopra illustrates what happens when people do not realize that there are choices to be made every day.

> Any time choice seems to be cut off, some form of illusion is operating. Thousands of years ago the greatest of Indian sages, Shankara, declared, "People grow old and die because they see others grow old and die." It has taken us centuries even to begin to catch up with this extraordinary insight. As a physical process, aging is universal and, to all appearances, inevitable. A steam locomotive doesn't wear out over time and fall apart because it sees other locomotives doing the same thing. The only conditioning that affects any machine is simply wear and tear, certain parts get worn down faster than others because they absorb the most impact or friction. Our bodies also absorb impact and friction, various organs and tissues wear out before others. This physical picture looks so much like mechanical wear and tear that we are blind to Shankara's deeper point — the aging body is responding to social conditioning. (p. 53).

Disclosing our feelings to another person who is nonjudgmental can be therapeutic. Using writing as a means of disclosure of innermost thoughts (some may call it confession) can measurable improve physical and mental health. Pennebaker (1990) has demonstrated that keeping a journal of your innermost feelings can improve your health, but mood, immune functioning, and health are improved only if facts and feelings are disclosed.

e) **Intellectual Stimulation, Problem Solving, and Creativity**

Montagu (1981) believes thinking is primarily a problem-solving process. The need to think soundly is accompanied by a cluster of traits characteristic of the developing child, such as "the need to know," the "need to learn," the "need to organize," "curiosity," and a sense of wonder. Explorativeness, experimental-mindedness, flexibility, open-mindedness, imagination, and creativity are additional intellectual conditions and characteristics that enable the person to master the environment and pursue mental, artistic, and productive activities that challenge thinking and produce satisfaction.

Maslow found that creativity was a universal characteristic of self-actualizing people. They demonstrated a special kind of creativeness, originality, and inventiveness. Although such characteristics have commonly been observed in children researchers and personnel working with older persons have noted how involving them in intellectually stimulating and creative tasks has the effects of regeneration and rejuvenation. Being mentally active and creative enriches the quality of life along with the longevity (Pelletier, 1981).

f) Sense of Humor

Humor, particularly when it is accompanied by laughter, promotes physiological, psychological, and social change. The skeletal muscles become more relaxed, breathing changes, and the brain is believed to release certain chemicals that are positive to our well-being, serving as an analgesic, a relaxant, or energizer. Humor creates an open flexibility for problem solving, reduces defensiveness, and improves communication while neutralizing stress (Cousins, 1979; Loehr & McLaughlin, 1986; Moody, 1978). Psychologically, the right kind of humor overrides negative emotions associated with "unsound" thinking, dissipating such thoughts at least for a time, and opens the possibility to changes in perception (Mosak, 1987).

Adler (1954) believed that in addition to specific training, therapists should have "a jovial attitude...blessed with cheerfulness and good humor..." (p. 201). Mosak (1987) and Fry and Salameh (1987) have described the benefits of humor in counseling and psychotherapy. Humor is seen as being useful in establishing a relationship, making assessment, turning the client around, and acting as a criterion in termination.

g) Physical Fitness and Health Habits

A landmark study that showed the significant relationship between health habits, health, and life expectancy was conducted with approximately 7,000 adults in Alameda County, California (Belloc, 1973; Belloc & Breslow, 1972). Seven factors were found to be significantly related to health and life expectancy:

1. Three meals a day at regular times and no snacking

2. Breakfast every day

3. Moderate exercise two or three times a week

4. Adequate sleep (7 or 8 hours a night)

5. No smoking

6. Moderate weight

7. No alcohol or only in moderation

Exercise. The benefits of exercise were summarized early in the 1980s by Cooper (1982). Exercise contributes to our well-being through such benefits as the following: more personal energy, greater ability to handle domestic and job-related stress, less depression and "free-floating" anxiety, fewer physical complaints, better self-image and more self-confidence, bones of greater strength, slowing of the aging process, more restful sleep, and better concentration at work and greater perseverance in all daily tasks. Sime (1984) noted that the association between exercise and a state of mind show the following:

1. A positive relationship with mental well-being

2. A decrease in state and trait anxiety

3. A decrease in mild to moderate depression

4. A decrease in muscular tension along with anxiety.

Nutrition. Nutritional research has demonstrated that there is a relationship between what we eat, our health, our moods, and our performance (Wurtman, 1986). Five nutrients are necessary for good health — proteins, carbohydrates, fats, vitamins, and minerals. Water is the sixth.

Dietary Guidelines for Americans (1990) provides sensible guidelines for nutrition and health:

1. Eat a variety of foods

2. Maintain healthy weight.

3. Choose a diet low in fat, saturated fat, and cholesterol.

4. Choose a diet with plenty of vegetables, fruits, and grain products.

5. Use sugars only in moderation.

6. Use salt and sodium only in moderation.

7. If you drink alcoholic beverages, do so in moderation.

Eating habits are established early in life and consequently become difficult to change with increasing age. When serious deficiencies or imbalances occur in any of the basic nutrients, optimal health is sacrificed and diseases are likely to occur. Two diseases that have dietary components are heart attacks and cancer. What we eat affects our health, mood, and perform-ance. (Witmer & Sweeney, 1992).

LIFE TASK 3: Work

Work is a fundamental life task that provides economic, psychological, and social benefits to the well-being of the individual and to others. The inability to fulfill this life task was regarded by Dreikurs (1953) as a serious symptom of illness.

The definition of work broadly encompasses everything we do to sustain ourselves and contribute to the sustenance of others (Adler, 1954). This includes not only gainful employment but also childrearing, homemaking, volunteer services, educational endeavors, and innumerable other activities that engage individuals in activities meaningful to themselves and others. Witmer & Sweeney also include the play of children and many leisure-time activities of adults as an extension of Adler's concept of work as a life task.

Herr and Cramer (1988) note psychological purposes include self-esteem, self-efficacy (control), identity, a feeling of mastery or competence, and commitment (meaning in life). Social benefits include a place to meet people, a feeling of being valued or needed by others, social status, and potential friendships. Economic purposes include the obvious resources to purchase goods and services, evidence of success, and assets to purchase leisure or free time.

Another measure of the importance of work can be derived by examining the effects of unemployment. Pelletier (1984) reported, "During periods of economic slump there is a marked increase in murder, suicide, mental illness, heart disease, alcoholism, divorce, domestic violence, family fights, and childhood abuse" (p. 129).

Dinkmeyer and Eckstein (1995) specifically apply Adlerian theory in work environments in their book, *Leadership by Encouragement.*

LIFE TASK 4: Friendship

Social Interest and Connectedness

Friendship is used to describe all those social relationships that involve connection with others either individually or in community, but do not have a marital, sexual, or familial commitment. Relationships that are formed on the basis of a commitment to one another and involve emotional intimacy, sexual intimacy, or both, including a family, are discussed under the fifth life task of love. Differences between the two life tasks are defined according to the nature of the relationship, the level of emotional attachment, and the extent of self-disclosure (Witmer & Sweeney, 1992).

Adler (1954) considered "social interest" or "social feeling" as innate to human nature (i.e., we are born with the capacity and need to be connected with each other and in a cosmic relationship). Therefore, the broad meaning of social interest is a "sense of fellowship in the human community" (p. 38). Empathy and altruism are manifestations of social interest. Montagu (1955) has applied the concept of social interest in support of his own view that "life is social and man is born to be social, that is cooperative — an interdependent part of a whole" (p. 185). The healthy persons in Maslow's (1970) research had deep feeling, sympathy, and affection for human beings in general as well as deep, profound, interpersonal relationships.

Social Support, Interpersonal Relations, and Health

Schaefer, Coyne, and Lazarus (1982) write that three functions are served through social support, namely a) emotional support — attachment, reassurance, being able to rely upon and confide in a person; b) tangible support — involving direct aid such as loans, gifts, and services (e.g., doing a chore or caring for someone who is ill); and c) informational support — providing information or advice and feedback.

In summarizing the research between social support and various health dimensions, Cohen (1988) noted the potential connections between social support and health behaviors, positive and negative affect, self-esteem and personal control, neuroendocrine response, and the immune system. In the absence of friendships, illness, a shorter life expectancy, and less satisfaction in life are likely companions to those individuals who fail to master the opportunities and responsibilities of friendships.

LIFE TASK 5: Love

The life task of love tends to be intimate, trusting, self-disclosing, cooperative, and long-term in commitment and often includes sexual relations (Witmer & Sweeney, 1992). Flanagan (1978) found that spouse, children, and friends were found to be the top three contributors to overall satisfaction of life for women and men. Well-being research by Argyle and Furnham (1983) found that women derive more satisfaction in the emotional support area and from friends and family; men get more satisfaction from spouses and work superiors. Older people derive more satisfaction from family and neighbors, younger people from friends and work associates.

Research reported by USA Today ("A Wife Adds..." 1988) noted that married men were almost twice as likely to outlive never-married men and were three times more likely to live longer than divorced men. Husbands had a lower depression rate than did people of any other marital status.

Major studies by Berkman and Syme (1979) and Lynch (1977) confirmed the health benefits of intimate relationships. Nonmarried persons always had higher death rates, sometimes as much as five times higher than did those of married individuals. Vaillant (1977) examined the linkage between loving and health in following 200 Harvard graduates for 30 years. The healthier men reflected a friendlier disposition and closer relationships with their children and were happily married over time and revealed better sexual adjustment. He concluded that being able to love one's friends, wife, parents, and children were predictors of good mental health. He also found that altruistic behavior was associated with better mental health, especially so during times of stress in people's lives. This study and the others reported support the position that trust, intimacy, caring, companionship, compassion, and similar qualities of a loving relationship promote good health and longevity (Witmer & Sweeney, 1992).

Thus, Step One in a life-style interpretation involves an exploration of how the client is functioning in the five basic existential life tasks.

Family Atmosphere

Family constellation theory and the projective use of early recollections are two of Adler's most significant contributions to psychology. In this section, family atmosphere will be examined. Specific sub-topics will include birth order research relative to personality and the projective use of literature in life-style assessment.

Shulman & Mosak (1988) use the following three qualities in describing family atmosphere: **mood, order,** and **relationships.** *Mood* refers to the overall emotional tone present within the family. It is most often the expression of one or both parents. Specific contrasting qualities of mood are **calm/anxious, placid/excitable, friendly/hostile, hopeful/discouraged,** and **cheerful/ unhappy.**

Order relates to the structural hierarchical relationships within the family. Patriarchal, matriarchal, authoritarian, pampering, and inconsistent discipline or limit-setting are all examples of structural relationships. Frequent changes either by moving, divorce or death of a parent all affect family stability. Specific contrasting qualities of order affecting an individual's life-style include: **orderly/chaotic, democratic/authoritarian, consistent/inconsistent, logical/arbitrary, clarity/confusion,** and **ethical standards/"might makes right."**

Shulman & Mosak define *relationships* as the consistent forms of interaction present within the family. Power struggles, approval or disapproval, withholding love, openly affectionate, and "double-blind" messages ("Come here and I will slap you" vs. "Why are you so afraid to get close to me?"), are all relationship examples. Contrasting relationships issues affecting one's lifestyle include: **intimate (affectionate)/distant, cooperative/competitive, accepting/rejecting, understanding/blaming, openness/concealed feelings,** and **harmonious/conflictual.**

Parental Influence

Naturally one or both parents or parental figures are infinitely important in the development of a child's own view of the world. The first masculine and feminine adult role models and their interrelationship are reflected in the parents. One of the highest correlates to adult marital happiness is still the young child's own perception of his or her own parents' marital happiness.

Since modeling and imitation have been shown to be key factors in learning theory, parental models can be of a positive or negative impact. "I vow *never ever* to treat my own children that way," is a frequent conclusion based upon negative parental role modeling.

Shulman & Mosak provide the following parental behavior and probable responses by the child:

1. **Accepting**— positive self-image
2. **Rejecting**— negative self-image, or may look elsewhere for acceptance
3. **Authoritarian**— submits, seeks to please, rebels, or seeks power
4. **Laissez-faire**— seeks guidance and limits
5. **Available**— feels closer to parent
6. **Unavailable**— feels isolated or looks elsewhere

130

7. **Consistency**— more trust

8. **Overprotection**— fearfulness or resistance to limits

9. **Excessive strictness**— seeks to please, rebels, or covertly rebels

10. **Lack of faith in the child**— tries to prove self to parent and/or loses faith in self.

It is important to avoid a "stimulus-response" type of fatalistic parental conditioning model. Many children continue later in life to blame their parents with a "He made me this way" or "She caused me to be _____." Certainly accepting, nurturing, available, and warm parenting styles are *highly correlated* with children's later mental health. But that does not mean that parents cause their children to be happy or unhappy. Ultimately it is the child's *own personal response* or decision that dictates their own happiness or unhappiness.

For example, one classic study the authors remember (but have been unable to reference) explored children of schizophrenic parents. One childhood decision was to incorporate the mental dysfunction and later to become hospitalized. These children were defined as being made of **glass**, as they too emotionally shattered and became schizophrenic. A second childhood decision was to be functional on a normal basis but that under stress they become neurotic. This was defined as a **plastic** child, who "dented" under duress.

But the final type of child of schizophrenic parents was described as being made of **steel**. These children used their parents as an example of what they would *not* be. Such children all had a **private place** somewhere in their environment. For example, it may have been building model planes in the basement, or an attic where one would read or keep a journal, or some other similar place to which one could retreat when his or her parents "went crazy." A second characteristic of such children was that they *actively* sought out *other* adult role models such as teachers, neighbors, and priests or ministers. Thus, the last type of child succeeded despite a horrible parental atmosphere.

A similar phenomenon was described in an Associated Press newspaper article (1991). It focused on what researchers are calling child "transcenders," children who succeed despite severe and abusive family atmospheres. Consider the following case history of Elizabeth as reported by Karen Northcraft, a psychiatric social worker:

> Abandoned by her mother, raised in a small, West Virginia town by an abusive aunt and a lecherous uncle, Elizabeth didn't seem to have a chance.

But when her impoverished family couldn't even provide a bathtub and a school counselor complained she was dirty, she made the swim team so she could get a daily shower.

Too poor to ever dream of owning a clarinet or violin, she joined the school band anyway, playing whatever instrument the school had to offer...

Elizabeth told Northcraft of bone-breaking beatings by her aunt, who had once stripped her naked and dunked her in a vat of scalding water. She told of the night when she was eight, that her uncle got into her bed and sexually molested her for the first time in what would be five years of assaults. Her aunt often told her that her mother had sold her for $25.

Elizabeth gained admission to college and was told she was dyslexic and should drop out. But she worked her way through school, earned a graduate degree and became a family therapist. (*The Arizona Republic*, Oct. 17, 1991, p. B-12)

The critical turning point for Elizabeth came in the fourth grade. One of her secret joys was her long blond curls. But when her aunt shaved her head, the deep well of pride, anger and determination buried within her broke through. She was then able to reject what her aunt was saying and to emotionally "insulate" herself from her. Northcraft believes that "life for 'transcenders' is often short, sharp, and brutish, but they do well in situations anyone else would find crushing."

Research indicates that such transcenders are smart, resourceful, and independent thinkers. They succeed because they are able to seek out other role-models and make personal decisions to rise above their adversity.

Thus, it is important to note the particular conclusions which are reflected in a child's early recollections to determine the "life is _____; others are _____; therefore _____"formative conclusions a child makes about the family atmosphere.

The Naming Process

Much insight can be gained by asking the client how he or she came to be named. Who decided? Was he or she named for a special person? What different nicknames has the person been called through his or her life? What specific reactions does the individual have about such names? What new name does the person want (or have they actually obtained)?

Such background issues provide important clues as to such environmental issues as power of influence, religion, politics, etc.

For example, consider the name of the co-author, Daniel Gene Eckstein. His Biblical heritage is reflected by having parents who were ministers in the Salvation Army and who named him after Daniel "in the lion's den" from the Old Testament. He vividly remembers as a child his mother telling him, "As a child, you will be called 'Danny'; as an adolescent, 'Dan,' and as an adult 'Dr. Daniel.'" It was only when the co-author celebrated his fortieth birthday and began asking people to change the "Dan" to "Daniel" that he remembered his mother's accurate prediction.

The middle name "Gene" remains a mystery despite having asked his parents of the origin. Consequently, it is seldom used.

The last name "Eckstein" is both a source of pride and some indication of family values. The German translation is "cornerstone," prompting an adolescent friend to joke, "We always knew you were a **blockhead**, Eckstein." When "Roots" was a mini-television series, the co-author began to search for his own German ancestry. At a restaurant named "Gotlieb's" in Greenwich Village, New York City, the co-author mentioned that "Gotlieb" was his father's middle name. "Beloved of God" was the owner's translation.

When the co-author questioned the restaurant owner about the possibility of a Jewish heritage, he was told: "Oh yes, haven't you heard the story of your Eckstein family? When they fled Germany, half the family denied their Jewish heritage and settled in Pittsburgh while the other half affirmed their Jewish ancestry and settled here in New York." Indeed, the co-author's grandfather was born in Pittsburgh, and when asked about possible Jewish heritage, he responded with, "It's best for you not to know or ask about such things."

It was a source of family concern when the co-author changed the pronunciation of his last name from "Eckstine" to "Ecksteen" to reflect his own pride in the Jewish tradition.

Concerning nicknames, he was also dubbed "Dumbo" as a child for his large ears, and "Dynamo Dan" as a participant in the 1968 Coaches All-American football game.

Thus, the three names reflect much of his cultural, religious, and family values. The naming process should be considered as a projective technique in and of itself.

Family Values

Family values are generally established by both parents. They reflect what is prized, esteemed and to be sought after as primary motivators. There is no "escaping" the judgment (positively or negatively) for a child. Consider for example, a common source of stress relative to a parental (family) value of "religion," which frequently is synonymous with being in church or synagogue every week. "But Mom, my cathedral is nature — I worship God outside" is simply unacceptable and thus rejected as an acceptable value by many parents. There is no neutrality on the issue of a family value. A sibling is either "in" or "out" on such an issue. Too often children feel a conflict between being one's self and losing parental approval versus compromising one's beliefs for such acceptance.

Often a child confronts what Walker & Belove (1982) describe as a loyalty dilemma in which the parents model values directly opposed to the child's beliefs. Nonetheless, the child still wants to please and be accepted by them both.

Core family values are generally reflected in the family motto. These are frequent parental injunctions or proverbs such as "children are to be seen and not heard"; "never betray a family member"; or "go to church often, get married, and have several children."

Powers & Griffith (1987) provide a partial list of some of the following most frequently identifiable family values: education, religious observance, honesty, loyalty to family, order, deference to authority, obedience, independence, doing your best, being best/first, thrift, distrust of "outsiders," manners, service to others, achievement, perfectionism, not complaining, not losing face, and doing one's duty (the "right" thing).

They conclude that "family values refer to standards that are held up before all the children, with the implication (or explicit statement) that, 'These are the things that are important in this family, whatever others may think or do in other families.'"

This means that family values operate as imperatives. None of the children can ignore them; on the contrary, we see each child taking up a position toward them, whether in support or in defiance, either overtly or covertly. They are the issues that all children in the family had to deal with in the formulation of their life-styles." (p. 148)

Birth Order (Family Constellation)

One of the most influential factors to be considered in the development of a person's life-style is family constellation, the order of birth of children living within a family and the dynamic relationship between siblings and other members of the family group. Dreikurs, Grunwald & Pepper (1971) state that in the life-pattern of every person, "there is the imprint of his position in the family with its definite characteristics. It is upon this one fact — the child's subjective impression of his place in the family constellation — that much of his future attitude toward life depends." (p. 46)

From the moment of birth, the child acts in a way in which he or she hopes to achieve significance or superiority in the family. Actions that are not productive in achieving these goals will be discarded and replaced by new behaviors aimed at the same goals.

Description of Siblings

To illustrate the concept of family constellation a hypothetical individual and his family will be used. The first step is to list all siblings in descending order, including our subject, Robert, in his ordinal position. The age of each sibling in our case study and a brief description follows. If there had been any deceased siblings, they would be noted in their respective position and identified in some way such as with a broken circle, e.g. (Bob.)

The age and sex of each sibling are extremely important as a family with an unbalanced sibling sex distribution may have special problems. For example, a boy with four sisters would probably have a different outlook on life than a boy with four brothers.

In Robert's case he had an older sister, a younger brother, and a younger sister. He was the oldest male, and the second of four siblings. In families where males are given preference, this fact would have decidedly influenced him, but in Robert's family neither males nor females are given preference.

Another important factor to consider is the age difference between siblings. Competition can be extremely keen between siblings that are close in age. This is especially true with a younger female who developmentally may "surpass" a slightly older brother. Conversely, siblings separated by several years may feel little, if any, competition. If the age difference is five or more years, the siblings are considered to be in two different "sub-families."

A diagram of Robert's family would look like this:

Mary	Robert	Fred		Susan
19	17	15		8
Sub-family				*Sub-family*

135

A look at the diagram suggests that Mary, Robert and Fred belong to one sub-family and Susan belongs to a second sub-family. If it is difficult to determine the sub-group in which a sibling belongs, ask the person which sibling was most different from him or her and who played with whom. The siblings mentioned will usually be in the individual's own sub-group.

We can guess that the competition between Robert and his older sister (Mary) and younger brother (Fred) would probably be quite intense. For example, if Mary was a good student, Robert might be a poor student. This phenomena is commonly referred to by Harold Mosak as the "teeter-totter" effect — meaning that when one sibling excels in an area the other does poorly and vice versa. In this family, if Mary were a musician, Robert might be an athlete. Because the competition is so intense, Robert would probably not participate in areas in which Mary was competent unless he thought he could do better. It is almost as if he concedes or defaults certain areas to Mary, claiming others for himself. Of course, if Robert does poorly in an area which his parents value intensely, problems are almost inevitable.

Mary 19	Robert 17	Fred 15	Susan 8
Good student	Poor student	Average student	Cute
Musically inclined	"Nice Guy Type"	Interested in sports	Long curls
Had few friends	Athlete	but not as much	Sweet
Thought I was a	One of the gang	as me	Sucked her fingers
loudmouth	Devilish	Had a few friends	Gentle, helpless
Called me fat	Irresponsible	Tried hard to please	Pleasant smile

Because of competition, usually the first and third siblings have more in common than the first and second. However, in Robert's family, because the first sibling is a girl and the third sibling a boy, there is a high probability that he would have more in common with his brother than with either of his sisters.

When one sibling is physically or mentally handicapped, the other siblings are usually affected. They may be required to assume many of the responsibilities that would normally be carried out by the other sibling were (s)he possibly not handicapped.

A difficult situation arises when one of the siblings dies during childhood. Normally the parents will tend to be over-protective of siblings born after the death of the child. Parents may also tend to compare the remaining sibling with the deceased child, by statements like, "Why aren't you as smart as our sister was?" or, "I wish you were more like Johnny used to be." This is an extremely difficult situation because a child cannot compete with a sibling who, in the parent's eyes, is approaching sainthood. It's difficult enough to compete with mortal siblings, but "angels in heaven" are untouchable.

When a half-brother or sister, cousins, or other children live with the family for an extended period of time, they become part of the family constellation. Usually the children will align themselves by age rather than the blood relationship to each other. This can be a traumatic experience for a child who has become accustomed to a particular place in the family constellation (especially oldest or youngest) and suddenly another child has that place. This is especially common when two divorced people with children marry, as in the former television program *The Brady Bunch.*

It is important to have the subject describe the siblings. Such descriptions will be very helpful in determining how the subject viewed relationships in one's first social group —the family. The fact that the siblings may be described inaccurately is not important; we are most concerned with the individual's subjective description of family members.

In the classic text *Maintaining Sanity in the Classroom,* Dreikurs, Grunwald and Pepper (1982) emphasize that an understanding of a child's classroom behavior can be helped by an exploration of the characteristics of the family constellation. The relationships that the children form within the family contribute greatly to their personality development and to transactions in the world outside the family. In the family each child develops his or her frame of reference through which (s)he perceives, interprets, and evaluates the world.

This early relationship with other members of the family establishes a personal approach to others in an effort to gain a place in the group. All strivings are directed towards achieving or maintaining a feeling of security, a sense of belonging, and a certainty that the difficulties of life will be overcome and that he will emerge safely and victoriously. A child cultivates those qualities by which he or she hopes to achieve significance or even a degree of power and superiority in the family constellation.

The authors also note that: "With the birth of each child the situation changes. The parents may become older and more experienced or more discouraged if they have had difficulties with their first child. During each child's formative years the financial situation of the family may have changed, the parents may have moved to another neighborhood or city or even country, or their marital status may have changed. These and other possibilities may affect one or the other. A sickly or crippled child, a child born just before or after the death of another, an only boy among girls, an only girl among boys, an obvious physical characteristic, an older person living in the home, or the favoritism of the parents toward a child — all these may have a profound effect on the child's environment." (Dreikurs, Grunwald, Pepper, p. 59).

In the following section we will explore the birth-order characteristics for the following five ordinal positions: *first, second, middle, only* and a*dopted.*

There are certain characteristics that are common to each of the sibling positions within the family constellation; however, the characteristics represent a composite, so not every detail will apply in all cases. We are making guesses aimed at probabilities. It is also important to note the difference between ordinal position and *psychological birth order.* For example, a person may have been chronologically sixth in a ten-person family, but psychologically perceived him/herself to be the first-born in a sub-group of three siblings. So, counselors should always ask clients, "Did you personally perceive yourself to be a first, second, middle, youngest, only, or adopted child? For what reasons?" Much criticism of birth order and lack of significance in research studies is partially due to limiting the scope of the inquiry to "ordinal" position and not "psychological" birth order.

Some general characteristics of various ordinal positions include the following:

Oldest Child

The oldest child has a unique situation in a family. Being born first entitles such a child to the parents' undivided attention, at least until another sibling is born. Usually an oldest child will conform to the parent's standard because he or she doesn't want to lose their favor. Such children tend to be very responsible because of their desire to meet the adult standards of their parents. When another sibling is born they often initially feel "dethroned." Usually because they are bigger and more capable, the threat of the new arrival will diminish with the passing of time. However, if the second child is very close in age to the first, there is a chance that the second might be more capable than the older. The situation of the second sibling permanently dethroning the first is most frequent when the older child is a boy followed very closely by a girl. Her accelerated rate of human growth and development makes such a "dethronement" more possible. Other frequent characteristics include preference for authority, dislike for change, conservative viewpoint, being "pacemaker" for the other children, ambitious, achievement-oriented, and having a tendency to relate better to adults than peers.

The Second-Born Child

Adler noted that second-born children often make the best counselors because they are keen observers and they can often relate to the "underdog" role. Such children come in on "the second act of the play." Having a "lap car" or a "moving rabbit" ahead of them often stimulates more rapid development.

Second-born are often keen observers. Roy Kern uses the following vivid example in his workshops:

First-born: *"Mom, can I go out tonight?"*

Mother: *"No, son. It's a school night and you must do your homework — you know the rules."*

First-born: *"Aw, Mom — come on — you never let me have any fun!"* (stomps off — second-born observing all the while.)

Two days later, the second-born approaches the mother.

Second-born: *"Mom, what are you doing? You're knitting — that's just great. Why, I've even got on the socks you knitted for me last month...Mom, I know it's a school night, but my friends just called me to go out for a pizza. I've finished all my homework — it would really mean a lot to me if I could go just for one hour — can I go, please, Mom?"*

And the answer usually is *"Yes, of course,"* much to the chagrin of the oldest.

According to Dreikurs, Grunwald and Pepper, the second child has somewhat of an uncomfortable position in life. Mostly, the child also takes a steam-engine attitude, trying to catch up with the child in front, often feeling under constant pressure. It is not unusual to see these youngsters move right on past their older and more perfectionistic-minded first-borns.

The parents, however, are more calm and relaxed with a second child, less strict, and less preoccupied with child-rearing. The second child is usually more socially oriented, more aggressive and competitive, and quite often rejects rules and regulations.

The second child may exhibit these characteristics:

1. Never having the parents' undivided attention.

2. Always having in front another child who is more advanced.

3. A feeling that the first child cannot be matched, which disputes equality.

4. Acting as if in a race — hyperactive and pushy.

5. If the first child is successful, more likely to feel uncertain and doubt one's own abilities.

6. Being the opposite of the first child (if the first child is dependable and "good," the second may become undependable and "bad").

7. Less concerned about winning adult approval than about winning peer approval.

8. The child may frequently be a rebel.

Middle Child

The middle child will usually try to overtake the first as a result of what Harold Mosak calls the "Avis Complex" ("because I'm second I'll try harder"). Usually the middle child will choose to compete in areas in which the oldest child is not proficient. If oldest children are good students, athletes, or models of good behavior, then middle children will probably be poor students, uninterested in athletics, and discipline problems; however, they might be good musicians, artists, or strong in an area where the oldest isn't skilled. Whereas the oldest child is the "center of the universe" the subsequent children must "slip in on the second or third act."

Middle children tend to be sensitive to injustices, unfairness, feelings of being slighted or abused, or of having no place in the group. When a younger sibling is born into the family, the middle child often feels dethroned, because of the new competition from the youngest child. The middle child also has a standard bearer in front and a pursuer in the rear and is surrounded by what is often perceived as competitors.

Such children may:

1. Feel they have neither the privileges of the youngest nor the rights of the oldest child.

2. Hold the conviction that people are unfair to them.

3. Feel unloved.

4. Become extremely discouraged and a problem child.

5. Replace their family if they do not feel as if they belong by becoming overly involved with a peer group. (Dreikurs, Grunwald, Pepper (1982)).

Youngest Child

Youngest children have the unique situation that they have never been dethroned. They are generally the most powerful persons in the family because of the many ways of getting the parents and other siblings to do things for them. Youngest children frequently are not taken seriously because they are the smallest, and as a result, they may be spoiled by others. However, it should also be noted that youngest children should have good sibling models from which to observe and learn.

Dreikurs, Grunwald and Pepper (1982) believe such children may:

1. Get more attention from the family.
2. Not get as much parental pressure as their older siblings.
3. Be punished less.
4. Retain the baby role and place others in their service.
5. Feel often like an only child.
6. Usually have things done for them.
7. Has most decisions made for them by others and responsibility taken away from them.
8. Not be taken seriously.
9. Become the "boss" in the family.
10. Often ally themself with the first child.
11. Attempt to excel and overtake the older siblings.

Single Child:

Single ("Only") children usually develop in one of two basic directions: either they will try to meet the adult level of competence or they will remain helpless and irresponsible as long as possible. Usually single children will have better relationships with people much older or much younger than they are, rather than with their peer group. Single children may refuse to cooperate when their every wish is not granted. They are similar to youngest children in that neither have ever been displaced. Single children are often loners, not very sharing-oriented, and may expect a "special place" without having earned it. They have also never had a sibling rival.

Other possible characteristics include being self-centered, feeling insecure because of being reminded, "you are all we have,"; may become too adult-centered and have difficulty relating to peers; usually accepts the values of the parents, and are often ambitious and achievement-oriented.

141

Adopted Child:

An important issue relates to the parental attitude regarding the decision to adopt a child. For example, many parents overprotect and/or pamper adopted children by means of a "We couldn't have any of our own, but this child will have the finest of everything" attitude. Another issue involves whether there are other siblings biologically born to the parents. "In" and "out" groups of siblings often result from such a situation. Of course, the advantages surrounding an adoption include the child's having been planned and desired by the parents and the adoption agency's having conducted a thorough investigation of the home environment prior to the child's placement in the home.

In large families there can be several sub-families. In Robert's case there are two sub-families: in one sub-group Mary would be the oldest child, Robert a middle child, and Fred the youngest child; and in the other sub-family, Susan would be a single child. Large families are frequently characterized by less competition among the middle siblings. Parents usually have less time to spend with each sibling, so there is often very little for which the siblings may compete.

Joan Drescher (1993) has written a creative book for children entitled *The Birth Order Blues* in which she describes the phenomenon that so often happens in children —that each birth order feels the other positions are more favorable than themselves. In a humorous way, she illustrates some of what most children say in a very concrete manner about their respective benefits and liabilities of the respective positions. The chart on the following page summarizes her own words from the vantage point of a child.

OLDEST — ADVANTAGES	OLDEST — DISADVANTAGES
You get to stay up later & talk to grownups.	You get the blame when everything goes wrong.
You get to see a TV show others can't.	Too bossy.
You get to bring in the cheese & crackers when company comes.	Other children invade my room. They get into my clothes & records & secret stuff.
Because you're born first, you always get to go	If you're born first, you get old first.
MIDDLE — ADVANTAGES	**MIDDLE — DISADVANTAGES**
You get to be older & younger at the same time. Sometimes I'm a little sister, and sometimes I'm a big sister.	I get my brother's hand-me-down bike instead of a new one.
	It's like being the baloney hidden in a sandwich, or the hole in a donut.
	People don't look up to you like they do with the oldest, or say you're cute like the littlest. You're just plain in the middle.
YOUNGEST — ADVANTAGES	**YOUNGEST — DISADVANTAGES**
My brothers & sisters teach me things, like how to skateboard.	I get worried that no one will notice me, so I make sure everyone knows when I'm around.
My friends & family are my very own cheering squad.	I didn't even get recorded in the baby book. I guess everything I do is a rerun.
	You get everyones' old toys & clothes, and the older kids boss you around like crazy.
	You are lucky if there's any space left on the
ONLY — ADVANTAGES	**ONLY — DISADVANTAGES**
You do get to have your own room, but when it's a mess, you can't blame anyone else.	When it's dark, there's no one to talk to.
My pictures get the whole refrigerator door, and I'm the only kid opening presents in our house.	There are no brothers & sisters to ask advice when you don't want to ask your parents.

Adapted from Joan Drescher's *The Birth Order Blues*.Viking Press, NY: Penguin of Penguin Books,1993.

Sibling Ratings and General Life-Style Themes

As Shulman & Mosak (1988) note, rating siblings comparatively on specific traits has several advantages. Specific questions often help define specific differences between themselves and other siblings. The comparative ratings also indicate specific areas of perceived success and failure. The concept of "180 degrees across the circle" indicates that siblings define themselves not only by who they are, but also by who they are not. By knowing how other siblings were perceived different or similar, we also are gaining valuable information about the individual.

Although each person has a unique life-style, Mosak (in Nikelly, 1972) has identified fourteen common life-style themes. They are included here to form a beginning summary of family constellation. We have also devised a specific chart comparing possible sibling ratings to such general life-style themes. Such general life-style themes can provide the rapid identification of commonly observed recurring syndromes. The counselor should also seek the specific unique manner in which the individual employs such broad life-style patterns.

1. The **"getter"** actively or passively manipulates life and others by employing charm, shyness, temper, or intimidation to put others into his/her service.

2. The **"driver"** is the person perpetually in motion, the over-conscious, over-ambitious person constantly striving to complete a goal. Each day is viewed in terms of how best to get the "most mileage" with as few "pit stops" as possible. Life is a perpetual "race" for such persons, although the goal or finish line is seldom attained. As one individual stated, "I don't know where I' going, but I've got my foot to the floorboard."

3. The **"controller"** either wants to control life or is afraid that it will dominate him or her. Surprises are disliked, spontaneity controlled, and feelings largely masked or hidden from others. Intellectualism, rightness, orderliness and neatness are favored actions. Such a person is always concerned about "saying the right thing at the right time."

4. Persons who **need to be right** scrupulously avoid making errors. Should they be caught in an error, they often will rationalize that others are wrong more often than they are. "Being right" becomes their obsession.

5. People who **need to be superior** may refuse to enter life tasks in which they cannot be the "center" or the "best." Such people may engage in such socially nonconstructive activities as seeing how many consecutive times they can jump on a pogo stick for the purpose of breaking the world record. "If I can't be first or best, then I'll settle for last or worst" often characterizes such individuals.

6. People who **need to be liked** to "please everybody all the time," are sensitive to criticism, and feel crushed when not enjoying universal and constant approval. They are adept at discovering how to be accepted by others, and feel that such opinions are the only measure of their personal worth.

7. People who **need to be "good"** prefer living by higher moral standards than their peers. Such extreme goodness may serve as an instrument for moral superiority, so that such persons not only elevate themselves over others, but may actually discourage the "inferior" person. As Mosak notes, this is a frequent device of the "model child" or the alcoholic's wife.

8. People who **oppose everything** rarely can be found to be for something. They are quick to identify faults, constantly finding themselves opposed to the programs or desires of others.

9. The **"victim"** innocently or actively becomes a "disaster chaser," characterized by feelings of nobility, self-pity, resignations, or proneness to accident. Seeking the sympathy or pity of others is also commonly employed by such people.

10. The **"martyr"** is similar to the victim, except that his or her "death" is for a noble or righteous cause. Moral indignation or silent suffering at the hands of "unjust" others are common actions.

11. The **"baby"** finds a place through the use of charm, cuteness, and the exploitations of others. Often (but not always) the youngest in the family constellation, such persons may have high pitched voices and childlike mannerisms employed to put others into their service.

12. The **"inadequate" person** can do nothing right, being thoroughly awkward or clumsy. Often activities are limited to those in which some success is guaranteed, and assuming responsibility generally results in failure. Such a person loudly proclaims his/her own inadequacies, a living symbol of an "inferiority complex."

13. People who **avoid feelings** believe that logical thinking and rational living can solve all life's problems. Their most prized characteristics consist of their logic, rationalization, intellectualization, and "talking a good game."

14. The **"excitement seeker"** despises dull, routine activities, preferring constant thrill and motion. In searching for excitement, others are often employed in providing new exhilaration. "Let's party tonight" is a frequent theme. Self-excitements of fears or masturbation may also be employed.

Suggested Templates for Sibling Ratings and General Life-Style Themes

Generalized Life-Style Theme	Rated Themselves Most When Compared to Other Siblings	
Getter	Selfish Having own way Temper tantrums	Materialistic Rebellious Sensitive
Driver	Hardest worker Critical of others Best grades in school	Idealistic Standards of accomplishment
Controller	Critical of others Rebellious Intelligent	Sensitive — easily hurt Having own way Least spontaneous
Need to be right	Critical of others Conforming Best grades in school	Sensitive — easily hurt Trying to please
Need to be superior	Selfish Temper tantrums Strongest Attractive	Most athletic Having own way Idealistic
Need to be liked	Trying to please Considerate Conforming Attractive	Punished Sensitive — easily hurt Helping around the house

Suggested Templates for Sibling Ratings and General Life-Style Themes — *Continued*

Generalized Life-Style Theme	Rated Themselves Most When Compared to Other Siblings	
Need to be good	Conforming Critical of others High standards of accomplishment Most athletic	Hardest worker Idealistic
Opposed to everything	Rebellious Temper tantrums	Spoiled Sensitive — easily hurt
Victim	Idealistic Sensitive — easily hurt	Punished
Martyr	Punished Trying to please	Sensitive — easily hurt Idealistic
Baby	Having own way Temper tantrums Selfish	Attractive Spoiled
Inadequate person	Trying to please Low intelligence	Sensitive — easily hurt Low standards of accomplishment, etc.
Avoids feelings	Intelligent Conforming Best grades in school	High standards of accomplishment
Excitement seeker	Sense of humor Rebellious Selfish	Spoiled Idealistic Spontaneous

Guidelines for Sibling Ratings

The interrelationship of people allows an opportunity to extend the information which the individual has given in data collection portions of the life-style process. The way in which this happens is that behaviors are retained in an individual's repertoire because they are useful means of dealing with others. If a behavior lacks utility, it is soon dropped in favor of other actions.

One has only to note the behavior of a child of deaf parents discarding the sound of crying yet retaining the physical manifestations of crying. In the same way we retain what works for us.

The following ratings are used as examples of utility of behaviors and are taken from the ratings section of the life-style investigation guide. People rating themselves as highly sensitive and easily hurt use this set of behaviors in a special way. One guess about the use of this behavior would be that the individual exerts a great deal of control over his/her environment. Few persons would verbally attack an individual who is easily hurt or sensitive. In this way an individual may exert profound control over a situation or an environment. Such individuals have found a way to limit access to themselves by others and limit the types of feedback about behaviors which the environment has to offer. Therefore, being sensitive and easily hurt generates a socially powerful position rather than a socially weak position.

Another descriptive characteristic could be a high rating on considerateness. An individual who is considerate is by many standards a desirable person to interact with in social situations. But if the behavior is over-used, it can be an attention-getting mechanism. Being considerate can be used by an individual with a need to be the center of attention, as shown by the "model husband." The "model husband" is considerate, kind, gentle, etc., at all times except when drinking. At this point he becomes suspicious and argumentative in demeanor. How can such apparently opposite behaviors co-exist in one individual? A person can employ socially useful and socially useless behaviors to effect their overall goal-directed behavior. The situation of drinking or not drinking merely represent two occasions to be the center of attention which are affected by differing methods at each respective time. Being considerate is one side of a two-faced coin. While in a drunken state, being argumentative attains the same objective of being noticed.

The Use of Literature in Life-Style Assessment

Favorite stories, fairy tales, television characters, etc. are other useful ways to find out about one's formative experiences. Literature has had a decided influence upon Adlerian psychology in general and on life-style assessment in particular. For example, Adler (1933) noted that:

> Our knowledge of the individual is very old. To name only a few instances, the historical and personality descriptions of the ancient peoples, the Bible, Homer, Plutarch, all the Greek and Roman poets, sagas, fairy tales, and

myths, show a brilliant understanding of personality. Until recent times it was chiefly the poets who best succeeded in getting the clue to a person's life-style. Their ability to show the individual living, acting, and dying as an indivisible whole in closest context with the tasks of his sphere of life rouses our admiration for their work to the highest degree.

Adler (1956) also wrote that :

Someday soon it will be realized that the artist is the leader of mankind on the path to the absolute truth. Among poetic works of art which have led me to the insights of individual psychology, the following stand out as pinnacles: fairy tales, the Bible, Shakespeare, and Goethe. (p. 329)

Eckstein (1984) describes how he integrated the projective use of literature and life-style assessment in a graduate counseling course. A student described the impact of literature on her personal "pilgrimage" in the following manner:

The word "pilgrimage" evokes in my mind images of ancient pilgrimages across northern Spain to the sanctuary at Santiago de Compostela. These pilgrimages are superbly described in James Michener's *Iberia*. In the year 1130, a French priest, Aymery de Picaud, who lived along one of the pilgrim routes, described the incredible dangers faced by the pilgrims. But for those who made it, the glories seem worth the hardships. It was said that only those who made this terribly hazardous trip to Compostela truly deserved to be called pilgrims. Thus a pilgrimage symbolizes to me a mixture of pain and pleasure.

In a sense, literary experiences can be compared to a pilgrimage. Literature encompasses all of the thoughts and emotions common to man. Written words have the power to reach into the darkest recesses of my mind and force me to take a look at the unlovely thoughts that lurk, as did the robbers who lay in wait for the pilgrims, just beneath the surface. Written words also have the power to bring to my awareness the parts of my mind that are bathed in the sunlight of love, sunlight such as the pilgrims experienced as they overcame each difficulty to demonstrate an expression of their devotion. Each word that I absorb brings me a little further along the path, with roadblocks and detours scattered along the way, leading me to my ultimate destiny (p.145).

The woman then concludes her own summarizing literary pilgrimage as follows:

With grief for Bambi I did weep;
An appointment at Treasure Island I did keep.
I entered the magic land of Oz;

For the miserable poor, I glorified in Robin Hood's cause.
The Bible was a lamp unto my feet:
Les Misérables my anger did heat.
Rebecca's misery in Gothic gray
Was lightened by a Shakespearean play.
I felt with Admiral Perry the bone-chilling cold;
I galloped with Revere on his midnight ride so bold.
I gloried in the myths of ancient Greece and Rome,
As on the magic carpet I traveled from home.
I watched in the night with the Highwayman's black-haired Bess;
And trekked with Daniel Boone in the untamed wilderness.
The legends of Beowulf, Roland and El Cid
And the poetry of Longfellow in my heart I hid.
I journeyed with Frost down the road not taken;
and marveled at the essays of Francis Drew;
The Robe my faith did renew.
I traveled Death's journey with Thanatopsis;
And so thus ends my "novel" synopsis.

What do all these past readings mean to me in a psychological sense? They have become a part of me because in my development as a human being, these books, and many others, have stirred my blood. My mind was, and is, like a sponge soaking up knowledge. Every book has the potential power to change my mind and to alter the direction of my development. (p. 146)

Thus, another means of exploring one's childhood is to ask about important stories, proverbs, Bible verses, or key teachings of the child's own particular religious beliefs. Like early recollections, there is a selective and projective nature to such memories which are a valuable potential "window" into the inner early childhood formative events.

Early Recollections Interpretation Guidelines

When we have a pretty clear picture of what an individual's early life was like, we move into the area of early recollections. These ER's are essential to life-style analysis because they are used to validate our hypotheses of how an individual views self, other people, and life in general based on the family constellation information.

The following guidelines should be considered in obtaining and interpreting ER's:

1. Employ *unstructured*, standardized statements such as "Think back as far as you can, and tell me the first thing you remember."

2. Be certain to write down all the events *exactly* as stated by the individual.

3. Distinguish between an early recollection and a report. An ER should be a specific event such as "One day I remember..." Conversely, a report is more global, typified by: "We used to..." or, "Many times I..."

4. Look for *recurring themes,* such as whether the person is alone or with others, active or passive, cooperative or competitive, plus relationships with peers, adults, males, females, etc.

5. ER's are not reasons. Rather, they are hints indicating movement toward a goal or they reveal what obstacles are to be overcome.

6. Note whether the person is interested in the useful or useless side of life. For example, a person seeking attention may obtain it by excelling in school or by stealing automobiles.

7. A desire to be with others does not always indicate a genuine interest in their welfare. For example, Adler (1937) describes the following ER: "I remember playing with my sister and two friends one day." However, the same person indicated her greatest fear was that of "being left alone." Rather than a genuine concern for others, such an individual was more characterized by a lack of independence.

8. The sequence of events does not have to be in the chronological order in which they occurred. It is more important to note the order in which the person presents the memories.

9. Pampering should be considered in recollections where the mother appears frequently. Feelings of neglect may be indicated in ER's where the mother never appears.

10. Remembering the birth of a younger sibling is a good indication of later sibling rivalry.

11. Nikelly (1971) suggests that the persons mentioned in the ER's may not necessarily be the actual ones involved in the client's life; for instance, "mother" may refer to a sister, teacher, or female peer.

12. Passive persons often recall observing others playing or working, while outgoing individuals mention self-activity and initiative in their ER's.

13. Physicians often recall people being sick or a series of accidents, while artists mention the color of clothes and scenery.

14. Athletes often cite sports and games in their recollections, and those having academic problems are apt to remember difficulty with writing and reading. The same applies with religious or sexual concerns, marital conflicts, self-concept, etc.

15. Encourage the person to share as many ER's as he or she can remember. A minimum of three and a maximum of ten are good guidelines.

16. Give more emphasis to initial recollections than the latter ones. Similarly, more importance should be placed on "less spectacular" events. For example, almost everybody would remember their house burning down, but how many people would remember "sitting in the corner by myself stacking blocks"?

17. Always get both the *content* and the *affective feeling* concerning the ER. After an individual shares a memory, always ask: "And how did you feel?"

18. ER's will change before and after counseling just as the individual's attitude about the environment, others, and self change.

19. Don't be afraid to guess about the meaning of ER's. If you're correct the person will let you know by means of a "recognition reflex," a slight smile or nod of acknowledgment. If you're incorrect, he or she may look confused or puzzled. But even when you're "wrong," the person has still defined himself or herself even if it's to disagree with a particular interpretation.

20. Separate ER's may be considered as individual beads comprising a necklace. Finding unifying themes provides the string which couples or explains seemingly inconsistent, separate ER's.

21. Shulman & Mosak (1988) note the following common thematic topics found in ER's: *dethronement* (the birth of a younger sibling or another person entering who takes center stage), *surprises, obstacles, affiliation, security, skill tasks dependency, external authority, self-control, status, power, morality, human interactions, new situations, excitement, sexuality, gender, nurturance, confusion, luck, sickness,* and *death.* The second part of the ER, the subject's feeling and identifying what was most vivid about the ER, gives valuable insight into what the person concluded about the event, the "therefore...". Shulman & Mosak provide the following list of representative response themes: *observer, problem-solving, compliance or rebellion, a call for help, revenge, suffering, manipulation, seeking excitement, pretense, denial, resolve, competence, social interest, activity, distance-keeping, cooperation, overconfidence, self-aggrandizement, criticism* and *feeling avoidance.*

22. Powers & Griffith (1987) summarize ER's utilizing the three major factors of sequence, similarity, and symmetry. "*Sequence* means the arrangement of the entire set of early recollections, and the relationship of each to the ones before and after it in the series. *Similarity* means a repetition of (or a variation upon) ideas or themes in applying various early recollections... *Symmetry* means correspondence between two early recollections as they balance one another, or are juxtaposed as if to represent two sides of an issue." (p. 266)

23. Other general guides for ER interpretation are summarized by Adler in Ansbacher & Ansbacher (1956):

    a) Much comes to light through the choice of presentation of a 'we' or 'I' situation. b) Much, too, comes to light from the mention of the mother. c) Recollections of dangers and accidents, as well as of corporal and other punishments, disclose the exaggerated tendency to keep in mind particularly the hostile side of life. d) The recollection of the birth of a brother or sister reveals the situation of dethronement. e) The recollection of the first visit to the kindergarten or school shows the great impressions produced by new situations. f) The recollection of sickness or death is often linked with a fear of these dangers, and occasionally with the attempt to become better equipped to meet them, possibly as a doctor or a nurse. g) Recollections of a stay in the country with the mother, as well as the mention of certain persons like the mother, the father, or the grandparents in a friendly atmosphere, often show not only a preference for these persons, who evidently pampered the child, but also the exclusion of others. h) Recollection of misdeeds, thefts, and sexual misdemeanors which have been committed, usually point to a great effort to keep them from occurring again. (p. 8)

In seeking common interpretive elements for both ER's and dreams, Adler's (1936) advice is important:

We need to warn ourselves that we cannot explain a dream without knowing its relationship to the parts of the personality. Neither can we lay down any fixed and rigid rules of dream interpretation. The golden rule of individual psychology is: "Everything can be different." We must modify each dream interpretation to fit the individual concerned; and each individual is different. If we are not careful, we will only look for types or for universal symbols, and that is not enough. The only valid dream interpretation is that which can be integrated with an individual's general behavior, early memories, problems, etc. In each case the contents of the dream should be gone over with the patient and as many associations elicited from him as possible. (pp. 13–14)

So, we cannot interpret dreams without first knowing the dreamer.

24. Kaplan (1985) suggests the following ten questions be answered relative to ER's:

a. Who is present in the recollection?

b. Who is remembered with affection?

c. Who is disliked in the recollection?

d. What problem(s) is (are) confronted in the recollection?

e. What special talent(s) or ability is (are) revealed in the recollection?

f. Is the recollection generally pleasant or unpleasant?

g. What is the client's level of activity in the recollection?

h. What emotion does the client feel and/or show pertaining to the recollection?

i. What does the recollection suggest to you about the client's social interest?

j. What fictional goal(s) is (are) implied in the recollection?

Sample Early Recollections with Pertinent Descriptions

Prior to interpreting ER's on your own, perhaps it would be helpful to see some memories complete with relevant comments from successful psychologists. In the following case-history ER's, Alfred Adler (1958) discusses important considerations and demonstrates the wealth of information available from seemingly insignificant memories:

"One big event stands out in my early childhood. When I was about four years old my great-grandmother came to visit us." We have seen that a grandmother usually spoils her grandchildren: but how a great-grandmother treats them we have not yet experienced. *"While she was visiting us we had a four-generation picture taken."* This girl is very much interested in her pedigree. Because she remembers so strongly the visit of her great-grandmother and the picture that was taken, we can probably conclude that she is very bound-up in her family. If we are right, we shall discover that her ability to cooperate does not go beyond the limits of her family circle.

"I clearly remember driving to another town and having my dress changed to a white embroidered one after we arrived at the photographer's." Perhaps this girl, too, is a visual type. *"Before having the four-generation picture taken, my brother and I had ours taken."* Again we come across the interest in the family. Her brother is a part of the family and we shall probably hear more of her relations with him. *"He was placed on the arm of a chair beside me and was given a bright red ball to hold."* Here again she remembers visible things. *"I stood by the side of the chair and was given nothing to hold."* Now we see the main striving of this girl. She says to that her brother is preferred to her. We might guess that she felt it disagreeable when her younger brother came and took away her position of being the youngest and most pampered. *"We were told to smile."* She means, "They tried to make me smile, but what did I have to smile about? They put my brother on a throne and gave him a bright red ball; but what did they give to me?"

Then came the four-generation picture. *"Everybody tried to look their best but me. I would not smile."* She is aggressive against her family because her family is not good enough to her. In this first memory she has not forgotten to inform us how her family treated her. *"My brother smiled so nicely when asked to smile. He was so cute. To this day I detest having my picture taken."* Such remembrances give us a good insight into the way most of us meet life. We take one impression and use it to justify a whole series of actions. We draw consequences from it and act as if the consequences were obvious facts. Clearly enough, she had a disagreeable time when this photograph was taken. She still detests having her picture taken. We shall generally find that any one who dislikes something as much as this chooses a reason for his dislike; selects something from his experiences to bear the whole burden of justifying it. This first memory has given us two main clues to the personality of the writer. First, she is a visual type; second, and still more important, she is bound to her family. The whole action of her first memory is placed within the family circle. She is probably not well adapted for social life. (pp. 82–84)

Although ER's should be consistent with each other, it is important to realize that individual recollections will not always convey the same meanings. For example, Plewa (1935) notes that:

> It is not always possible to extract the entire facets, and it is only when one is able to study an individual for a long time that one notices in him the tendencies to be seen in the recollections with their multitude of variations. Therefore, no matter how many interpretations one recollection lends itself to, each of these substantiates the unity of the personality. (p. 97)

As noted earlier in the interpretive guidelines, apparent ER contradictions need to be examined within their total context. To that end, Mosak (1958) notes that:

> Occasionally the contradiction merely states that under a certain set of conditions, actual or perceived, the individual will respond in one manner and to another set of circumstances in a second way. An illustration of this type of "contradiction" appears in the following recollections of an adult woman.
>
> **ER** — I remember that I was under three and the lady next door picked me up over the fence to take me home.
>
> **ER** — My uncle gave my sisters ten cents to kiss him. Then he made me the same offer. I ran out the back door and all the way home.
>
> **Interpretation** — In the first ER people are depicted as supportive while in the second, they appear to be threatening. Actually the contradiction is resolved when one observes that the supportive person is a woman while the threatening person is a man. Thus, this woman only has a place in the woman's world. The masculine world, especially because it involved sexual behavior, is threatening and she must avoid it. (p. 6)

Mosak suggested a helpful method of obtaining significant information from ER's is to consider the memory as a newspaper story. Your job is then to compose the "newspaper headline" to present the story in the paper. In other words, read the story, then summarize the key points in a sample newspaper

156

bold print heading. For some practice, read the following ER's and compose your own newspaper headline for each story. In your headlines, use general references rather than specific persons. For example, use "adults" or "women" for "mother," "peers" instead of specific names of friends. etc.

1. **Age 3:** "My father put me on my sister's two-wheeler — I didn't trust him — I was terrified — felt I was too young to ride. He then took me off, knowing I was too scared. Later I went back and pretended I was riding.

   Feeling: "Scared; relieved when I finally got off."

   Headline: _____

2. **Age 3:** "My sister dressed me up in a fancy costume — she took me into the backyard and took pictures. I liked it because my hair was fixed like grandmother's. My sister then put her jewelry on me."
   Feeling: "In my glory; neat."

   Headline: _____

3. **Age 3:** "Mom said I could take ballet or go to kindergarten. I figured kindergarten would end in one year, so I chose ballet. I remember my first day in ballet. I had been downtown with mom. She said I could start ballet, but I didn't have a ballet outfit. The teacher said I could dance. I then walked into the room — it was the biggest I had ever seen. Scared and thrilled me — it was so unbelievably big."
   Feeling: "Liked it: Thought it was neat; knew I would like ballet. But it scared me because it was a new situation and I didn't know the other girls."

   Headline: _____

Read the observations below after completing your headlines.

In the first recollection, we see a person who is terrified because of a number of possible reasons. It may be the thought of coping with a new experience. Can you think of some others? A second part of the ER involves others (adults, or adult males) "rescuing" her in a time of trouble. Therefore, the headline might reflect the idea of fear in dealing with new experiences, adults coming to her rescue, and her subsequent relief. There are many possibilities, but a few possible headlines might include: "Girl terrified by new experience rescued by adults"; or "Girl wants to be grown up, but isn't ready, yet." (A first-person headline could also be employed.)

The second recollection indicates an interest in materialism, a concern for neatness and fashion. We might guess that these concerns are still important considerations for her. Some sample headlines include: "Girl enjoys special attention, recognition, and possessions." We might also note that in both ER's she is being acted upon rather than actively shaping her environment. (As a vocational predictor, it should be noted that this person is now an artist.)

The third ER contains an "approach avoidance" type situation where the vastness and newness of a situation both frightens and awes her. Our headline would probably want to convey both the thrill of the moment plus the apprehension of making new friends. We might also want to follow-up on her reactions to her mother and her teachers (adults) when compared with her fear of making new friends (peers).

Additional Early Recollections

In contrast to the above ER's of a white female artist are the following ER's of a black male in a correctional setting. As in the above examples, it would be most beneficial for you to write your own "newspaper headline" for each ER. Then read the comments.

1. **Age 5:** "My brothers and I picked on a midget; we called him 'midget', 'shorty,' etc. He got mad, but laughed. He called us bad names, then we'd run him down the street. He'd try to get the police on us, but we'd hide."
   Feeling: "Thought it was fun."
   Headline: _____

Here is an individual who enjoys having fun at the expense of others. There is a marked lack of social interest with peers rather than adults being involved. One possible headline might be: "It is satisfying to get the best of other people, especially those whom I consider inferior."

2. **Age 5:** "I remember running down the alley throwing down trash cans and making noise. Someone called the police. They snuck up on my brothers, taking us all to the station. We wouldn't talk, and they warned us if we were caught again we d be locked up. When we got

home, dad wanted to whip us, but mom wouldn't let him."

Feeling: "When throwing cans, felt happy; it was fun; liked playing; when caught, was still happy; didn't know what was happening; when home, still laughing — just followed the gang."

Headline: _____

Again we can see a lack of social interest, including enjoyment at the expense of others. There is a lack of regard for the rules, and, even when caught, nothing serious happens. Having fun continues to be important, especially with his friends. It is also interesting that when punishment was imminent (dad), someone else (mom) intervened on his behalf. A sample series of first-person headlines include: "I can do as I please, and don't have to worry about the threats of others, nor do I have to abide by the rules of the game," or enjoy having fun at the expense of others."

3. **Age 4:** "My brother and I were playing in the house — he hit me — I became cross-eyed — people started making fun of me — I didn't understand how I got cross-eyed."

Feeling: "Didn't like it — wasn't laughing when I came up.

Headline: _____

The proverbial "shoe is on the other foot" typifies this ER. Here, the individual is the subject of the laughter, and he doesn't like it at all. A sample headline might state: "Boy upset when others laugh, (belittle, make fun of) him."

In just three memories concerning his childhood, this person has told us a lot about himself. When included with other life-style information such as ordinal position, and family atmosphere, we could make some "educated guesses" about the way he views life, others, and self.

Perhaps you had different ideas from the preceding ER's — that's fine. We all need to form "hunches," be willing to guess at the meaning and, as Dreikurs often noted, "to have the courage to be imperfect." You may also feel totally incapable or inadequate at "finding" any underlying themes. Each of the authors have had to wrestle with his own feelings of inadequacies also. We would like to encourage you to practice interpreting ER's. And, there's nothing like being "on target" with a client to encourage additional use of ER's.

Additional guidelines for using ER's are presented in Appendix A on the use of the Willhite technique, and in Appendix B, Eckstein and Kern's "Early-recollection Role-reversal" process.

Mansager et.al. (1995) utilizes group interactive discussions of ER's with other adolescent peers in substance abuse groups. Within 2–3 clinical intervention sessions they use the following format:

1. **Introduction to ER's (20 minutes).** General discussion of how a child might view the world and the conclusions that might be drawn.

2. **Gathering of ER's (30 minutes).** Specific focus steps involve the group by:
   a) focusing on the presenting substance abuse challenge;
   b) identification and awareness of the emotion;
   c) the actual recording or writing down the memory; and
   d) collection of the papers for use later.

3. **Client guesses about generic ER's (20 minutes).** Sharing general adolescent ER's and having the group brainstorm and free associate to possible needs/themes/values expressed in such a memory.

4. **Client guesses about each other's ER's (20 minutes).** Specific ER's from the actual group members.

5. **Giving/Receiving Feedback about the accuracy of Guessing** — the adolescent then responds to the feedback given by his/her peers.

The Number One Priority and the "Top Card"

To complete this section on interpretation techniques, we conclude with what paradoxically may also be an initial first-step forming initial impressions, along with Mosak's 14 general life-style themes. The number-one priority is determined on the basis of the person's answers to the questions "What is most important in my quest for belonging?" and "What must I avoid at all costs?" Kefir (1972) originally defined four number-one priorities: **comfort, pleasing, control** and **superiority.** Dewey (1978) also credits Rudolf Dreikurs and William Pew with the same four priorities. She notes that although it is often difficult for an individual to determine his or her own life-style, the relative order of priorities is generally recognizable.

The following chart compares the four priorities with what is to be avoided at all costs:

Number-one priorities:	To be avoided at all costs:
Comfort	Stress
Pleasing	Rejection
Control	Humiliation
Superiority	Meaninglessness

Although people seldom give up their number-one priority, it is possible to become more aware through insight and to "catch oneself" being over-involved in each priority. Kefir & Corsini (1974) propose that a quick assessment of one of a client's life-style and core convictions could be accomplished by a clinical investigation of the person's number-one priority. The priorities are further defined as follows:

Comfort

Self-indulgence and immediate gratification characterize the comfort priority. The price for pleasure is often in diminished productivity, since they will not risk frustration and do not want responsibility. Being able to delay immediate gratification is necessary for such vocational fields as medicine and graduate school, as they require many years of training prior to completion. Some stress is also helpful in providing a positive motivator. For example, it is a grain of sand which motivates an oyster to form a pearl. Undue comfort is often correlated with lethargy and diminished risk-taking.

Pleasing

Pleasers often are challenging in respecting themselves or in receiving respect from others. The price the pleaser pays is stunted growth, alienation and retribution (Dinkmeyer, Dinkmeyer & Sperry, 1987). Pleasers are good at tuning in to what others want and need. Pleasers are characterized by an "external locus of control" using Rotter's (1980) term where one's happiness is in someone else's hands. Pleasers especially have difficulties in the political arena because there is always someone who disapproves of their actions. Pleasers often choose perfectionistic role models with whom they vainly jump through countless hoops, almost always in vain, as the "Good Housekeeping Seal of Approval" simply will never be granted.

Control

There are two sub-types of control: control of others and control of self. By striving for, and perhaps even attaining control, the negative consequence is that feelings of challenge and resistance in those around them are often evoked. Control of self is characterized by being "on edge," "uptight," and "hyper." Diminished spontaneity, creativity, flexibility and an inability to "go with the flow" are additional emotional costs for overcontrol.

Superiority

Being competent, being right, being useful, being a victim, or being a martyr are some of the specific manifestations of superiority. First-borns often expect to be "number-one" and are subjected to a feeling of meaninglessness when "dethroned." Such strivings also lead to undo competitive behavior. There is a profound parable relative to getting to the top described in Trina Paulus' (1972) *Hope For the Flowers*. It is a story of an aggressive caterpillar who literally steps on top of others in his single-minded quest to get to the top of a "caterpillar pillar." His own awakening occurs when his former partner appears to him as a brilliant yellow butterfly. He then leaves the vertical pillar to begin his own metamorphosis by being willing to let go of his former self, or "die," to enter a cocoon for his own transformation.

The "price" paid for superiority is over-involvement, over-responsibility, fatigue, stress, psychosomatic illnesses, and uncertainty about one's relationships with others.

Steve Cunningham adapted Eckstein's life-style animal typologies and created what he called one's "Top Card." In *Positive Discipline in the Classroom,* Jane Nelsen and Lynn Lott creatively adapt his "Top Card" to the #1 Priorities. Specific strengths and potential blind spots or liabilities of one's early style are illustrated in the chart on pages 164–165.

The Five Animal Types representative of the five life-style traits:
Aggressive — Tiger; Conforming — Chameleon; Defensive — Turtle;
Individualistic — Eagle; Resistive — Salmon

TOP CARD

If You'd Like To Avoid:	Then Your Top Card is:	And Perhaps You:	Assets:
Rejection and Hassles	Pleasing (Chameleon)	Act friendly. Say yes & mean no. Give in. Worry about what others want more than your needs. Gossip instead of confronting directly. Try to fix everything & make everybody happy.	Sensitive to others. Have lots of friends. Considerate. Compromiser. Nonthreatening. Likely to volunteer. People count on you. Usually see positives in people & things.
Criticism, Humiliation, and Ridicule	Control (Eagle)	Hold back. Boss others. Organize. Argue. Get quiet & wait for others to coax you. Do it yourself. Stuff your feelings. Cover all the bases before you make a move.	Good leader & crisis manager. Assertive. Persistent. Well organized. Productive. Law abiding. Get what you want. Able to get things done & figure things out. Take charge of situations. Wait patiently
Meaninglessness, Unimportance & Stupidity	Superiority (Lion)	Put down people or things. Knock yourself. Talk about the absurdity of life. Correct others. Overdo. Take on too much. Worry about always doing better. Operate on "shoulds."	Knowledgeable. Precise. Idealistic. Get a lot done. Make people laugh. Receive a lot of praise, awards & prizes. Don't have to wait for others to tell you what to do to get things done. Have a lot of self-confidence.
Stress and Pain	Comfort (avoidance) (Turtle)	Make jokes. Intellectualize. Do only the things you already do well. Avoid new experiences. Take the path of least resistance. Leave sentences incomplete. Avoid risks. Hide so no one can find out you aren't perfect.	People enjoy being around you Flexible Do what you do well. Easy-going. Look out for self & own needs Can count on others to help. Make others feel comfortable.

Problems:	Someone Can Be A Friend To You By:	What I Really Want Is:
Invite revenge cycles & others to feel rejected. Feel resentful & ignored. Get in trouble for trying to look good while doing bad. Not having things the way you want them. Reduction in personal growth. Lots of sense of self & what pleases self.	Telling you how much they love you. Teaching you a lot. Showing approval. Showing appreciation. Letting you know you won't be in trouble if you say how you really feel.	To do what I want while others clap. For others to like me, accept me, and be flexible. For others to take care of me & make hassles go away.
Lack spontaneity. Social & emotional distance. Want to keep others from finding weak spots. Invite power struggles. End up sick. Avoid dealing with issues when you feel criticized. Get defensive instead of open. Sometimes wait for permission. Critical & fault finding.	Saying "OK." Giving you choices. Letting you lead. Asking how you feel. Giving you time & space to sort out your feelings.	To be in control even though others can be better, smarter. To get respect, cooperation & loyalty. For others to have faith in me & give me permission to do what I want. To have choices & go at my own pace.
Overwhelmed, overburdened. Invite others to feel incapable & insignificant. Seen as a know-it-all or rude & insulting & don't know it's a problem. Never happy because you could have done more or better. Have to put up with so many imperfect people around you. Sometimes you don't do anything.	Telling you how significant you are. Thanking you for your contributions. Helping you get started with a small step. Telling you you're right.	To do it best. To get appreciation & recognition from others & a spiritual connection. To be told I'm right.
Suffer boredom. Lazy, lack of productivity. Hard to motivate. Don't do your share. Invite special attention & service. Worry a lot but no one knows how scared you are. Lose out on the contact of sharing. Juggle uncomfortable situations rather than confront them. Wait to be taken care of instead of becoming independent. Invite others to feel stressed.	Not interrupting. Inviting your comments. Listening quietly. Leaving room for you. Showing faith. Encouraging small steps.	For things to be as easy as they look. To be left alone. To have my own space & pace. I don't want to argue.

Adapted from the manual, *Positive Discipline in the Classroom,* by Jane Nelsen and Lynn Lott. Fair Oaks, CA: Sunrise Press. (Phone 800-456-7770)

Research Studies

In a theme issue of *The Counseling Psychologist* devoted exclusively to the theory and practice of individual psychology, Allen (1971) noted that more empirical studies validating core Adlerian concepts were needed. Since that time there has been a significant increase — in *Individual Psychology,* the principle Adlerian-oriented journal, C. Edward Watkins, Jr. (1982, 1983, 1986) has summarized core Adlerian research articles and developed a bibliography based on four core Adlerian concepts, including: 1) Birth order, 2) Social interest 3) Early recollections, and 4) Life-style.

Some of his overall conclusions are that research articles in *Individual Psychology* have indeed flourished. From 1970–1981, birth order studies predominated; investigations of social interest have increased substantially since 1977.

A family atmosphere related study involves Chandler & Willingham's (1986) research comparing perceived early childhood family influence and the patient's later established life-style. They found that the following five factors explained a significant portion of the variance: 1) Parent relationship/parent-child relationship, 2) Mother's characterization, 3) Father's characterization, 4) Sibling inter-relationship, and 5) Subject's childhood characterization.

Research on ER's and life-styles has been limited but has seen increase in the past decade. Much research has been conducted on a college population exclusively or on some other type of students (elementary, high school, etc.), but more studies on actual clinical populations and the general adult population are recommended.

Three formative doctoral dissertations at the University of South Carolina, under the supervision of then NASAP President Frank Walton, led to the development of an Early Recollections Rating Scale (Rule, 1972; Quinn, 1973; and Altman, 1973).

Eckstein (1976) used the ERRS to empirically validate a core Adlerian idea that ER's change as a result of therapy. For example, Dreikurs (1967) writes that:

> The final proof of the patient's satisfactory reorientation is the change in his basic mistakes, indicated by a change in his early recollections. If a significant improvement has taken place, new incidents are recollected, reported recollections show significant changes, or are in some cases completely forgotten. (p. 71)

Eckstein's major finding was that "ER's do appear to change significantly as a result of long-term therapy." He also found that global ratings based on all combined ER's was more effective in demonstrating change than separate ER ratings, again consistent with Adler's reference to the total context ("Zusammerhang") of the whole individual. High inter-rater reliability gave additional credence to the use of Altman's ERRS in research studies. (Changes in ER's is a needed area for additional empirical clinical studies.)

John Zarski (in Baruth & Eckstein, 1981 and with Sweeney & Barcikowski, 1977) provides further validation of the ERRS. Dutton & Newlon (1988) used the ERRS to discriminate sexual fantasies of adolescent sex offenders. They found significant correlations on the mistreated vs. befriended, threatening vs. friendly, and depressing vs. cheerful sub-scales. A significant difference between the means was found on the scale threatening vs. friendly.

Savill & Eckstein (1987) used the ERRS to demonstrate changes in ER's within a state mental hospital as a function of mental status. They found a significant change toward higher mental status and higher social interest from time of admission to time of discharge as measured by the ERRS when compared to a control group which showed no such changes. They also found a significant correlation between the ERRS, a social interest sub-scale of the NOISE-30, and the Zung scale, the highest correlation being on the "be-friended/mistreated" ERRS sub-scale.

Some actual pre/post ER changes from both the Eckstein (1976) and the Savill & Eckstein (1987) research studies help to identify for the beginning life-style assessor a dramatic difference in the "feeling tone" of the ER's.

This following example was described earlier in this chapter — it is noteworthy in that the same memory is recalled but with a much higher conclusion of social interest after nine months of therapy.

Pre

"My father put me on my sister's two wheeler — I didn't trust him — I was terrified — I screamed at the top of my lungs — felt I was too young to ride.

Post

"My father was trying to teach me to ride a two-wheeler — he was trying to teach me to ride — He then took me off, knowing I was too scared. I should have been more cooperative. Later I went back and pretended I was riding. He wasn't hurting me; Felt I should have "been more cooperative."

Kern, his students, and associates, as discussed earlier, have produced the Kern Lifestyle Scale with Interpretive manual, the Lifestyle Questionnaire Inventory (Appendix C), and the BASIS-A (Basic Adlerian Scales for Interpersonal Success). After some 17 years of research and some 20 studies, the authors of the BASIS-A, Wheeler, Kern, and Curlette, have not only produced the instrument, but in addition the interpretive and technical manuals to assist the user to employ the lifestyle assessment tool in clinical, as well as research settings (available through CMTI Press, Coral Springs, FL 33075 (305-345-7057, FAX 345-2052) and TRT Associates, 65 Eagle Ridge, Highland, NC 28741 (704-526-9561). For additional information, one can consult *Test in Print* and the most recent Burro's *Mental Measurement Yearbook.*

Thorne (1975) and Thorne & Piskin (1975) administered a 200-item questionnaire to seven sample clinical populations including incarcerated prisoners, alcoholics, and chronic undifferentiated schizophrenics from a state hospital. A factor analysis of their scores yielded the following five clinical life-styles differentiations:

1. Aggressive-domineering

2. Conforming

3. Defensive withdrawal

4. Amoral sociopathy

5. Resistant-defiant

In an effort to provide a more encouraging approach to the clinical descriptions of the five factors, Driscoll & Eckstein (1982) developed a life-style questionnaire utilizing the following animals to represent both the strengths and weaknesses of each style: **tiger, chameleon, turtle, eagle,** and **salmon.** A revision of that questionnaire formed the basis of Eckstein's questionnaire near the end of Chapter 2.

Substantial clinical experience with early recollections by Adlerians, and some others, has strongly established their value "as the basis of Adlerian personality assessment, or understanding of a person's life style" (Ansbacher, 1973, p. 135). Clearly early recollections are of extreme value in investigating "a personality".

Nomothetic research, the search for general principles, in investigations of personality, per se, theories and types of personalities, is, however, a very different kind of endeavor. Some information from early recollection analysis relevant to ascertaining the particular and unique aspects of an individual's life-style is necessarily lost in the quest for the common elements in personalities of subgroups of people, an enterprise from which other benefits in understanding are derived.

The authors suggest additional pre-post outcome studies with clinical populations. A longitudinal study exploring the change or constancy of ER's in general of 5, 10, 15, and 20 years is also needed.

Chapter Summary

The purpose of this chapter has been to present introductory interpretation skills in analyzing life-style data. Specific focus has been on the family atmosphere, the family constellation, birth order, and early recollections. Empirical research validating core Adlerian life-style theory was also presented. Chapter 5 explores the goal of reorientation by focusing particularly on the counseling relationship.

REORIENTATION

Reorientation consists of encouraging changes in attitudes and/or behaviors. It should occur after first: a) establishing an effective **relationship**, and b) conducting a **psychological investigation** including a life-style assessment. In reorientation the counselor and client work together to consider alternative beliefs, behaviors, and attitudes — a change in the client's life-style.

The purpose of this chapter is to integrate life-style assessment into a therapeutic context. Adlerian techniques for recognizing and changing self-defeating behaviors plus encouragement to reclaim one's personal power will be the focus. According to Murphey (1984), Adler was one of the first theorists to emphasize personal responsibility for one's behavior. Adler (1973a) stressed the patient's active, responsible role in psychotherapy when he stated, "The actual change in the nature of the patient can only be his own doing." According to Adler, "From the very beginning the consultant must try to make it clear that the responsibility for his cure is the patient's business" (p. 336).

Core Adlerian therapist attitudes include mutual trust and respect, and a client/therapist relationship based upon equality and friendliness. Viewing Adlerian psychotherapy as a "cooperative educational enterprise," Mosak (1979) stressed the client's responsibility and active role:

> Therapy is structured to inform the patient that a creative human being plays a role in creating one's problems, that one is responsible (not in the sense of blame) for one's actions, and that one's problems are based upon faulty perceptions, and inadequate or faulty learnings, especially of faulty values. If this is so, one can assume responsibility for change... From the initiation of treatment, the patient's efforts to remain passive are discouraged (p. 65).

The following section will explore general counseling implications relative to the issue of client change. Specific interpretative guidelines for Adlerian Life-style assessment will then be introduced.

The Paradox of Change — Considerations for Counselors

Abstract changes in beliefs and behavior are fundamental goals of counseling. The following section addresses such specific concepts as:

1. "Legacy," impressions — ("seeing beyond Z") and the tendency of the now
2. Paradigm shifts
3. The paradox of therapy
4. "Intent and outcome"
5. Who is the "Perceiver I?"

Illustrations and implications for client change will also be included. *"Impressions of the now"* are formed by one's early developmental experiences. Such impressions are literally etched like an engraving on the human mind and soul. Early recollections provide a valuable prospective insight into one's formative impressions created in childhood when each person makes core decisions or conclusions about life, others and one's self.

Such impressions may of course be either positive, or "negative," or a combination of both. These etchings create a literal groove on one's mind. Unfortunately, most people are unaware of such etchings of the mind because they are formed at such an early age the child has no conscious cognitive awareness or "container" to know such markings on the mind.

"Impressions of the now" then lead to legacy which can be defined as the resulting habitual remnants or pattern resulting from such things. Legacy is the consequence or result of impressions and forms what Shulman (1973) calls a "pre-working hypothesis."

The *"tendency"* is the consequence of such unified, holistic, deeply-grooved largely unconscious impressions — patterns which come to characterize one's basic life-style. Piaget (1972) uses the term *"assimilation"* to refer to the process where a person filters new information through a pre-formed hypothesis — over many years, habitual ways of acting result in tendencies or predispositions of beliefs and behaviors.

Although most people who come to counselors usually say they want to change, the paradox of therapy is that clients typically resist change (called *accommodation* or changing one's inner belief by Piaget) to adapt to new "external" information. Such factors as fear of change, fear of the unknown, comfort in one's predictable, breakable habitual patterns often create client resistance to have the courage to change the known for the "road less traveled" in the unknown, unexplored future.

Intent and Outcome

The difference between intent and outcome is an important change-related concept. ***Intent*** is what one *says* he or she wanted to happen (e.g., "I intended to be on time for our meeting"). The *outcome* is what actually occurred ("I was talking on the phone"). Counselors can gently confront such "I intended 'this' but a different 'that' happened" outcome *occurred* by asking clients to consider that what actually happened (outcome) is precisely the desired result that was wanted all along. Simply stated, an outcome is *saying* one thing but *doing* another. Or, as Adler said, "Trust only movement."

A ***paradigm*** is a systematic organized pattern, similar to what Piaget called a *scheme.* We all have broad categories ("computer programs") on such concepts as love, friendship, helping, self-love, women, men, work, abuse, change, etc. Paradigms are necessary to help organize separate, discrete disconnected bits of information. But unless paradigms are open to change or modification (accommodation) then one continually recycles through a "washing machine with dirty water and no rinse cycle." In such a case, one becomes a prisoner or slave to one's rigid, habitual unexamined patterns.

Personality disorders (i.e., borderline, narcissistic, being schizoid, dependent, etc.) are basically distorted schemes. Specific examples such as: "I am enraged because I was never truly loved," are preoccupied with, "me, me, me." "I avoid intimate/close relations," or "I must be in a relationship and approved of by significant others" are representative broad conclusions corresponding respectively to the above-listed personality disorders. Cognitive therapists such as Albert Ellis identify and confront such broad overgeneralized irrational beliefs.

A vivid example of a rigid scheme or paradigm involves the Swiss watchmakers. In the 1960's they had 60 percent of the world watch market and 80 percent of the profits. One day a technician adapted the quartz crystal to keep time. Excitedly he took his invention to his Swiss superiors. "It has no moving parts — it's not a watch at all!" they ridiculed him. The quartz crystal idea was considered so unimportant that it was not even patented.

Later at an international watch conference, the quartz crystal idea was openly displayed at a booth by the Swiss. Personnel from Texas Instruments and Seiko walked by the table — they liked what they saw. Their ability to see beyond the previous "this is a watch" paradigm helped create a new product. Only ten years later, Texas Instruments and Seiko had captured 80 percent of the international watch market.

Change: Creating New Impressions

In order to create new tendencies (paradigms) one must form new impressions. Telling an "old" story in a "new" way is one example of "reframing." To reframe is to create a new version of the habitual story. For example, a spiritual disciple once went away from his home and family. During his trip his father and all other members of his family were slain by a rival warring tribe. "My father violently abused me," he lamented to his spiritual teacher. "I feel guilty but I'm glad he's dead," he added. "What a great opportunity for you to be more compassionate to others because you have suffered such abuse," came the surprise reframing reply from the sage. "You are grander for the experience — you have new, greater power to help others," he concluded.

"You seek problems because you need their gifts — there is no such thing as a problem without a gift for you," Richard Bach wrote in Illusions (1977). In The Search For the Beloved (1984), Jean Houston notes that wounding is a core component of being able to have empathy for others.

Thus, a new reframed story is an assertive first step to changing old paradigms into new impressions.

The Gospel of Change According to Reverend Ike?

Reverend Ike puts it very succinctly. As an impoverished inner city child, he frequently would leave his neighborhood and visit another part of the city where "uppity folks" were dining in fine restaurants. He would stand outside the window watching what they ate, how they acted; he imagined their feelings, their conversations, the taste of their food— all the while telling himself that someday he, too, would be inside that fine restaurant. "When you see someone in a new Cadillac, instead of being jealous, say, 'someday that will be me,'" he suggests.

Such positive impressions help "seed" new tendencies. Paradigms, creativity, positive change — all are the consequence of the paradox involving simultaneously maintaining the best of established, stable personality traits (assimilation), coupled with the openness to new experiences (accommodation).

A "City of Refuge" — Counselors and Change

The Role of Counselors in the Change Process

In the Old Testament, there was what was known as a "City of Refuge" where one could go and be nurtured by others when life's challenges seemed overwhelming. In this century the natives on the "Big" island of Hawaii created a similar "City of Refuge" — even if criminally guilty of murder, if they could make it safely to that place, then they would be safe from harm's way. In a similar manner, it is possible for clients to feel such a safe and caring environment in the presence of counselors.

The counseling process itself involves dialogue between two or more people ideally is conducted in an atmosphere of trust and safety, and so can be an important conduit of client change. Plato formulated and refined his personal philosophy through meaningful dialogue with others. Specific counseling techniques previously described such as "stroke and spit," "reframing a perceived minus into a perceived plus," encouragement, acting "as if," etc., are part of the "doing" component. "Being" involves a counselor attitude of openness, honesty, genuineness, warmth, understanding, etc.

Because we are all "encapsulated" within ourselves and our often unconscious conditioning, counselors can help provide a more encouraging and empowering "reflection" to the client of him/herself.

"Man of La Mancha" is a poignant musical about Don Quixote, a "madman" knight who battled "windmills" he perceived to be "the Great Enchanter." But in his delusional state there was a purity of spirit and an innocence of heart much like the contemporary Forrest Gump. Along with his loyal sidekick Sancho Panza, Don Quixote encounters a country inn and tavern which he perceives to be a castle. There he sees the woman of his dreams, Dulcinea. He is instantly smitten by her radiant beauty and sings to her:

"I have dreamed you too long,
  Never seen thee, or touched, but know thee
  with all of my heart..."

His beloved Dulcinea quickly corrects him that her name is Aldonza and that she is "no kind of a lady":

"I was spawned in a ditch by a mother who left me there,
  naked and cold and too hungry to cry...
  I never blamed her, I'm sure she left hoping
  that I'd have the good sense to die!
  For a Lady has modest and maidenly airs

and a virtue I somehow suspect that I lack;
It's hard to remember these maidenly airs
in a stable laid flat on your back!
If you feel that you see me not quite at my virginal best,
Cross my palm with a coin and I'll willingly show you the rest!"

Then Don Quixote exclaims, "Never deny thou art Dulcinea," to which Aldonza replies:

"Take the clouds from your eyes and see me as I am!
You have shown me the sky, but what good is the sky
To a creature who'll never do better than crawl?
Of all the cruel bastards who've badgered and battered me,
You are the cruelest of all!
Don't you see what your gentle insanities do to me?
Rob me of anger and give me despair!
Blame and abuse I can take and give back again,
Tenderness I cannot bear!
So please torture me now with your "sweet Dulcineas" no more!
I am no one! I'm nothing! I'm only Aldonza the whore!"

Again Don Quixote asserts, "And forever thou art my lady Dulcinea!" (in Wasserman, 1966). She stomps away yelling at his madness. And yet on a more subtle level a seed had been planted, a new impression germinated in this reflection of her beauty. The *perceiver I* of Don Quixote saw the woman of his dreams. The "perceiver I" of her own self-worth was of "Aldonza, the whore," but it was Don Quixote's external reflection of beauty that helped her rediscover it within herself so that at the end of the play she called herself Dulcinea. Such a profound reorientation of her own self-assessment was influenced by someone else.

Who Is The "Perceiver I?"

In like manner counselors have the opportunity to be the "perceiver I" that reflects beauty, love and harmony in a myriad of personal strengths within the client. Profound behavioral and belief shifts thus are facilitated.

Through an optimistic orientation, Carl Rogers steadfastly maintained that counselors who help create a favorable environment by sending "powerful invitations" (reflections) help clients rediscover the traits within themselves. Obviously such an idealistic perspective does not always occur in the "real" world, however.

Robert Carkhuff (1987) concluded that "counseling can be for better or worse" for clients. Sexism, racism, ageism and other counselor prejudices negatively impact the "perceiver I" reflections being sent to clients. Consider the following different perceptions of the same person.

Eliza Doolittle to Colonel Pickering in George Bernard Shaw's Pygmalion:

...The difference between a lady and a flower girl is not how she behaves but how she's treated. I shall always be a flower girl to Professor Higgins because he always treats me as a flower girl and always will; but I know I can be a lady to you because you always treat me as a lady and always will.

Often our most profound wisdom is stated in childlike innocence. In Dr. Seuss (1971) describes new paradigms this way:

Said Conrad Cornelius o'Donald o'Dell,
My very young friend who is learning to spell:

"The A is for Ape. And the B is for Bear.
The C is for Camel. The H is for Hare.
The M is for Mouse. And the R is for Rat.
I know all the twenty-six letters like that ...

...through to Z is for Zebra. I know them all well."
Said Conrad Cornelius o'Donald o'Dell.
"So now I know everything anyone knows
From the beginning to end. From the start to the close.
Because Z is as far as the alphabet goes."

Then he almost fell flat on his face on the floor
When I picked up the chalk and drew one letter more!
A letter he never had dreamed of before!

"In the places I go there are things that I see
That I never could spell if I stopped with the Z.
I'm telling you this 'cause you're one of my friends.
My alphabet starts where your alphabet ends!"

After introducing his friend to an entirely new vocabulary featuring such letters as "Yuzz," as in "Yuzz-a-ma-Tuzz"; "Wum" as in "Wumbus"; and "Fuddle" as in "Fuddle-dee-Duddle," Dr. Seuss concluded:

The places I took him!
I tried hard to tell
Young Conrad Cornelius o'Donald o'Dell
A few brand-new wonderful words he might spell.
I led him around and I tried hard to show
There are things beyond Z that most people don't know.

I took him past Zebra. As far as I could.
And I think perhaps, maybe I did him some good...

Because, finally, he said:
"This is really great stuff!
And I guess the old alphabet
ISN'T enough!"
Now the letters he uses are something to see!
Most people still stop at the Z...
But not HE!

Behavioral or attitudinal change is possible when expanded "tendencies" result in new impressions of the now. "Who is the perceiver I?" basically explores specific issues of self-love (or the lack thereof). Such self-assessment can paradoxically be facilitated in a therapeutic dialogue with a caring person who genuinely "reflects" the "impossible dream" of "Dulcinea" awaiting transformation from "Aldonza."

The late John F. Kennedy frequently quoted George Bernard Shaw's "You see things as they are and you ask, 'why?' But I dream dreams that never were and ask, 'why not?' Caring counselors can help create an environment where positive client change coupled with core stable traits or temperaments become the "possible dream."

Interpretative Guidelines

A first step involves what Nystul (1985) calls "motivation modification" as contrasted with behavior modification. "The Adlerian counselor is not preoccupied with changing behavior; rather he is concerned with understanding the individual's subjective frame of reference and the identification of the individual's mistaken goal, or goal within that framework. Indeed, the behavior of an individual is only understood when the goals are identified." (Sonstegard, Hagerman & Bitter, 1975, p. 17)

Adlerian theory is initially based on the client gained insight, or a recognition into one's own style. But as Kurt Adler (1989) notes, insight alone is not enough.

> In order for change to occur at all... the patient must learn to understand something — about his life, his relations to others, his behavior — that he did not understand before. One would say, perhaps, this is a new insight. But insight alone is not enough; there must be, in addition, a sort of artistic penetration and permeation of the patient's life attitudes with this newly understood more social behavior. (p. 62)

Mistaken Beliefs

The "private logic" of a client often contains faulty conclusi(
overgeneralizations. Utilizing the "basic mistakes" of Adler, the "irra
beliefs" of Ellis (1973), and the "cognitive deficiencies" of Beck (1970), Kern,
et al. (1978) compiled the following list of faulty cognitions:

1. **Casual Inference.** Making an unjustifiable jump in logic by drawing a
   conclusion from evidence that is either insufficient or actually contrary to the conclusion reached. ("I made an A- on the test; I am not
   smart.")

2. **Blowup.** Tending to exaggerate or magnify the meaning of an event
   out of proportion to the actual situation; generating a general rule from
   a single incident ("I made a mess of my relationship with Ellen. I guess
   you could consider me a real social bust.").

3. **All-or-Nothing Thinking.** Thinking in extremes; allowing only two
   possibilities — good or bad, right or wrong, always or never ("People
   never have a good time with me").

4. **Responsibility Projection.** Failing to assume responsibility for one's
   emotional state ("This course is causing me to have a nervous breakdown!"), or for one's personal worth ("If my parents had only made
   me study in high school, I'd have been able to qualify for college").

5. **Perfectionistic Thinking.** Making idealistic demands on oneself ("I
   made a D on that test; I'm so stupid!").

6. **Value-Tainted Thinking.** Couching a statement in such terms as
   "good," "bad," "worthless," "should," "ought," or "must" ("I must get
   into medical school or I won't be able to look my father in the eye").

7. **Self-Deprecation.** Focusing on punitive self-statements rather than
   task orientation ("I hate myself for not being able to break this habit").

Once clients discover the illogical aspect of their thinking, they generally
are motivated to make changes in their personal private logic that will render
it more functional. According to Kern, et al. (1978, pp. 21–22), the correction
of self-defeating, private logic includes the following steps:

1. Asking the client to describe only the **facts** of the actual situation that
   gave rise to an expression of the faulty thinking ("I made a 78 on my
   freshman composition exam") and to omit the self-defeating statement ("...and I know I'm just going to flunk out of college"). In this

179

way, the reality of the situation is separated from the individual's personal conclusion.

2. Asking the client to generate **alternative explanations** for the situation that triggered the illogical conclusion. The student making the 78 on the composition exam could have concluded, "I made a high C when I'm used to making A's, and this discrepancy is disappointing. I guess I'll have to study much harder if I am to meet my expectations."

3. The client is told to avoid being the direct object or the subject of a passive verb. In the case of responsibility projection, the personal statement is to be reconstructed in such a way that the client becomes the subject of an active verb. For example, the statement "My roommate makes me so mad when she doesn't hang up her clothes" could become: "When my roommate doesn't hang up her clothes, I become very angry because I'm telling myself that she should meet my expectations and something's wrong with me since I can't get her to do better. Clearly, my roommate is not doing it to me — I'm doing it to myself!"

4. Asking the client to design a positive course of action based on the more reasonable of his or her alternative explanations. This technique is used to assist clients to recognize the poor fit between many of their fictions and reality and to practice a more responsible kind of self-talk.

Lingg & Kottman (1991) suggest a technique of changing mistaken beliefs through visualization of early recollections. They define basic mistakes as follows:

> Basic mistakes are *basic* because they are the original ideas a child develops to fulfill the needs of belonging and significance. They are considered *mistakes* because they are faulty conclusions drawn from a child's perspective while the child is engaged in the struggle to establish a place in the world. As Dreikurs & Soltz (1964) indicated, "Children are expert observers but make many mistakes in interpreting what they observe. They often draw wrong conclusions and choose mistaken ways in which to find their place." (p. 15)

One of the goals of counseling is to identify basic mistakes and bring them to the client's awareness. It is the counselor's responsibility to discover those early, erroneously developed convictions and to help the client see how those ideas are false and how they can interfere with effective social and personal functioning. Manaster & Corsini (1982) refer to the process of psychotherapy as uncovering the basic mistakes and correcting them. (p. 256)

The specific technique involves beginning with some basic relaxation techniques, such as closing one's eyes, focusing on the breath, and imagining oneself to be in a caring, nurturing place. The counselor then asks the client to visualize a specific incident such as an early recollection to represent the particular mistaken belief. With the eyes still closed, the incident is then described, along with the scene and the feelings to it.

In order to change the mistaken belief, the counselor asks the client to visualize himself or herself as an adult actually entering the scene. The adult self is then encouraged to show support to the child with statements as to how valuable, important and loveable he or she is. The counselor then suggests that the visualized adult help the child reconsider any mistaken beliefs about what is necessary to achieve significance, a feeling of belonging, and increased social interest. The counselor should allow quiet time and encourage the adult's "inner creative problem-solver to come forth" with whatever words, phrases, colors, suggestions, etc. are appropriate and for the highest wisdom of all concerned in that moment.

Visualization is a powerful technique for changing mistaken notions, because clients often are willing to suspend the usual linear rationale mode of viewing the world and thus allow greater creativity as a valuable *partner* with logic. Hypnosis and trance work are closely related to the use of visualization for encouraging life-style change. An entire issue of the *Journal of Individual Psychology* (December, 1990) is devoted to Adlerian applications of hypnosis. There Carich, Sperry, and Fairfield also present specific induction techniques and case studies illustrating the role of hypnosis in depth personality change.

Distorted Thinking Styles

Negative thinking can very often be identified as distorted thinking. Becoming aware of thinking distortions makes one able to actually change negative thoughts to positive ones, effectively eliminating the depression and anxiety that these thoughts create.

Distorted thoughts can be easily identified because they 1) cause painful emotions such as worry, depression, or anxiety, and/or 2) cause you to have ongoing conflicts.

The following fifteen distorted thinking styles are examined by McKay, Davis and Fanning (1981).

1. **Filtering** entails looking at only one part of a situation to the exclusion of everything else.

2. **Polarized thinking** involves perceiving everything at the extremes, as either black or white, with nothing in between.

3. **Overgeneralization** reaches a broad, generalized conclusion based on just one piece of evidence.

4. **Mind reading** takes place when one bases assumptions and conclusions on an "ability" to know other people's thoughts.

5. **Catastrophizing** involves expecting the worst-case scenario.

6. **Personalization** results in interpreting everything around you in ways that reflect on oneself, and one's worth.

7. **Control Fallacies** involve feeling either that the events in your life are totally controlled by a force outside of oneself, or that the individual is responsible for everything.

8. **Fallacy of Fairness** is based on the trap of judging people's actions by personally created rules about what is and what isn't fair.

9. **Emotional Reasoning** is the mistaken belief that everything an individual feels must be true.

10. **The Fallacy of Change** is the assumption that others will change to suit oneself if they are pressured long enough.

11. **Global Labeling** is making a broad judgment based on very little evidence.

12. **Blaming** involves the belief that bad things that happen are someone's fault, either of the individual him/herself, or of someone else.

13. **Shoulds** entail operating from a rigid set of indisputable rule about how everyone including oneself should act.

14. **Being Right** involves continually needing to justify a personal point of view or way of behaving.

15. **Heaven's Reward Fallacy** is the belief that if one always does the right thing, he or she will eventually be rewarded(even if doing the right thing means ignoring your personal needs).

Copeland (1992) suggests the following four-step process for eliminating distorted thoughts:

1. What emotion (or emotions) are you feeling now?

   I am feeling angry, tense, and anxious.

2. Describe, in detail, the event or situation that gave rise to your emotion. For example:

   I went to my friend Peter's house at 4:00 p.m., as previously arranged, to go for a walk and have dinner together. He was not home when I got there.

3. Describe your thoughts, and identify any distortions in your thinking.

   Because Peter wasn't there, I decided he really didn't want to spend the time with me, that he really doesn't like me and doesn't respect my feelings.

4. Refute the distortions.

   There was only one piece of evidence, his not being there when I arrived, that was the basis for my distortion. The truth is, Peter and I have been close friends for a long time. All evidence indicated that he likes me a lot. An emergency may have come up, he may have gone to do an errand that took longer than anticipated, he may have misunderstood the plan that we made or he may have forgotten that we made a plan (or I may have misunderstood) — any of which are acceptable reasons and do nothing to lend credence to my distorted thought. The best course of action for me would be to wait on his porch (doing relaxation exercises) until his return; or leave him a note asking him to call me when he gets in.

Copeland also suggests "Thought Stopping" as a way of confronting one's own self-defeating beliefs (Adler's "spitting in the soup" concept).Thought stopping is a simple way to bring thoughts to consciousness and eliminate them. By eliminating a negative thought, you can eliminate the emotions and feelings that go along with it.

After identifying a negative thought for target practice, the following self-reflective questions should be asked:

1. Is this thought realistic or unrealistic?
2. Is the thought productive or counterproductive?
3. Is this thought easy or hard to control?
4. How uncomfortable does this thought make me feel?
5. How much does this thought interfere with my life?

Sample Thought-Stopping Exercise

Bothersome Thought:
I'm afraid I'll have another deep depression and need hospitalization.

Is this thought realistic or unrealistic?
It is realistic,because I've had deep depressions before for which I needed to be hospitalized. However, the circumstances of my life have changed significantly since then. I understand depression. I have an excellent support system of health care workers, family members, and friends. I watch for early warning signs and get help early. Several related medical problems have been appropriately treated. I use relaxation techniques, exercise regularly, and carefully manage my diet. I have eliminated sugar and caffeine from my diet. There is limited stress in my life and I have learned to handle stress that is unavoidable.

Is the thought productive or counterproductive?
Definitely counter-productive.

Is this thought easy or hard to control?
At times this thought is very hard to control.

How uncomfortable does this thought make me feel?
Very uncomfortable!

How much does this thought interfere with my life?
It interferes a lot, because it makes me depressed and discouraged. Based on the answers to these questions, it is clear that I would benefit from eliminating this thought from my mental repertoire.

Secondly, Copeland recommends dwelling on the thought by bringing it to the level of consciousness and by focusing on it for several minutes. Next, the undesirable thought should be interrupted by means of such a powerful response as forcefully saying, "STOP!"; wearing a rubber band on one's wrist to snap when unwanted thoughts come up, pinching one's self or digging the nails into the palms on one's hands.

Lastly, a positive or assertive thought should be substituted for the negative one.

Affirmations

An affirmation is a statement that describes the way one would want his or her life to be utilizing a best-case scenario. Some examples include such phrases as:

I think and act with confidence.
I am strong and powerful.
I fully accept myself as I am.
I have many accomplishments to my credit.
I am healthy and energetic.
I deserve the time and space to heal.
I have all the resources to do what I want to in my life.
I am loved by many people.
I am a very valuable person.
I am safe and protected.
I am effective and efficient in stressful situations.
I am peaceful and serene at all times.
My relationships are happy and fulfilling.
I am in charge of my life.
I look and feel wonderful. (Copeland, p. 216)

"Stroking" and "Spitting": Two Core Adlerian Counseling Skills

The skillful blending of both encouragement and confrontation are described by Nikelly (1971) as "stroke and spit tactics." Stroking is synonymous with encouragement, caring, and other "powerful invitations" for client growth. Dreikurs (1967) described Adler's vivid metaphor of "spitting in the soup" by noting that a bowl of soup will not be enticing to a soup lover if someone contaminates it with spittle.

An additional analogy — when we were children it was a rare treat when our parents would give us sparkling ice-cold soda pop on a hot summer day. The first few sips were pure ecstasy, but ultimately the command came to "share it with your brothers and sisters." Inevitably our siblings would grab the soda pop in one hand and a pack of crackers in the other. After a few "swigs" the half empty bottle would be returned to us, complete with a mixture of cracker crumbs floating on the top. We called it "backwash," and it certainly changed the meaning of the cold drink for us. What had once been so desirable was instantly made much less gratifying.

Allen (1971) also describes a technique known as "sweetening the pot." For example, a 37 year-old single male client was avoiding asking any women out for a date because he feared his mother would not approve of any them. The counselor's intervention consists of having the man imagine a "great big smile of delight over his mother's face because her little boy was not going to leave home" the next time he avoided asking a woman for a date.

Encouragement is a core component to "tapping creative personal power." Key factors contributing to reorientation are the client's recognition of a personal power, an ability to make decisions, and the ability to choose directions (Dreikurs, 1967). Personal power arises from a creative ability which lies in each person. "In consideration of the influence of the environment, the therapist must take into account the creative ingenuity by which events are perceived. Based on an innate striving to succeed, the influences existing in the environment, and a unique creative power, the individual establishes a personal style of living which directs thinking, feeling and acting. The creative schema through which an individual orients the self to the world is a personalized sense of meaningfulness, significance, or power." (Chandler, 1991, pp. 222–223)

Chandler then suggests the following three major components of the therapeutic process of reorientation: 1) assessment of the current life-style, 2) interpretation of the creative forces of the life-style, and 3) the creation of new realities.

Kopp & Kivel (1989) describe confronting client resistance. The paradox of therapy is that although clients purportedly seek counseling to change, they also have a nonconscious investment in maintaining their particular symptoms for the protection it affords the self-esteem and the life-style. This threat to the self-esteem generates a fear of change, rooted in what Adler (1964) termed the fear of being proven worthless. He notes that "all neurotic symptoms have as their object the task of safeguarding the patient's self-esteem and thereby also the lifeline [later, life-style] into which he has grown" (in Ansbacher & Ansbacher, 1964, p. 263).

A core confrontation often involves the clients overtly stated desire for change as contrasted with his or her desire to maintain **homeostasis**, a balance or the status quo in order to protect one's own self- esteem.

Shulman (1973) noted that the client's fear of disapproval — of being exposed and found defective — may interfere with the counseling relationship.

He listed the following defenses used by clients to "defeat" the counselor or to "save" their self-esteem:

1. **Externalization:** *The fault lies outside me,* including:

   ✧ Cynicism: *Life is at fault.*

   ✧ Inadequacy: *I am just an innocent victim.*

   ✧ Rebellion: *I cannot afford to submit to life.*

   ✧ Projection: *It is all their fault.*

2. **Blind Spots:** *If I don't look at it, it will go away.*

3. **Excessive Self-Control:** *I will not let anything upset me.*

4. **Arbitrary Rightness:** *My mind is made up; don't confuse me with facts.*

5. **Elusiveness and Confusion:** *Don't pin me down.*

6. **Contrition and Self-Disparagement:** *I am always wrong.*

7. **Suffering as Manipulation:** *I suffer to control others.*

All such defenses have the potential for destroying the counselor-client relationship. Allen (1971) humorously calls this "avoiding the client's tar-baby," which he describes in the following manner:

> The Adlerian recognizes all too well that as self-defeating and incommodious as a particular modus vivendi or 'identity' may be, it remains, in the eyes of the client, his best bet — and accordingly, he will defend it. As dismal as his set of expectations for himself in the world may be, they at least enable him to make sense out of the "blooming, buzzing, confusion" and perhaps even entitle him to certain concessions. So, he will struggle to maintain their claim to validity...

> For example, some clients attempt to annoy the counselor in order to establish the validity of his thesis that he is an unlikable person (see, even my counselor whose job it is to like all sorts of people, dislikes me). Other clients will try to discourage the counselor in order to validate the hopelessness of their position or the wisdom of their decision to do nothing about it. In effect the counselor's sense of discouragement is used by such clients as license to curse the darkness and to avoid the unpleasantness involved in the attempt to generate any light by their own efforts. (p. 43)

The skillful use of confrontation of discrepancies coupled with the power of encouragement are two essential global Adlerian counseling skills which should permeate the entire process. Specific development approaches and Adlerian counseling techniques follow.

Suggested Sequences of Adlerian Counseling

Morrow & Kopp (1988) suggest the following seven steps of Adlerian therapy:

1. **Aligning the goal.** This includes communicating empathy for the client's own creative movement for significance, intentions and beliefs. This may include assessing whether the goals are realistic.

2. **Discussing the role, tactics, and strategy.** Specific methods of how the client attains significance are discussed. The role generally involves how a person reaches a goal (usually lacking in some form of social interest) by using particular strategy and tactics.

3. **Encouraging creativity.** This encourages an "unfreezing" of a client who is "stuck" in a habitual mode of functioning. (The visualization process described earlier in the chapter is a good technique.)

4. **Confronting nonconstructive tactics.** (Such as those described earlier in this chapter.)

5. **Stimulating a social "strategy" — encouraging contributions to the needs of the situation.** Often clients are absorbed in narcissistic "self" oriented myopic vision. The counselor encourages a return to the original problem by considering a more socially useful approach.

6. **Reorientation — stimulating socially interested "tactics."** The therapist now asks the client if he or she would be willing to consider other tactics which would result in an effective pursuit of the goal and an effective resolution of the problem. (Dreikurs, 1967)

7. **Exploring alternatives and obtaining a commitment for socially interested action.** The client is now made aware that insight has little value in and of itself. It is only a prelude to action. **Outsight** — moving ideas into action is the real aim of the process (Dinkmeyer, Dinkmeyer & Sperry, 1987). In dealing with depressed patients Adler (1958) advised "You can be cured in fourteen days if you follow this prescription. Try to think every day how you can please someone."

Reorientation involves what Carkhuff (1969) describes as the "action" phase of counseling. The initial therapeutic style is suggested as **facilitation**, being receptive and encouraging a "downward, inward" self-exploration. Conversely, the action phase is an "upward, outward" focus.

Specific action-oriented homework assignments may include **bibliotherapy,** derived from the Greek words *biblion* (book) and *therapeia* (healing). (See Rubin, 1978 for more information.) Popular self-help books and other audio-visual aids can be used.

Journal writing (Progoff, 1980) is also an effective method for clients to record their personal feelings and reactions in a reflective manner. Carich (1990) describes seven specific action-oriented tasks:

1. **Cognitive oriented** — involving beliefs/thoughts, perceptions, etc. These include guided imagery, practicing specific self-talk, etc.

2. **Cognitive/behavioral** — both thought and physical activities such as letter writing (anger, forgiveness, acceptance, guilt, good-bye, self- and other love), keeping journals, writing likes/dislikes, goal and expectations and relaxation exercises.

3. **Behavioral** — reinforcement strategies, punishment, aversive conditioning, exercising.

4. **Metaphorical/symbolic** — stories, anecdotes, puns, riddles, metaphors.

5. **Strategic/paradoxical tasks** — paradoxical (self-contradictory meanings), prescriptions, experiences and messages.

6. **Absurd/ambiguous tasks** — assignment of deliberate absurd tasks with an indirect meaning or experience.

7. **Social directives** — tasks that involve or promote social interest, cooperation and interactions.

Nikelly (1971) summarizes other action-oriented interpretive techniques in the following manner:

> An effective and practical approach is to encourage the client to interpret his own behavior and then to consider alternative solutions which might prove effective. In other words, he is encouraged to search his life pattern and to suggest alternative behavior to reach his goals rather than to seek for deep and hidden drives. The therapist can sift out unacceptable or inappropriate explanations and help the client gain insight into those that are actually interwoven into his lifestyle...

> Humor can be effective in helping the client relate more positively toward the therapist... Humor can help to disarm the client provided that the therapist is fair and honest with him and that the humor is built upon mutual respect and trust... The technique of overstatement, for example,

may show the client that he is deciding (by avoiding anxiety and interaction) to see the world as a hostile jungle. 'Let's see if we can make it even worse' exposes this maneuver and yet allows for an acceptance of the person...

The Midas technique ostensibly attempts to gratify the client's psychological demands. However, since giving in to his demands never solves his basic problems, he continues to remain unsatisfied and comes to understand that his fundamental outlook and style of living must be altered so that he will no longer rely on others for attention and gratification. (pp. 87–89)

Another technique includes **role-reversal**, where the person is encouraged to assume the position of "significant others" in the environment to assess the effects of his/her behavior on them.

Other techniques include what Adler termed "anti-suggestion," similar to what Viktor Frankl (1971) called "paradoxical intention." Here the person is encouraged to do the very things which has been feared by him or her. It is also done with as much humor as possible. For example, a person afraid of losing consciousness may be asked to try "passing out." Bringing humor into the situation, the counselor then adds, "Come on now, pass out all over the place..." People, discovering they cannot intentionally do what they had feared would happen to them, often laugh at the situation also. Of course the counselor then attempts to assure such persons that since it is impossible to "pass out here on purpose, then you cannot pass out any other place if you try." Frankl said such a situation "takes the wind out of the sails" of fear.

Additional Specific Counseling Strategies

Several Adlerian counseling techniques or strategies have been described already in this chapter. These include: encouragement, spitting in the client's soup, paradoxical intention, humor, and avoiding the client's tarbaby. Other strategies include:

1. **Immediacy** — using the present here and now interaction between the counselor and client as a "slice of life" a microcosm of one's macrocosm.

2. **Acting "as if"** — Adler created the "as if" technique based on Hans Vaihinger's "as if" philosophy (Ansbacher & Ansbacher, 1956). It can be defined as a cognitive, behavioral intervention in which the client anticipates, pretends, and/or enacts a futuristic event, belief, or desired

behavior. The client can also be asked to act or behave "as if" the problem is resolved (Mosak, 1979). Carich (1989) concludes that the "as if" technique is a pretend intervention which alters cognitive factors (guiding fiction, private logics, etc.) and behavior as the client engages in pretend experiences.

3. **Catching oneself** — as clients gain insight into their own goals they are invited to "catch themselves" falling into dysfunctional patterns. Often this awareness initially comes after the fact; however, as greater insight is developed, it often can even precede the actual event. Coupled then with "spitting in one's own soup," "catching oneself" is a valuable first step to awareness and then the freedom to choose an alternative behavior or attitude.

4. **The therapeutic memoir technique** — described by O'Reilly & Edgar (1987) and involves the use of childhood photographs. The selection description of specific childhood pictures is another valuable means of gathering formative childhood information.

5. **The push-button technique** — described by Mosak (1985); clients are asked to close their eyes to visualize an event in their life that made them very *happy*. They are then asked to re-experience the good feelings they had on this occasion. Next, clients are requested to visualize an unpleasant event such as when they felt humiliated, and are again asked to re-experience those feelings. Then they are asked again to visualize and re-experience the happy incident and the associated positive feelings. The goal is for clients to learn they can create their feelings by the thoughts they choose to have.

The Counselor as Philosopher: The Philosopher as Pastor/Priest

In a sense, the presenting problems of therapy are similar to the basic philosophic and existential questions confronting all human beings. "Who am I? Why am I here? What is my purpose? What is valuable? What is ethical and moral? What is truth?" are representative questions reflecting such philosophic modes of inquiry as identity, epistemology (knowledge), and axiology (values). Therapists need to see specific presenting problems in a larger, more existential or spiritual quest for higher meaning or purpose in one's life. Such a spiritual quest is not synonymous with religion which often is associated with blind adherence to a particular set of rules. However, spirituality often includes one's own religious preferences as part of it.

Many Adlerians are uncomfortable with the word "spiritual." Baruth & Manning (1987) address God, religion and the five life tasks. They include personal communication from Alfred Adler's son Kurt relative to his father's view. They conclude that Alfred Adler felt that the idea of God only meant that humankind posited an ideal to emulate or for which to strive, as it represents the idea of perfection.

Pancner & Pancner (1988) use the creative analogy of *The Wizard of Oz* by L. Frank Baum (1900) to illustrate a representative pilgrim (Dorothy) and her spiritual quest along the "therapeutic" yellow-brick road. Selected passages follow:

> Twentieth century America offers a standard of living and a wealth of material goods unsurpassed by any other known civilization. And yet, in this society which is so oriented to consumption and instant gratification, happiness and balanced living seem to elude many. The rise of crime, increase of alcoholism and drug addiction, and escalating suicide rates are evidence that although people are living in a nation of plenty, many still are struggling and searching for more.

> As therapists, we may begin to sense our enlarged task and responsibility in taking the patient's symptoms as metaphor or allegory for defining and exploring broader issues and questions. Many of the patient's presenting problems can be interpreted as revealing deeper issues and discordances on the spiritual level. Although unable to do the actual changing for the patient, the therapist can be a teacher and guide

> ...Psychology is derived from the Greek word psyche, meaning soul and life. One of the founding fathers of psychology, William James, strongly advocated and focused on the psychological as well as the spiritual nature of man. Modern psychology has emphasized the psychological side of man, while almost entirely negating the spiritual aspect. Because the spiritual nature is not addressed in most clinical training institutes, the clinician is very hesitant to deal with this facet of a person. And yet, if the whole person is to be the focus, this spiritual area has profound impact on the personality and therefore has to be recognized and incorporated into the psychological therapeutic process ...(p. 159)

Pancner & Pancner then address the specific story of the *Wizard of Oz* and apply it as being like the journey of counseling:

> ...As the story opens, Dorothy, in gray, barren, arid Kansas, finds herself being sucked up and whirled away in the eye of a cyclone. She, her dog

Toto, and the house are quite literally blown out of Kansas. Her fear rages as greatly as the storm. Wondering if she will be dashed to pieces, she senses she is on an uncharted, unplanned journey.

So it is with many people coming into psychotherapy. The onset of their symptoms may be experienced as occurring quite suddenly, coupled by a feeling of having little or no control over what is happening, and being at the mercy of the unknown. With disorientation and disruption either due to symptoms or upheaval in one's environment, the orderly, predictable life-pattern is abruptly changed. The person is thrown into another dimension of dealing with altered perceptions, frightening medical intervention, perhaps physical incapabilities, and a new, uncharted "cyclone" experience is begun ...

Similarly clients find themselves dumped into an alien land of helpers. Many clients believe that their great hope of returning to the way it used to be hinges on the magic and wizardry of the therapist whom they then can perceive as guru or god. In psychotherapy, one of the initial tasks for the therapist and patient is to define expectations and goals for treatment. At this point, many clients do not sense any power from within to solve the dilemma and lean heavily on the therapist ... (p. 160)

Reproduced from Pancner, K. and Pancner, R., "The Quest, Gurus, and the Yellow Brick Road," *Individual Psychology*, V. 44, No. 2, 1988, 82-85.

Pancner & Pancner then specifically focus on the process of psychotherapy and the relationship to the spiritual/existential task of life. Their philosophy would appear to be consistent with Teilhard de Charden who wrote that "We are not human beings having a spiritual experience. We are spiritual beings having a human experience." (in Corey, 1989)

...The path of spirituality parallels the course of psychotherapy in that they both explore the steps involved in knowing or discovering oneself. Both are a journey inward, and, like Dorothy's quest, usually there is intense upheaval. The path can become a long, arduous journey like the yellow brick road, having many bumps and potholes ...

Through psychotherapy, an awakening process can begin, and coming to terms with one's individuality puts one on the path of growth. As one senses more freedom, the chains of robotic deadness can be loosened and the awakening process can begin ...

...In the final analysis, clients must realize they have the energy, source of power, and locus of control to live out life in a balanced way. Within a person lies the capacity to travel one's own yellow brick road, search for answers to questions and problems, and drown the witches of fear, negative thinking, and destructive living. Therapists and teachers are important for the introduction of new concepts and techniques, clarification and redefining of perceptions and current situations; however, if one continues to only look outside oneself, seeking out solutions, happiness, and balance from others, one's answers will remain obscure. It is by turning inward and acknowledging one's inner depths and resources that one realizes that answers and power come from within. At that point of discovery one realizes that outer 'gurus' have clay feet, are merely mortal, and are sorely lacking in answers for another's life journey, and so, "physician heal thyself" can be aptly applied in stating, 'client, heal thyself.' One must become one's own wizard or guru, realizing that the power lies within, not emanating from external sources. This then is the task of the therapist: to guide patients to seek within themselves. (pp. 163–165)

Counselors need to be aware of the physical, mental, emotional and existential/spiritual needs of their clients. The ultimate encouragement is for clients to discover those gifts within themselves. Despite different levels of mental health or mental illness, each person is striving for some type of significance. And, as Lovejoy (1961) observes, "Though not everyone can occupy the top of every tree, there are, in fact, many trees ...

Force-Field Analysis

Kurt Lewin (1969) developed the Force-Field analysis model to assist in problem solving and planned change. In his model, the term *force* does not refer to a tangible, physical force; rather it serves as a metaphor for a broad range of interpersonal influences affecting the system. For example, some influences on couples might include such issues as religious beliefs/preferences; financial considerations; fear of change itself; mistrust; sex-role stereotypes; division of responsibilities (role perceptions); competitive behavior between the couple; and basic personality differences such as being introverted or extroverted.

Basically Lewin believes that there are both *restraining* forces and *drawing* forces arrayed against each other within a force field. The interaction between the restraining forces that work *against* change and the drawing forces that are "pushing" or motivating toward change. If the desired change is not coming about, then the *restraining* forces are collectively stronger than the drawing forces. Conversely, change will occur when the collective driving forces are greater. The benefit of the model for couples is that it provides a way to analyze the various "push/pull", drawing/restraining forces; it also can assist a couple in developing strategies for causing change.

In *The Encouragement Process in Life-Span Development,* Eckstein (1995) presents the following specific activity that can be utilized by counselors to clients. It is intended to help couples in exploring the issues involved with considering a change. For example, many times counselors are contacted because one or both members are considering separation or a divorce.

Being more aware of the issues which say "yes" as well as the factors which say "no" to any change being considered by the couple can help focus the issues. The following questions can be completed by one or both members of the couple. It is often useful if both persons are completing the form to answer the questions independently, then to compare the responses together.

Force-Field Analysis Activity

1. Write down a specific issue or situation which you feel needs to be *changed* (e.g., moving, changing jobs, having children, separation or divorce, etc.) below.

   _____

   _____

   _____

2. List below the issues which are *restraining,* saying "no" to the considered change (e.g., too risky, too expensive, etc.).

   _____

   _____

   _____

3. List below all the factors which are *driving* or motivating you to say "yes" to the possible change (e.g., emotional pain, unhappiness, better opportunity, etc.).

   _____

   _____

   _____

4. Does this situation remind you of a previous decision or issue? If so, briefly describe the incident, including the decision and the outcome.

_____

_____

_____

5. What are the *benefits* to you of **not** making this change right now?

_____

_____

_____

6. What are the costs (emotional and/or financial) to you of **not** deciding right now?

_____

_____

_____

7. Review your list of **restraining** forces in #2. Rank each in order of priority by assigning a rating from 10 being the highest to 1 being the lowest value in terms of importance to you. For example, "too risky" might be rated an "8" for a fairly high value to you, whereas "too expensive" may be only a "4" because of being a moderate to low issue. Now rank order your priorities with your 1–10 rating beside it.

Issue   **Rating**

_____   _____

_____   _____

_____   _____

_____   _____

8. Do the same thing as #7 for your ***driving*** forces. For example, "emotional hurt" might be ranked a "10", whereas "better opportunity" might be a "7."

   Issue   **Rating**

   _____   _____

   _____   _____

   _____   _____

   _____   _____

9. What are your reactions/feelings/opinions to your responses in #7 and #8? How likely do you feel it is for a ***change*** to occur?

   _____

   _____

   _____

   _____

10. What would be a specific "game plan" necessary for the change to actually occur?

    a. _____

    b. _____

    c. _____

    d. _____

Some specific examples of *restraining* and *drawing* forces include the following issues as adapted from Hargrove (1996):

Potential restraining ("no") factors within an organizational environment striving to make positive change include:

1. Most people are not experts in human nature.

2. Most communication does not represent a true personal calling and is stated in a way that does not capture people's imagination.

3. A credibility gap is created because most managers don't walk their talk.

4. The goals, objectives, and reward systems are not aligned with the message that the leader is trying to send.

5. There is often a massive amount of resignation or "giving up" in the organization.

6. Managers may talk about change but stay in the comfort zone.

7. Leaders underestimate the degree of difficulty involved in communicating a new message and tend to give up too soon when confronted with the reality of what it takes.

Conversely, specific examples of *amplifying* ("yes") factors include:

1. All executive communication is created in terms of a context — one that becomes the vision, culture and spirit of the organization.

2. The generation of "new" conversations moves people beyond fear and the comfort zone, eliciting their commitment to make a difference, to bring forth a breakthrough.

3. New conversations are based on a big idea that shapes products, services, and organizational processes.

4. When top executives dare to take a stand, their speaking and listening can make a difference.

5. Spearheading a breakthrough creates a structure for fulfillment for the message.

6. An idea picks up force and speed to the extent that it is translated into action.

7. A rigorous active inquiry into the organization's issues makes the message sustainable once it is delivered, understood, and acted on.

Chapter Summary

Reorientation has as its therapeutic goal long-term client behavior or attitude change. This chapter has explored core mistaken beliefs, and specific Adlerian counseling techniques for use in life-style interpretations were identified. Force Field Analysis was presented as an example of one specific structural approach to identifying both the restraining and driving forces relative to the issue of change in one's life. A systematic case study and a recommended systematic life-style interpretative guide are presented in the next chapter.

Chapter 6

A SYSTEMATIC CASE STUDY
and Recommended Life-Style Interpretive Summary Form

In this section we will attempt to assimilate all previous chapters by means of a systematic summary of a case history. You will then be invited to write an interpretation for your own life-style interview.

Robert is a 17-year-old high school junior. In a hypothetical situation, if Robert were to seek counseling services, the high school guidance counselor would probably already be familiar with him, having previously been of assistance in class scheduling and registration. She may have also heard some of the teachers refer to him as a minor "discipline problem."

Upon recommendations of his friends, Robert concludes that the guidance counselor is an "okay person" and decides he would like to "talk a few things over" with her. He then pays her a visit and begins to share some of his concerns. Utilizing an Adlerian orientation, the counselor's developmental goals in establishing some type of ongoing experience would include the process of establishing a relationship, a psychological investigation, providing possible interpretations, and lastly, some type of reorientation or change in attitude and/or behavior.

The Relationship

Although Robert has never before requested actual counseling services, previous interactions by the counselor with other students have been important. The core characteristics described in Chapter 1, including unconditional positive regard, genuineness, empathy, self-disclosure, and concreteness are now crucial if the counselor is to "earn" the trust of Robert.

In the opening remarks, the counselor might be warm and supportive, primarily responding to information which Robert presents. To facilitate further self-exploration, the counselor should maintain eye contact and make general comments in response to the specific information as presented by Robert. "Active listening" to discern important self-references, body language, and other variables would also be essential.

In establishing a relationship, crucial "micro-counseling" skills as described by Ivey (1972) should be employed. For example, an open invitation to talk might consist of "how have things been going?" Such statements should provide a maximum amount of latitude for Robert to explore personal areas of concern. Minimal encouragements to talk might consist of statements like "Can you tell me more about that?", "Can you give me an example?", etc. Here the counselor would attempt to encourage more self-exploration in pinpointing problem areas. By establishing a relationship of mutual trust, a more precise discussion of Robert's concerns should surface.

Psychological Investigation

Having established a base of effective communication, the counselor would become more "directive" in helping Robert explore specific problem areas. In the "objective situation" Robert would be asked how he is functioning in such areas as work (or school), friendships, relationships with the opposite sex, etc. His typical comments might be: "In school, I really like playing on the football and baseball teams, but my grades aren't too good. I can't seem to get along with some of my teachers. I really like the mechanics course and mechanical drawing class, but math is a hassle. My friends are very important to me, and I'm treasurer in the Letterman's Club. On the weekends, we are rebuilding an old Model-T. I date some, but I haven't been very close to any one girl for quite a while. It seems I get 'fired up' about them, then, things just kinda 'cool off' after a while."

An investigation of the "subjective situation" would focus upon specific complaints or problems Robert was experiencing. His response might be: "I'm kinda concerned because I'm not dating much ... I'm also having some problems with Miss Pennington, the new English teacher. She's been discussing women's liberation too much and making us read 'radical literature' by those kind of women. We've had some heated debates during class, and today I stayed after the bell rang to tell her I thought it was all a bunch of baloney."

When asked the question, "How would things be different if all these problems were solved?," Robert would reply: "I wouldn't have to put up with unreasonable demands by adults. I would be happy like my friends ... no hassles."

At this point the counselor could suggest a life-style investigation in attempting to determine Robert's subjective "life is — others are — I am" themes. A complete summary of Robert's life-style is given in the following table.

Life-Style Interview Guide

(Example for Robert Johnson)

Write the name and age of each sibling (including yourself) in descending order beginning with the oldest. Include deceased siblings. When you have listed all the siblings, describe each sibling, including yourself.

Your Name: *Robert Johnson*

Sibling 1	Sibling 2	Sibling 3
Name: *Mary* Age: *19*	Name: *Robert* (Our subject) Age: *17*	Name: *Fred* Age: *15*
Description: *Good student* *Musically inclined* *She thought I was a* *loudmouth*	Description: *Poor student* *"Nice guy" type* *Athlete* *Had few friends* *Tried to please*	Description: *Average student* *Interested in sports, but* *not as good as me* *One of the gang* *Devilish*

Sibling 4	Sibling 5	Sibling 6
Name: *Susan* Age: *8*	Name: Age:	Name: Age:
Description: *Long curls* *Sucked her fingers* *Sweet* *Cute smile* *Helpless*	Description:	Description:

Following each adjective or description indicate which siblings demonstrated that characteristic most and least. If you are at neither extreme, show in which direction you were inclined by pointing an arrow. An example might be:

Characteristic	Most		Least
Idealistic	*Mary*	⟶	*Fred*

This would indicate that with regards to idealism Mary was more idealistic, Fred was least idealistic, and Robert tended to be on the least idealistic end of the continuum. If you are a Single Child, rate yourself in comparison to the peer group you associated with as a youth.

Now respond to each of the following characteristics:
(Note: M=Mary, R=Robert, F=Fred, and S=Susan)

Characteristic	Most		Least
1. Intelligence	M	⟶	F
2. Hardest Worker	F		R
3. Best Grades in School	M		R and F
4. Helping Around the House	*(Everyone helped, although reluctantly)*		
5. Conforming	M		R
6. Rebellious	R and F		M
7. Trying to Please	*(None of us)*		
8. Critical of Others	R		M
9. Considerateness	M and R		F
10. Selfishness	*(All pretty selfish)*		
11. Having Own Way	F		R
12. Sensitive — Easily Hurt	R	⟶	F
13. Temper Tantrums	M		F
14. Sense of Humor	R		M
15. Idealistic	R		M and F
16. Materialistic	*(None of us)*		
17. Standards of Accomplishment	M		R and F
18. Most Athletic	R	⟵	M
19. Strongest	F		M
20. Attractive	R		F
21. Spoiled	S	⟵	M
22. Punished	*(No one in particular)*		
23. Spontaneous	S	⟵	M

Further Sibling Descriptions

Answer the questions below as accurately as possible.

1. **Who was most different from you? How?**

   Mary. She organized things. I never did. She seemed so involved in doing things — just about everything. She spent time talking with mom and dad and it was somehow different. She would pass their message to rest of us.

2. **Who was most like you? How?**

   Fred. He and I fought over the same things. We both did athletics. I could move faster and he had enough brute strength to be good. We played together a lot.

3. **Did you have many or few friends? Describe your relationship with them.**

   I had a small group of six or seven friends. I wasn't the leader — just one of the gang.

4. **Who fought and argued?**

   Fred and me.

5. **Who played together?**

   Fred and me.

6. **Who took care of whom?**

   Mary took care of all of us — especially Fred.

7. **Who had a handicap or prolonged illness?**

   None of us.

8. **What were the most important family values?**

   Work hard, maintain a neat appearance, get along with others, and cooperate.

Description of Parents

Father

Current Age: *51*   **Occupation:** *Teacher*

Description of father: *Quiet, well-liked, responsible, good-looking, hard worker, firm, intelligent, understanding.*

Father's favorite child? Why? *Mary. She was hard working and did well in school.*

Ambitions for children? *Work hard. Study hard. Do what is right.*

Relationship to children? *Interested in what the kids were doing. When he spoke, you listened.*

Sibling most like father? How? *Mary. Seemed to value the same things in life.*

Mother
Current Age: *47*   **Occupation:** *Housewife*

Description of mother: *Neat appearance, supportive, hard worker, outgoing personality, gentle, always there, tried to please, sometimes critical.*

Mother's favorite child? Why? *Susan. She was always giving mother things.*

Ambitions for children? *Behave and make her proud.*

Relationship to children? *Usually supportive. Sometimes critical of our behavior.*

Sibling most like mother? How? *Fred. Tried to please others.*

Describe the nature of your parents' relationship: *Very supportive. Mother was responsible for the home and raising the children. She was sometimes critical of father. He would just remove himself without saying anything.*

If there were other parental figures in your family, describe the effect they have had on your outlook on life: *No other parental figures.*

Early Recollections

Think back as far as you can and describe the first specific incident that you remember. Tell how old you were and what feeling you had. Make sure it is a specific situation and not a generalization. When you have completed the information on the first incident, do the same with the second situation. Try to do this for at least four or five statements.

1. **Age 5:** *I remember going to kindergarten twice. Once I went with my sister on her first day of school; the second time, I went alone for my first day of school.*

   Feeling: *Somewhat confused the first time, but secure with my sister. The second time, I felt alone and afraid.*

2. **Age 7**: *I dreaded getting my report card — I had all 'satisfactories' but one 'S -'. I erased the minus, but got caught. The teacher told the entire class I had all satisfactories, but erased the minus.*

   Feeling: *Guilty: afraid to let my parents find out what I'd done.*

3. **Age 6**: *I remember my friends and I spent several weeks building a treehouse. One day while we were playing in it, I fell out of the treehouse. I was scratched and bruised a bit, but I wouldn't accept any help from the guys. I said I was okay, so we went back to playing.*

   Feeling: *Kinda foolish for falling out of the tree, but proud I was able to take care of myself.*

4. **Age 6**: *I remember my brother's birthday. He was having a party with all his friends from school. I remember many gifts that he received, especially a paint-by-number set. I also remember that he got extra ice cream and cake.*

   Feeling: *Upset because he was getting special favors.*

5. **Age 7**: *I remember playing 'witch' with the guys in the dark one night; a cop came up and told us to go home. We went behind the bushes and called him a few names, but we finally went home.*

   Feeling: *It was unfair that we had to stop playing; we gave up too easily.*

6. **Age 7**: *I remember my father and I were always working on the car together. One day I remember he bought a new kit designed to let us change the oil ourselves. He let me do it all by myself.*

   Feeling: *Liked working on the car with dad; proud I was able to change the oil by myself.*

Family Constellation Summary

From the initial portion of the *Life-Style Interview Guide* we learned that Robert was the second born in a family of two boys and two girls. Psychologically we would assume he was the second child in a subfamily of three, consisting of two boys and one girl (Mary, Robert, and Fred). Robert's interactions and competitions are with an academically-achieving, well-mannered, conforming older sister and a rebellious, self-centered, critical younger brother. Robert chose peer-oriented, athletic behaviors as his way of interacting and being noticed. He also ascribed to the family values of hard work, sociability, and being neatly attired.

As we view the sibling descriptions and ratings, we find Robert attaching traditional views to the female members of the family (i.e., making good grades, conforming, having high standards of academic achievement, being verbally skillful, and being highly emotional). Conversely, Robert chose the "all male" areas in which to excel (i.e., athletics, considerateness, sense of humor, being one of the gang, and idealistic). Robert developed his skills in relating to peers while his older sister developed the art of interacting with the adults in the family. It appears that Robert possessed characteristics and developed attributes similar to those of his father such as being good looking, hard-working, well-liked, and cooperative. But in situations where authority was involved, he was rebellious, devilish, and, by self-description, irresponsible. Robert, a "squeezed" middle child, found an outlet for positive social interactions with his peers, while at the same time exhibiting antagonistic tendencies toward authority. Having an openly rebellious younger brother may have lead Robert to adopt a "nice guy" image. His rebellion seems to have been of a more covert nature.

As for his parents, Robert appears to have viewed them in traditional sex-role stereotyped functions. His father was seen as hard-working and assertive, while the mother was more passive, though verbally critical. In Robert's view, the parents seemed to be content in their roles, and to regard their marriage as a happy one.

It is interesting to note that Robert was the only sibling not mentioned as the favorite of either parent, or the sibling most like either parent. Such a "left out" situation probably contributed to the importance of peer relationships for Robert.

Early Recollections Summary

In the first ER there seems to be a feeling of security associated with a female (sister) and insecurity when Robert was left on his own. One possible headline might be: "I am willing to trust peers in a situation as much or more than I trust my own ability to handle the situation." The reference to the school situation should be especially noted in this regard.

In the second ER, Robert is acting on his own and being caught breaking the rules. The critical comments of others (authority) to the peer groups (entire class) really disturb him and threaten his status. One possible reaction might be a desire to avoid doing things wrong, the "nice guy approach." One headline might read: "Guilt is a big burden to carry. I don't want to be a disappointment to self or others." A similar headline might be: "In trying to please others (adults), I 'fudge' a bit, getting caught and humiliated in the process."

In the third ER, Robert's peer group again appears in a slightly traumatic situation which turns out all right. Again the theme of inadvertently making a mistake is disappointing to his self-image, but he receives support from others and takes care of himself in his opinion.

The fourth ER depicts Robert's concern with being the center of attention. It is as though Robert feels he should get special treatment, whereas in other ER's it seems that Robert doesn't especially want to be the center of attention. In ER 2 and 3 special attention is "hurtful" for Robert. It might be assumed that an ideal situation would be one where no one is the center of attention, everyone being on an equal basis. A newspaper headline might be "Equality is established; Happiness reigns."

The fifth ER focuses on the unfairness of authority in relation to Robert's peer group. In this case a more covert reaction takes place (hiding behind bushes) but authority wins in the end. A possible newspaper headline might be "Peers receive unfair treatment by authority figures."

The sixth ER denotes a cooperate interaction in the absence of authority. Robert has the chance to work in a setting where he can show his competence, allowing him to feel good about himself. Work is linked to good feelings. A newspaper headline might read "Boy mechanic makes good."

In the sixth ER we also noted an authority figure present, but Robert works independently at the task. There is a difference between this ER and the preceding ER's where authority figures were associated with domination and critical statements. This apparent conflict might be resolved by noting the behavior of the adult. If the adult is dominant and critical, the result is negative; if the adult allows Robert to do the work independently, then Robert reacts in a positive manner.

Life-Style Summary

In the following section the data from the family constellation and the ER's are combined into a format which focuses attention on three key statements of a life-style analysis. The crucial statements are, "I am.., they are.., and life is.." These statements are viewed in the framework of the three "life tasks" of love, work, and friendship. (See Dreikurs, 1950.) A systematic "first-person" summary of Robert viewed in these three areas compared with crucial "I am — others are — life is" themes follows.

I Am...*(Love)*

"I may not trust my own capabilities in a love relationship. While I am attractive, strong, cooperative, considerate, and kind, I tend to lean towards a series of relationships rather than a commitment to one person over a period of time. I am attracted by traditional women and shun the 'liberated,' aggressive females."

I Am...*(Work)*

"I am a hard worker, nice guy, and cooperative in situations where I am able to function on an equal basis with others. I also have good psychomotor ability and work well with my hands."

I Am...*(Friendship)*

"I am covertly rebellious of authority outside of the home. I am cooperative and don't feel the need to be the center of attention in situations where I perceive a co-equal relationship with others. I am considerate and sensitive, a 'one-of-the-gang' type. I will not allow others to push me around."

Others Are...*(Love)*

"Females are conforming, intelligent, good grade getters, and have a more passive orientation in life. They do what is expected of them." (In such a situation, which might be construed as discouraging, love might not flourish. Love is an active state with two people participating fully.)

Others Are...*(Work)*

"Other males sometimes are the center of attention but these times are for special reasons. Others are helpful and considerate, hard working and playful. Females in work situations are likely to be intelligent with high standards of achievement and will conform to the expectations of supervisors."

Others Are...*(Friendship)*

"Others are helpful and playful in recreational situations. Authority can be critical even in friendship interactions. It is difficult to be friends with those in authority, for they often make unfair rules and punish me unjustly."

Life Is...*(Love)*

"Life is a place where I am distant from one strong relationship."

Life Is...*(Work)*

"Life is a place where I don't lead. However, I do expect a co-equal relationship with men and women engaged in traditional sex-stereotyped functions. Each sex will contribute different expertise to the work situation. In most situations my hard work and cooperative nature will allow me to be the center of attention at times. Good feelings will predominate in this situation."

Life Is...*(Friendship)*

"Life is a place where authority is to be challenged. I don't question my behaviors closely enough to do the right thing all the time. Safety and belongingness is found within the group.

Mistaken and Self-Defeating Apperceptions

- ✧ Robert tends to underestimate his ability to complete tasks successfully. He seldom volunteers to take on the leadership role even in a task which he knows he's capable of doing.

- ✧ Robert tends to develop feelings of inadequacy when facing a task unaided by others.

- ✧ Robert may overrate the dangers of new situations and tend to engage in familiar activities.

- ✧ Robert may overrate the injustice in situations involving authority figures.

- ✧ Robert may have difficulty in expressing his perceived injustices to authority figures.

Assets

- ✧ Robert is personable and considerate in most social situations.
- ✧ Robert is sensitive to people around him.
- ✧ Robert is a hard worker and is skilled at working as a team member.
- ✧ Robert is good looking and cooperative.

Reorientation

The life-style data and analysis is presented in an interpretation session commonly called the insight portion of the life-style process. The individual is allowed to react to all portions of the life-style analysis and encouraged to develop and deepen the concepts as they relate to his current situation. After this procedure the question to be answered is "What is standing in your way?" In reorientation we focus on selected areas, concentrate on goal setting and implement a plan of action. The following are some areas which a counselor and Robert might outline for improvement:

A project may be suggested which will provide Robert a heightened awareness of his potential to initiate and follow to completion a series of tasks. The focus of such a project would be upon specific tasks he finds agreeable as well as the way in which he proceeds in a task. The culmination of such a project may be an occupational or educational choice.

A project may be suggested which allows Robert the experience of a series of new situations. The learning involved may lead to more comfort and skills in this regard.

The counselor and Robert may further investigate the area of unfairness to find alternative choices for such situations.

A project may be suggested which allows Robert an opportunity to test his power of directly sharing his concern about injustices associated with authority figures. Role playing the situation prior to actual implementation might be useful.

And now it's time for your own
Life-Style Summary.
Use the following guide on the next
page to help focus your conclusions.

A Suggested Systematic Introductory Life-Style Summary

(Page numbers appearing in brackets [ ] denote location in the workbook where topic is addressed)

1. **Current Functioning in the Five Life Tasks** [pp. 116 – 129]

   A. Activities which bring joy to the client:

   _____

   _____

   B. Subjective concerns/complaints/illnesses/medications:

   _____

   _____

   C. Summarize the five life tasks:

   _____

   _____

   _____

   D. Integrate "the question" and formulate 3– 4 key areas of concern in the person's current life:

   _____

   _____

   _____

2. **Family Atmosphere** [pp. 115; 129 – 143]

   (Summarize overall impressions in the following areas)

   A. Issues regarding the "naming process":[p. 132]

   _____

   _____

   B. Mood:[pp.129 – 130]

   _____

   _____

C. Order:[pp. 129 – 130]

_____

_____

D. Relationships:[pp. 129 – 130]

_____

_____

E. Masculine and feminine role models:[p. 130]

_____

_____

F. Parental interaction and parenting style:[pp. 130 –131]

_____

_____

G. Family Values/Family Motto:[pp. 133 –134]

_____

_____

H. Psychological birth-order position and sibling ratings (list personality traits):[pp. 134 –142]

_____

_____

I. Influential stories, fairy tales, television characters,myths, etc.:[pp. 148 – 150]

_____

_____

J. Describe the impact of the person's cultural heritage:[pp. 26 – 31]

_____

_____

K. Any other significant factors (e.g.. significant deaths, additions or subtractions to family, divorces, ethnic or community values, etc.):[pp. 26 – 31]

_____

_____

3. **Summarize key aspects of the Early Recollections (ER's) [pp. 151 –160]**

    A. ER #1

      1. Newspaper headline:

         _____

      2. a. Who is present in the recollection?

            _____

         b. Who is remembered with affection?

            _____

         c. Who is disliked in the recollection?

            _____

         d. What problem(s) is(are) confronted in the recollection?

            _____

            _____

         e. What special talent(s) or ability is(are) revealed in the recollection?

            _____

            _____

         f. Is the recollection generally pleasant or unpleasant?

            _____

         g. What is the client's level of activity in the recollection?

            _____

         h. What emotion does the client feel and/or show pertaining to the recollection?

            _____

            _____

         i. What does the recollection suggest to you about the client's social interest?

            _____

            _____

215

    j. What specific needs or values are reflected in this E.R.?

_____

_____

B. ER #2

    1. Newspaper headline:

_____

    2. a. Who is present in the recollection?

_____

      b. Who is remembered with affection?

_____

      c. Who is disliked in the recollection?

_____

      d. What problem(s) is(are) confronted in the recollection?

_____

_____

      e. What special talent(s) or ability is(are) revealed in the recollection?

_____

_____

      f. Is the recollection generally pleasant or unpleasant?

_____

      g. What is the client's level of activity in the recollection?

_____

      h. What emotion does the client feel and/or show pertaining to the recollection?

_____

_____

      i. What does the recollection suggest to you about the client's social interest?

_____

_____

j.   What specific needs or values are reflected in this E.R.?

_____

C.   ER #3

1. Newspaper headline:

_____

2. a.   Who is present in the recollection?

_____

b.   Who is remembered with affection?

_____

c.   Who is disliked in the recollection?

_____

d.   What problem(s) is(are) confronted in the recollection?

_____

_____

e.   What special talent(s) or ability is(are) revealed in the recollection?

_____

_____

f.   Is the recollection generally pleasant or unpleasant?

_____

g.   What is the client's level of activity in the recollection?

_____

h.   What emotion does the client feel and/or show pertaining to the recollection?

_____

_____

i.   What does the recollection suggest to you about the client's social interest?

_____

_____

217

j. What specific needs or values are reflected in this E.R.?

_____

_____

D. ER #4

1. Newspaper headline:

_____

2. a. Who is present in the recollection?

_____

b. Who is remembered with affection?

_____

c. Who is disliked in the recollection?

_____

d. What problem(s) is(are) confronted in the recollection?

_____

_____

e. What special talent(s) or ability is(are) revealed in the recollection?

_____

_____

f. Is the recollection generally pleasant or unpleasant?

_____

g. What is the client's level of activity in the recollection?

_____

h. What emotion does the client feel and/or show pertaining to the recollection?

_____

_____

i. What does the recollection suggest to you about the client's social interest?

_____

_____

    j.   What specific needs or values are reflected in this E.R.?

    _____

    _____

E. Recurring Dream

    1. Who is present in the recurring dream?

    _____

    2. Who is remembered with affection?

    _____

    3. Who is disliked in the recurring dream?

    _____

    4. What problem(s) is(are) confronted in the recurring dream?

    _____

    _____

    5. What special talent(s) or ability is(are) revealed in the recurring dream?

    _____

    _____

    6. Is the recurring dream generally pleasant or unpleasant?

    _____

    7. What is the client's level of activity in the recurring dream?

    _____

    8. What emotion does the client feel and/or show pertaining to the recurring dream?

    _____

    _____

    9. What does the recurring dream suggest to you about the client's social interest?

    _____

    _____

10. What specific needs or values are reflected in this recurring dream?

_____

_____

11. Summarize the issues/wants/needs/values revealed by the "most memorable" adolescent observation:

_____

_____

F. Global ratings and impressions of all early memories:

_____

_____

_____

4. **Major Needs/Values of the Client** [pp. 106 – 108]

(Check all that apply)

___ Abasement	___ Deference	___ Rejection
___ Achievement	___ Dominance	___ Sentience
___ Affiliation	___ Exhibition	___ Sex
___ Aggression	___ Harmavoidance	___ Succorance
___ Autonomy	___ Infavoidance	___ Understanding
___ Counteraction	___ Nurturance	
___ Defendance	___ Order	

5. **Common ER Themes** [pp. 151 – 154]

(Check all that apply and briefly describe them)

___ dethronement (the birth of a younger sibling or another person entering who takes center stage) _____

___ surprises _____

___ obstacles _____

___ affiliation _____

___ security _____

___ skill tasks _____

___ dependency _____

___ external authority _____

___ self-control _____

___ status _____

___ power _____

___ morality _____

___ human interactions _____

___ new situations _____

___ excitement _____

___ sexuality _____

___ gender _____

___ nurturance _____

___ confusion _____

___ luck _____

___ sickness _____

___ death _____

6. **Major Life-Style Themes** [pp. 110 – 113; 144 – 148]

_____

_____

7. **Identify and summarize the importance of the #1 priority and the "Top Card" assets/liabilities** [pp. 160 – 165]

_____

_____

_____

8. **Create a "force-field analysis" relative to what issues impede ("no") or amplify ("yes") relative to a possible change in this person** [pp. 194 – 198]

_____

_____

_____

9. **Mistaken Notions and Self-defeating Beliefs/Behavior** [pp. 179 – 184]

_____

_____

10. **Assets/Strengths/Specific Areas To Be Encouraged** [pp. 185 – 187]

_____

_____

11. **Reorientation (Reframing a "perceived minus into a plus") Recommendations and Suggestions** [pp. 102 – 106]

_____

_____

_____

12. **Future Implications of Present Life-Style** [pp. 172 – 178]

_____

_____

(OPTIONAL)

After sharing your life-style summary with your client, answer the following questions:

13. What were the major "recognition reflexes" or areas of agreement by your client of your summary?

_____

_____

_____

14. What were the major disagreements? How did you handle them?

_____

_____

_____

15. What were your own issues that were brought up by your client's life-style? (e.g. similarities, differences, judgments, etc.) What were your own reactions to your summary?

_____

_____

_____

16. Any revisions or modifications to your original summary?

_____

_____

_____

_____

_____

_____

_____

17. Any other observations or reactions?

_____

_____

_____

_____

_____

_____

_____

☺

CONGRATULATIONS!

Chapter 7

THE NEXT STEPS —
A LOOK TO THE FUTURE

In a traditional doctoral dissertation the first four chapters follow a structured "stick-to-the-facts (data) please" format. But in the final chapter, the supposedly wiser "wannabe doctor" gets to speculate, to dream about a better future based on the significant contribution he or she has now made to the discipline. Thus, we approach the final chapter with an eye to the future, with all the hopes of an idealistic dreamer.

Jon Carlson (1979) correctly predicted what he called an "exciting re-birth" of the helping professions:

> Through the work of thousands of researchers and practitioners, we are about to rediscover the meaning of truly helping others to realize previously untapped states of health and wellness. This talent has remained latent because the helping professions have been plagued with the following problems: a) an emphasis on disease and problems; b) a lack of understanding about what health consists of and corresponding inability to recognize high-quality behavior; c) using a solely mental approach to helping that has not included the physical, nutritional, spiritual, environmental, and social realms; and d) not believing in our own ideas and theories enough to model or live a wellness life-style. (p. 85)

Such a rebirth starts in profoundly simple ways. As Lao Tzu said, "The journey of a thousand miles begins with a single step." We hope this workbook has aided you in taking that first step. Just watching expert swimmers demonstrate their proficiency is important, but there is no substitute for personal practice in gaining new skills. John Dewey aptly stated that "We learn by doing." In addition to encouraging you to read and observe additional "expert" life-style techniques, we have attempted to aid your active participation through this workbook. Don't just watch — get actively involved in the helping process in its rebirth.

Just as counseling can be "for better or for worse," so this workbook can be helpful or harmful. If the workbook is viewed as an introductory examination of life-styles, we feel that our purpose will have been accomplished. However, we do not intend that a person make a "parlor game" out of early recollections or family atmosphere after having read our workbook. If one believes that "a little learning is a dangerous thing," then the workbook could be harmful. But if our workbook is viewed as an introduction to life-styles, then we have succeeded in this venture. It is our hope that this workbook will be viewed as a catalyst for other persons to modify, expand, and improve.

There are many practical uses for a life-style investigation. For example, counselors and psychologists will find life-styles an integral aspect of a "mental status exam," with the inclusion of early recollections as another type of projective assessment technique. Social workers will also find the standard interview an invaluable tool in obtaining relevant family background and case history information. Marriage and family therapists can utilize life-style inventories with couples, as part of Jay Haley's (1976) interpersonal relation-ships fourfold typology consisting of: **personality differences, role perceptions, communication patterns,** and **problem-solving skills.**

Of course, inherent in all ethical standards for members of the helping professions is the important consideration to practice within the limitations of one's own skills and competence. As with any assessment technique, life-style investigation should be interpreted in a manner consistent with professional skills involving "depth psychology."

A limitation of the self-interpretive nature of the workbook is that personal "blind spots" may not be identified through "Self-Analysis" only. That is one reason we have encouraged a partnership approach. The reader may want to pursue additional life-style investigations by contacting local experienced qualified Adlerian counselors or by writing the North American Society for Adlerian Psychology (65 E. Wacker Place #400, Chicago, IL 60601; (312) 629-8801).

Other invaluable life-style texts on a more advanced clinical nature are Shulman and Mosak's *Manual for Life-Style Assessment* (1988), and Powers and Griffith's *Understanding Life-Style: The Psycho-clarity Process* (1987). A suggested overview to Adlerian therapy is Dinkmeyer, Dinkmeyer and Sperry's *Adlerian Counseling and Psychotherapy* (1987).

The journal *Individual Psychology* is an excellent quarterly publication featuring the latest in Adlerian ideas. It is available as part of the membership to NASAP.

Future Trends: Cultural Diversity

As for the future dream we share in Adler's own striving for increased interconnectedness through the enhanced social interest or humanistic identification. This has both personal and national implications.

On a personal level a commitment to respecting cultural uniqueness is an important step. Newlon and Arciniega (1983) have a helpful perspective regarding the process of cultural diversity.

> The acculturation process that occurs in all minority families is a movement toward belonging, of wanting to be a part of the whole in order to contribute. Minority families socialize their children to be able to survive in the majority culture.
>
> Albeit, at times this socialization is manifested by training children to deal with racism through anger. If counselors can understand the purpose of the anger, they can see that the ultimate purpose is actually a continuation of fighting to belong in spite of the social and economic obstacles placed before many minority groups. (p. 138)

Kogod (1992) summarizes some key trends being predicted by the United States Department of Labor. By the year 2000, white males will account for only 15% of the 25 million people who will join the workforce between the years 1985 and 2000. The remaining 85% will consist of white females, immigrants, and minorities (both genders) of black, Hispanic, and Asian origins. The Hispanic and Asian populations will each grow by 48%; the black population will grow by 28%; and the white population by only 5.6%. It is projected that sometime in the next century non-Hispanic whites will lose their majority status in the United States.

Quick, et al. (1992) describe a growing problem among top U.S. executives as being that of emotional isolation and loneliness. They feel the American culture which places so much value on independence is one of the chief causes of the problem. They note that many oriental cultures place much less importance on independence and individualism — instead the values they prize emphasize the family system and the group. Such a value system leads to a social process of attachment, a bonding in human relationships, not emotional isolation.

That is not to say that the oriental culture is superior, another twist in the vertical plane of competitive struggle. It is to say that the overemphasis on individualism can and often does lead to a feeling of aloneness and detachment from the total group. Such personal isolation has a national correlation.

Ward (1958) believes that "Total sovereignty is to the state what egoism is to the individual —the last, holiest, most treasured source of all disaster."

In Chapter 2, we introduced the concept of ethnocentrism, the cultural equivalent to personal superiority. Kogod (1992) describes it as follows:

> The greatest difficulty arises in a relationship when a person believes that "only my culture makes sense, espouses the 'right' values, and represents the 'right' and logical way to behave."

> This mode of thinking is called ethnocentrism. When two ethnocentric people from different cultures interact... common reactions to differing world views are anger, shock, and amusement. (p. 242)

Some of his recommendations for living in an increasingly culturally diverse world include:

1. Understand that cultural differences exist.

2. Acknowledge your own stereotypes and assumptions.

3. Learn about other cultures.

4. Be flexible; try to adapt to the style of the person with whom you are communicating.

5. Encourage constructive communication about differences.

Learning about differences reminds one of the authors (Eckstein) of a valuable lesson he learned during his first visit to Japan. His host was Sakan Yanagidaira, a well-known Adlerian consultant and businessman.

"Tell me how you perceive American and Japanese management styles as being different," Eckstein inquired.

"Tell me how a giraffe and a chimpanzee are different," came Mr. Yanagidaira's reply.

After hearing a few differences (i.e. heavier, faster, etc.) the Japanese host continued with, "Now tell me how they are similar."

That required a new cognitive functioning, a restructuring and reframing of a predisposition of finding differences. With a twinkle in his eye and a knowing smile on his lips, he concluded, "Most people seek the differences between American and Japanese traditions — I encourage people to seek the similarities instead."

Lydia Sicher (1890-1962) was a physician who studied closely with Adler during the 1920's and early 1930's. When Adler left Austria to move to the United States, he left Sicher in charge of The Viennese Society and all its activities, which she directed until Hitler closed them nine years later. In 1941 she moved to Los Angeles where she helped establish Adlerian clinics on the west coast. The influence of Adler and her own wisdom are reflected in a recently edited book by Adele Davidson (1991) entitled *The Collected Works of Lydia Sicher: An Adlerian Perspective.*

As we dream of a better future her words from several decades back remind us of the timeliness of Adler's original ideas. Some selected quotes include:

> Only if we think of ourselves as one with the surroundings will we establish relationships which not only benefit situations, but also benefit ourselves and this extrapersonal entirety. This means we have to be interested in the welfare of the *whole* just as much as in the welfare of others... Acting constructively can be seen in striving for something with an eye set on a future community of humanity which is yet to be, but could be established. (pp. 7–8).

> This is the problem: all of us are *immortal*. It is not immortality in the religious sense, but immortality because whatever we do sets a cause which has an effect. This effect becomes a new problem, either a soluble or a nonsoluble one ...(p. 11)

> If only we realized in all our human relationships how much our undeveloped sense of cooperativeness and sense of responsibility produce difficulties, such as prejudice, race, hatred, or nationality. Wars are based on the *fear* people have that their own prestige will be endangered. They are afraid that they will not be seen as *the* perfect individual, *the* perfect nation, if they cannot find someone whom they can tear down. If we could eliminate the idea of above and below, we could get along with people marvelously well. On a horizontal plane everyone has his own road, his own goal. We could then walk next to each other toward the very distant goal of evolution ...(p. 54)

> Cooperativeness and contributiveness are only part of it; they are two of the basic laws. It is the experience of *oneness* with the cosmos. In the cosmos, the human race and you are one ...(p. 54)

> It is interesting that the mistakes we make, the wars we create, are considered as 'human nature.' We forget that this is not human nature, but that we have not yet developed being really human. If we were *really human*, we would have this feeling of *connectedness*..." (p. 55) "If we really would once become human, we would not do all those things that are so inhuman ...(p. 55)

> We Individual Psychologists are not intent on reforming the world. We are intent on making, in our small circle, a nucleus of people who will perhaps

know in which direction to develop in order to reach their own self-fulfillment. (p. 56)

Sicher utilizes the following metaphor to graphically represent our interconnectedness on the horizontal plane of existence:

> I see the whole human race as an *orchestra*. Each player is important, of equal importance, as symphony or cacophony depends upon the full cooperation of all among themselves...I think of Haydn's symphony with the drum beat, the measure that represents the climax of the composition. And there sits the drummer, remote from the front row, almost disappearing behind the other instruments ...(p. 97)

Sicher then describes the drummer's possible inner feelings of competitiveness and jealousy of the first violinist, the concert master. "I am much better looking than him and would certainly make people applaud...if only I could make up my mind to study the violin. Life has been against me, but if I ever decide to study the violin the world for once will see what a concert master should be like," the drummer contemplates.

Sicher concludes her story by saying, "He sits and dreams, glorious dreams of elevation of self and belittling of the 'foe.' His measure comes and he *forgets to beat his drum*. The whole symphony falls flat, as flat as the world, because there are too many day-dreaming drummers among individuals, and groups, and nations, and races, and too few who have an interest in the symphony. But thanks to Adler, this too has been made understandable." (in Davidson, 1991 p. 97)

The twentieth century has been an age of *dreamers*. We trust that in some small way, this workbook will bring greater awareness of your limiting habitual patterns and, along with it, a renewed ability and freedom to chose to live with more happiness and more interconnectedness with your surrounding world.

Alfred Adler's visionary ideas dropped a small pebble into a vast pond. Many concentric circles continually reverberate toward the shore, circles of hope that a better way of personal and global living is a dream continually motivating us toward being together in harmony, as part of the extended family called humanity...

Imagine...

Appendix A

The "Willhite" Method of Early Memory Analysis

by Robert G. Willhite, M.S.W.

Excerpted from *The Willhite: A Manual Teaching a Method of Early Recollection Analysis*. Self-Care Books, Route 11, Box 489, Mountain Home, AR 72653. Used by permission of the author.

This is a manual of a process of Early Memory analysis developed by Robert Willhite. The purpose of this method of analysis is to see more in depth, what is happening in the thinking and feeling process of that particular individual, and reveal the particular set of biases consistent with his/her private logic.

The recollection reveals an intricate set of feelings and emotions generated to fulfill the intended goal. Adler said, "...emotions are generate to promote behavior to the degree, and in the direction of the intended goal." Using "The Willhite" method of recollection analysis, this intricate pattern is revealed.

The "Willhite" is a process to reach in depth into the early memory to find the emotional "steam engine" that drives the behavior, to fulfill the expectations of a person's private view of the world. The primary goal of the process is to reveal to the subject not only the emotions created that bring out the behavior, but also which specific set of feelings he/she needs to look at, to change the behavior. Too often we, as therapists, admonish the client to "change," but we do not give him/her the correct tool (understanding) of how to accomplish this. It is imperative that a new "set" of feelings be created, to support a new conviction about "outcomes" in life for believable changes to come about. We can have new "insights" about our behaviors, but if we stubbornly hold on to the old convictions, nothing is different. Likewise, if we do not create a new set of feeling behaviors to be consistent with the new insights, we are doomed to repeat the old dysfunctional patterns. This process is designed to break into the old pattern and present the hope that new behavior is attainable.

METHOD

The method used to analyze a recollection using the Willhite Method needs to be followed precisely to get the desired results. The method is designed to basically accomplish two things. One, to elicit precise data from the subject using his/her specific data, thus tapping into the subject's private view of the world. The second, and perhaps the most significant goal, is to keep the therapist's influence out of the data collecting process so as to keep from biasing the outcome. This is not meant to discount the importance and value of therapeutic interpretation and professional feedback. This, in fact, is why the person seeks professional help. The design is specifically constructed to get as much data from the private logic (personal biases) of the subject before the interpretations are made.

The method is as follows:

1. Ask the subject for his/her earliest memory. This can be at any age, even though many Adlerian theorists insist on memories at the age of five or earlier.

2. When you write the recollection, double space, as you will be adding data between the lines later.

3. In accepting data, write every word the subject gives, even parenthetical insertions.

4. Once the memory is reported, ask for the "stop action" or significant point of the recollection.

5. Read the material back to the subject for accuracy.

6. Now, go back over the memory and read it a line or phrase at a time, and ask the subject to respond to that data, giving a feeling or emotion. These can be emotions felt at the time of the memory, or feelings now. If there is a difference, write both down.

7. Number these responses in sequence all the way through, to and including the "stop action" response.

8. Now, list these feelings and emotions separately. This list proves to be the intricate pattern of emotions the subject uses at times to attain intended goals. The subject will immediately recognize the "private thread" for it has been obtained directly from his/her data, and it is impossible to deny.

Case Study

1. Sorry for self   2. Small   3. Curious
I had to walk to school. I was the youngest. The school was straight
                          4. Frustration
across a vacant lot from our house. Mom made me walk with my older
             5. Uneasy
brother and sister. We were never to cut across the field. One day,
6. Anticipation/Excitement
coming home from school, I decided to leave my brother and sister and
7. Gutsy   8. Horrified
cut across the field. Halfway across I stepped on a hive of bees.
9. Extreme pain   10. Hurt
They stung me. I ran home screaming in pain. As I got close to the house,
11. Anticipation/Relief   12. Shock/Painful
I saw mother waiting for me. She grabbed me and spanked me.
13. Hurt/Angry
I was hurt and angry.
                14. Sympathy/Small
STAND OUT: *Seeing mother waiting for me.*

1. Sorry for self	8. Horrified
2. Small	9. Extreme pain
3. Curious	10. Hurt
4. Frustration	11. Anticipation/Relief
5. Uneasy	12. Shock/Painful
6. Anticipation/Excitement	13. Hurt/Angry
7. Gutsy	14. Sympathy/Small

SUMMARY:

This person is obviously feeling sorry for herself partly from her feelings of inadequacy and smallness. One would guess that she is a spoiled child, being the youngest, and the fact that a spoiled child is a discouraged child. She also is obviously trying to break the mold — insisting that she can cross the field by herself, in spite of her mother's admonition.

The feeling sequence series suggests a number of things that should be checked out with her. Even though she feels sorry for herself, and sees herself as "small", she covers this up with a "curious" attitude and maybe a mischievous nature (this is purely a guess on my part). These two positions (small and curious) result in her feeling frustrated and uneasy.

Nonetheless, she follows by anticipation, excitement and gutsy, which even though this is a choice of hers, results in her feeling horrified, and if she takes this risk of being gutsy, she will suffer "extreme pain and hurt", (9 and 10). Having gotten herself in this position, she looks to someone bigger (mother) to get her out of this mess she has created. But to her shock and pain, the opposite occurs (she is punished) and she winds up feeling hurt and angry.

The stand out features of the memory reinforced the vicious cycle of her position in life — as long as she seeks sympathy, she will reinforce the position in life that she is small.

As Mary continued in therapy, she began to gradually change the view of herself from feeling small and feeling sorry for herself, to feeling proud that she could begin to take steps to being responsible in her decisions, and that in so doing, others would view her as competent and secure. She is now loved and cared for out of her own sense of adequacy and competency. As you look at the reconstructed material, you can see I was able to help her, using her own words and data (proud, secure, cared for, etc.).

Using "The Willhite" it is relatively simple to check where a client intends to reach out in terms of changing his/her behavior. I turn to the use of dreams, imagination or fantasy to make this point. The context of this theory suggests that one cannot fantasize something that is not consistent with their private logic.

Rather than asking them to make up an entirely new creation in fantasy, I ask them if they could change the recollection to have it come out any way they wanted, how would the story read? It is fascinating to watch in what areas change is made, and how blatantly consistent this change is with the private logic today. Let's see how this subject chose to change her story, and see how this reveals where she stands today in terms of her view of life.

Here is the reconstruction:

1. Proud   2. Small
I was able to walk to school by myself. I was the youngest.
3. Curious
The school was straight across a vacant lot from our house.
4. Smug
Mom told my brother and sister I could handle myself just fine.
5. Uneasy   6. Anticipation/Excitement
I was told never to cut across the field. One day, coming home from school,
7. Gutsy   8. Horrified
I decided to cut across. Halfway through, I stepped on a hive of bees.
9. Extreme pain   10. Hurt
They stung me. I ran home screaming in pain. As I got close to the house,
11. Anticipation/Relief   12. Safe/Secure
I saw mother waiting for me. She grabbed me and hugged me.
13. Warm/Cared For
She held me real close and comforted me.
                          14. Cared for
STAND OUT: *She comforted me.*

Let us look at what changes she chose and what these choices tell us about this person. First, she chose to be able to walk to school by herself — feeling proud. She continued to hold to thoughts whereby she feels small (I was the youngest). She could remain the youngest and still feel fulfillment about herself, (her choice). She chose "smug" to be told she could handle herself just fine.

The most significant part of the process comes when she makes a choice to step on the hive of bees. I remember asking her, with some amazement, if she was sure she wanted to keep this phrase. She did. It became clear why she did this. Her goal was to be held and comforted by her mother. She would go to any length to get this closeness. The bottom line for her is, rather than accept the consequences for her behavior and learn from them, she looks to be rescued and comforted — to the degree of setting situations up for this to happen. In continuing this behavior, she fosters dependency, thus reinforcing her feelings of smallness and feeling sorry for herself.

The final phase of "The Willhite" then involves seeing if the client can identify with a current life challenge which bears some relationship with the

ER. This is an excellent way to demonstrate how the pattern is being "played out" presently. The desired changes from the original ER can then be adapted to the current ER.

Thus, the Willhite procedure compares a past ER to a current Life challenge. It is then possible to use creative imagination to construct a desire future change. It is often insightful for clients to see how their past decisions' patterns are affected by their current life — desired changes can help concretize future goals. It also helps establish a rationale for seeing how early formative experiences impact present and future decisions and goals.

Summary

The "Willhite" is a structured way of viewing the relationship of emotions to the content of one's ER. It is also a process of identifying a client's "private logic" relative to desired changes, plus a way to see the correlation of such a formative event on one's present situation. It can also illustrate how one "uses" his/her emotions to obtain conscious or unconscious goals. Further goals and needed behavioral attitudinal changes needed can thus be identified.

Robert Willhite, M.S.W. is a retired Social Worker, living in Mountain Home, Arkansas. His expertise is working with individuals and families who have problems with addictions. He developed "The Willhite — a Method of Early Memory Analysis" and has made presentations of this model at several national seminars. He is also on the faculty of the Nebraska Adlerian Society in Omaha.

Appendix B

The Early Recollections Role Reversal Technique

by Daniel Eckstein, Ph.D., ABPP and Roy Kern, Ed.D.

Introduction

The use of Early Recollections (ERs) as a valuable projective technique is one of Adler's most significant contributions to the helping profession. Just as Freud called dreams the "royal road to the unconsciousness" perhaps it is fair to say that ERs represent a similar "royal road" to a person's "private logic."

Although the use of ERs is an essential component to Adlerian theory, they can also be used quite compatibly by such other closely related theories as: existential, gestalt, reality therapy and rationale emotive therapy. The following experiential activity can be used in "pure" Adlerian theory-oriented presentations as well as generic courses or seminars focusing on counseling theories or techniques.

Rudolf Dreikurs extended Adler's original "inferiority coupled with striving for success" theoretical premise to include what he called the "horizontal versus vertical plane" of interpersonal relationships. In contrast to the typical "better than" or "worse than" superiority/ inferiority relationship polarity. Dreikurs stressed the "horizontal" ("different than") relationships. For example, an apple is neither "better" or "worse" than an orange; it is merely different.

Such a equalitarian relationship approach can be extended into the classroom, workshop, or seminar setting by Adlerian education consultants or facilitators. The following experiential activity is a practical extension of an empowering approach to student/teacher or participant/trainer interactions. It creates a role-reversal to the typical volunteer who courageously shares his or her ERs somewhat as a type of "sacrificial lamb" so that peers can gain practical experience both collecting and making clinical inferences by observing an "expert" teacher interpret ERs.

The obvious disadvantage to the volunteer approach is of course, the unknown variable of the degree of discouragement, lack of social interest and/or level of pathology which may be reflected in the volunteer-generated ERs. Peers are often reluctant to identify such issues for fear of hurting the individual; instructors are often similarly uncertain about the degree of "ego-strength" necessary to receive feedback by others.

The following activity allows the advantage of using actual facilitator/instructor generated ERs. It identifies how the instructor/trainer can model self-disclosure and risk-taking. A further advantage of the activity is that it empowers the students as the "experts" in the process.

Procedures for The ER Role Reversal Technique

The following sequence is suggested for this experiential ER demonstration:

⬥ An initial first step is to collect all the students'/participants' names on 3x5 index cards. Following an overview to the introduction to the therapeutic use of ERs and to model facilitator self-disclosure should set the stage.

⬥ The second step is to provide a theoretical base for understanding ERs as well as standard collection techniques. The instructor first provides a theoretical input on guidelines for collecting and interpreting ERs.

⬥ Third, the instructor randomly calls a student's name from the index cards to collect the first ER from the instructor. A second and third ER is collected with a different randomly selected student. The students should verbally "gather" the ER with such instructions/prompting as, "And then what happened? What was most vivid about the memory? What were you feeling?"

⬥ Fourth, a student should post the ERs word for word on the flip chart/board so that everyone can read it. Gathering three ERs and one recurring or significant dream is suggested.

⬥ After collecting the ERs and dream, students may individually or in sub-groups generate such responses to the first ER as a headline, major themes, wants, needs, values, etc. This information is then solicited by the instructor selecting at random from the index cards students'/participants' responses.

✧ Another randomly selected student should share impressions respectively for ER #2, ER #3, and the significant dream. Then the facilitator should request a summary of the overall themes/needs/wants/values/strengths observed from these four incidents.

✧ To assist students' understanding as to how ERs can be operationalized into educational or therapeutic settings, the facilitator may randomly request students/participants to conclude the exercise by asking the following questions:

   ✧ If I were to come for career counseling, what would be some of your guesses about my vocational interests? What other suggestions or recommendations would you make?

   ✧ If this was my first counseling session with you and you had only collected these three ERs and one significant dream, what would you predict would be some of the possible presenting problems?

   ✧ If you were going to encourage the reframing of various "mistaken" or "self-defeating" beliefs and/or behaviors, how would you proceed?

   ✧ What particular theory(ies) or technique(s) would you use?

   ✧ What other observations/implications do you have for beginning a therapeutic relationship? For example, what type of resistance might be present? How receptive do you feel such a client would be to counseling?

A total class discussion should conclude the demonstration.

Variations

Instead of randomly selecting students, the instructor could seek volunteers for each respective consideration. Another option is to give the specific task to various sub-groups and have each group select a spokesperson — a combination of sub-group brainstorming plus random individual selection is yet another option.

Because of the personal nature of the ERs, it may also be a challenge for the instructor to switch roles from sharing ERs to then facilitating the experience. To avoid such a "dual relationship" another member or two of the group may be appointed or volunteer to facilitate the discussion.

Limitations and Conclusions:

The potential strength of having an instructor courageously model self-disclosure also has a potential weakness. Just as any therapeutic can be "for better" or "for worse," so too, the risk is that students will negatively judge or lose respect for the "crazy" teacher. Such high self-disclosure can both model openness while concurrently resulting in self-absorption. Instructors/trainers need to remember the major learning objective is for students to gain clinical experience. Personal insights, while useful, need to be a secondary agenda.

Clinically oriented students are adept at finding pathology ("the glass half empty") in contrast to the assets ("glass half full"). Instructors who have a high need for approval or to be pleasing to students might also be discouraged at the candor of some of the students' comments.

In conclusion, the Adlerian use of ERs is a valuable contribution. The present article introduces a specific technique whereby students/participants gain practical ER experience by working with instructor/trainer generated ERs.

It also is an interesting teaching tool to increase the probability that all members of the group stay "tuned in" to the experiential process since index cards are used as opposed to the more traditional raising of hands.

Roy Kern, Ed.D. is a professor in the Department of Counseling and Psychological Services of the College of Education at Georgia State University.

Appendix C

The Life-Style Questionnaire Inventory

By Roy Kern, Ed.D.

The *Life-Style Questionnaire Inventory* was developed by to provide practitioners involved in lifestyle assessment with a guide that would assist them in identifying patterns and reoccurring life-style themes in a more quantifiable fashion. To increase the probability that the instrument did indeed assist the user toward this goal it was systematically field tested by well known Adlerian experts conducting blind reviews on life-style questionnaire inventories on various clinical populations.

The LSQI consists of two forms. One for interviewing or collecting data with *siblings* and one for *only children.* It may be employed as a paper/pencil assessment or as a clinical interview guide. The questionnaire is included here, as it provides an opportunity for quantification and empirical research on the life-style interview process.

NOTE: *The LSQI form for "only children" is not included here, but may be obtained from the author.*

INSTRUCTIONS FOR USE AS CLINICAL INTERVIEW GUIDE

To use the inventory it is best to decide whether the client is long term or short term. It is not recommended to complete an extensive interview on life-style assessment if the client is only dealing with situational crisis which only requires good listening skills coupled with recommended problem solving strategies.

If one does decide to use this guide the following steps are suggested:

- ✧ Identify specifically the presenting concern via active listening and responding skills
- ✧ At the completion of this phase of the interview, the professional must decide whether to conduct the life-style assessment.

✧ If yes is the decision then the professional might wish to introduce the life-style questionnaire by stating:
"Each of us decide on what are the best ways to solve problems. For me, it is helpful to cooperatively explore with you how you have decided to solve the concern that you have discussed with me. I like to use the *Life-Style Questionnaire Inventory* to get at, not only how you solve problems, but also to assist you in understanding more about how you will deal with concerns in the future."

✧ At the conclusion of this intro or one that discusses the "reason" for the assessment, the professional should show the guide to the client and indicate that the client can accept or refuse answering any questions during the 1-1/2 hour interview.

✧ As the professional begins the interview they must keep reminding themselves on how does this individual in which you are conducting the interview use their life style to solve the presenting concern.

✧ At the conclusion of the interview the professional can choose to provide immediate feedback on presenting concern or delay feedback to the next session.

✧ Regardless of how extensive the feedback it is recommended that during future sessions with the client that the professional keep bringing back how their life-style information disclosed to them in the prior session is impacting their problem solving strategies.

✧ Use as take-home instrument strategy that would simply consist of giving the instrument prior to the interview and then reviewing with the client the reoccurring themes. This approach seems to be more applicable for research purposes and if time is a factor. However, our experience is that it is not as effective in educating the client as to personal life-style dynamics.

LIFE-STYLE QUESTIONNAIRE INVENTORY

By Roy Kern, Ed.D., Georgia State University, University Plaza, Atlanta, GA 30303. ©Roy Kern. Used by permission of the author.

Directions:

Below is a list of brothers and sisters starting with the oldest.

		SEX	AGE
1.	Older brother	M	28
2.	Older sister	F	26
3.	Me	M	25
4.	Younger brother	M	24
5.	Younger sister	F	21

You notice the descending order is numbered beginning with 1 (older brother and ending with 5 younger sister). The numbers will be used to rate brothers and sisters on a particular item.

This is not a test. There are no "right" or "wrong" answers. Take as much time as you need. Answer as fairly as you are able. Answer **every** item with the above numbers. Your responses will be held in **strictest confidence**.

EXAMPLE

Helping around the house

```
        5   4                 1       3       2
Least ──────────────────────────────────────────── Most
      0   1   2   3   4   5   6   7   8   9   10
```

In this example, the older sister is most helpful. You do not help as much, but you are more helpful than your older brother, younger brother and younger sister.

Turn to the next page. At the top of the page make a list of your brothers and sisters, starting with the oldest. Give their ages and sexes. Be sure to include yourself by indicating "me" and what your age and **sex** is.

NOTE:
This inventory may be used as an interview guide or a paper/pencil assessment for research purposes. When answering the following questions, think of yourself and your family when you were growing up, especially before your teenage years.

LIFE-STYLE QUESTIONNAIRE INVENTORY
PART I

Complete your list according to directions given on page one.

	Name	Sex	Age		Name	Sex	Age
1.	_____	_____	_____	1.	_____	_____	_____
2.	_____	_____	_____	2.	_____	_____	_____
3.	_____	_____	_____	3.	_____	_____	_____

Using the birth order number above (1, 2, 3, etc.) rank each family member on the traits listed below.

Intelligence

Least   0   1   2   3   4   5   6   7   8   9   10   Most

Grades in elementary school

Least   0   1   2   3   4   5   6   7   8   9   10   Most

Industries

Least   0   1   2   3   4   5   6   7   8   9   10   Most

Critical of others

Least   0   1   2   3   4   5   6   7   8   9   10   Most

Critical of self

Least   0   1   2   3   4   5   6   7   8   9   10   Most

246

Standards of accomplishment

Least   0   1   2   3   4   5   6   7   8   9   10   Most

Lived up to standards

Least   0   1   2   3   4   5   6   7   8   9   10   Most

Helpful at home

Least   0   1   2   3   4   5   6   7   8   9   10   Most

Friends

Least   0   1   2   3   4   5   6   7   8   9   10   Most

Felt sorry for self

Least   0   1   2   3   4   5   6   7   8   9   10   Most

Athletic

Least   0   1   2   3   4   5   6   7   8   9   10   Most

Physical looks (appearance)

Least   0   1   2   3   4   5   6   7   8   9   10   Most

Feminine

Least   0   1   2   3   4   5   6   7   8   9   10   Most

Masculine

Least   0   1   2   3   4   5   6   7   8   9   10   Most

Idealistic

Least   0   1   2   3   4   5   6   7   8   9   10   Most

Materialistic

Least   0   1   2   3   4   5   6   7   8   9   10   Most

Sensitive and easily hurt

Least   0   1   2   3   4   5   6   7   8   9   10   Most

Standards of right and wrong

Least   0   1   2   3   4   5   6   7   8   9   10   Most

Conforming

Least   0   1   2   3   4   5   6   7   8   9   10   Most

Made mischief

Least   0   1   2   3   4   5   6   7   8   9   10   Most

Covertly (hidden, secret) rebellious

Least   0   1   2   3   4   5   6   7   8   9   10   Most

Pleasing others

Least   0   1   2   3   4   5   6   7   8   9   10   Most

Charm

Least   0   1   2   3   4   5   6   7   8   9   10   Most

Assertive

Least   0   1   2   3   4   5   6   7   8   9   10   Most

Bossy

Least   0   1   2   3   4   5   6   7   8   9   10   Most

Demanded own way

Least   0   1   2   3   4   5   6   7   8   9   10   Most

Got own way

Least   0   1   2   3   4   5   6   7   8   9   10   Most

Considerate

Least   0   1   2   3   4   5   6   7   8   9   10   Most

Selfish

Least   0   1   2   3   4   5   6   7   8   9   10   Most

Daring

Least   0   1   2   3   4   5   6   7   8   9   10   Most

Easy going

Least   0   1   2   3   4   5   6   7   8   9   10   Most

Sense of humor

Least   0   1   2   3   4   5   6   7   8   9   10   Most

Temper

Least   0   1   2   3   4   5   6   7   8   9   10   Most

Complained at home

Least   0   1   2   3   4   5   6   7   8   9   10   Most

Punished

Least   0   1   2   3   4   5   6   7   8   9   10   Most

Spoiled

Least   0   1   2   3   4   5   6   7   8   9   10   Most

Over-protected

Least   0   1   2   3   4   5   6   7   8   9   10   Most

LIFE-STYLE QUESTIONNAIRE INVENTORY
PART II

Now continue to use the numbers in answering the following questions. Space is provided for brief comments. Use an extra sheet of paper if necessary. Try to answer every question.

1. Among your brothers and sisters who was most different from you? In what way?

     _____

2. Who, among your brothers and sisters, was most like you? In what way?

     _____

3. Who played together most?

     _____

4. Who fought and argued the most?

     _____

5. Who took care of whom?

     _____

6. Who had an unusual achievement? What was it?

     _____

7. Who had an unusual talent? What was it?

     _____

8. Who had a sickness (or surgery or accident)? At what age?

     _____

9. Did anyone in the family die? What was your age?

     _____

10. What was your role in the peer group? Leader, follower, outsider, etc.

     _____

11. What grade school subjects did you like best?

12. What grade school subjects did you like least?

13. What were your childhood fears?

14. What were your childhood ambitions?

15. What was your favorite story or fairy tale when you were growing up?

16. What was your family's position in the community? Middle class, working class, socially prominent, etc.?

17. What were the most important family values?

18. Which child was father's favorite? Why?

19. Which child was mother's favorite? Why?

20. What kind of person was your father?

21. What were his ambitions for the children?

22. What was his relationship to the children?

23. What sibling was most like father and in what ways?

24. What kind of person was your mother?

25. What were her ambitions for the children?

26. What was her relationship to the children?

   _____

27. What sibling was most like mother and in what ways?

   _____

28. Who were you most like — mother or father (if not already answered above)? In what ways?

   _____

LIFE-STYLE QUESTIONNAIRE INVENTORY
PART III

Use this page to write a description of yourself, including strengths, weaknesses, situations you find most comfortable and most difficult, etc.

_____

_____

_____

_____

_____

_____

_____

_____

_____

_____

_____

_____

_____

_____

_____

_____

_____

_____

_____

_____

_____

_____

_____

_____

LIFE-STYLE QUESTIONNAIRE INVENTORY
PART IV

Earliest Recollections

Directions:

Think back as far as you can to the first thing you can remember — something that happened when you were very young (it should be before you were seven or eight years old). It can be anything at all — good or bad, important or unimportant — but it should be something you can describe as a one time incident (something that happened only once), and it should be something you can remember very clearly or picture in your mind like a scene.

Write about an incident or something that happened to you. Make sure that it is something you can picture, something specific, and something where you can remember a single time it happened. Try to remember how you felt at the time or what reaction you had to what was going on? Write down that reaction or feeling. Explain why you felt that way or had that reaction? Which part of the memory stands out most clearly from the rest — like if you had a snapshot of the memory, it would be the very instant that is most vivid and clear in your mind? How did you feel (what was your reaction) at that instant? Be sure you include any other people who are in the memory and what the situation was in terms of time and place.

Write about at least three early recollections. Use an extra sheet of paper if necessary.

_____
_____
_____
_____
_____
_____
_____
_____
_____
_____
_____

Appendix D

An Instrument for Assessing Competencies in Establishing the Life Style

Betty Lowe
Raymond Lowe
Reprinted by permission of the authors.

Instructions

Following are a number of items identified as characteristics or qualities considered essential to conducting a life style analysis. The instrument is intended as a training device to direct attention to specific strengths or specific areas in need of attention.

The instrument may be used in a variety of ways. It may be completed by a student counselor for purposes of self-evaluation, by a supervisor, or by observers who wish to learn more about the process. When a student and supervisor are involved, it is suggested that optimum growth will probably result when both the supervisor and the student counselor complete separate instruments and subsequently use these as a basis for conferring. In whatever capacity the instrument is used—by student, supervisor, or observer—it should be completed following, not during, the analysis session.

Indicate on the scale provided the level you think the student counselor performed on each item.

Scale

1. *Decidedly lacking in competence.* Counselor is sufficiently uninformed or inexperienced that s/he must confer with his/her supervisor for additional training.

2. *Lacking in competence.* Counselor will probably improve with additional information or experience. S/he may wish to confer with his/her supervisor or the supervisor may wish to confer with the counselor.

3. *Competent.* Counselor is qualified to function with minimal supervision.

4. *Decidedly competent.* Conferring with colleagues rather than supervisors is indicated.

5. *Insufficient information.* The competency is appropriate to the session, but information is unavailable or inadequate to evaluate the competency.

6. *Not applicable.* The competency is not appropriate to this particular session.

I am using this instrument: Name of Student: _____

( )   As a supervisor.   Date: _____

( )   As a peer/observer.

( )   For self-evaluation.

PART I: ADLERIAN THEORY

Competencies expected of a counselor utilizing Adlerian Psychology as a theoretical basis for undertaking the life style analysis include:

PERSONAL CONGRUENCE
The counselor's posture, facial expressions, and gestures are   1 2 3 4 5 6
congruent with the client and the situation (1).

ASSUMPTIONS
The counselor articulates Adler's assumptions about human   1 2 3 4 5 6
behavior as they relate to the client's behavior (2).

LIMITATIONS
The counselor recognizes the adequacy of her/his knowledge of   1 2 3 4 5 6
Individual Psychology to the situation with which s/he is dealing (3).

GUESSI NG
The counselor:
integrates what s/he has learned (4), and   1 2 3 4 5 6
"guesses in the right direction" (5).   1 2 3 4 5 6

The counselor:

validates his/her "guesses" (6), and	1	2	3	4	5	6
in the absence of validation readily shifts the guessing process (7).	1	2	3	4	5	6

PRIVATE LOGIC

The counselor is aware of the client's private logic and the purpose it serves (8).	1	2	3	4	5	6

SOCIAL INTEREST

The counselor utilizes the notion of social interest in the helping process (9).	1	2	3	4	5	6

PART II: ADLERIAN TECHNIQUE

Competencies expected of a counselor utilizing Adlerian techniques in the analysis process include:

INTRODUCTION

The counselor easily orients the client to the analysis session (10).	1	2	3	4	5	6

SUBJECTIVE SITUATION

The counselor solicits the subjective situation (11).	1	2	3	4	5	6

OBJECTIVE SITUATION

The counselor explores the objective (current) situation in terms of the client's approach to the life tasks:

Work (12).	1	2	3	4	5	6
Society (13).	1	2	3	4	5	6
Sex (14).	1	2	3	4	5	6

THE QUESTION

The counselor appropriately raises "The Question" (15).	1	2	3	4	5	6

FAMILY CONSTELLATION

The counselor establishes the family constellation and draws appropriate inferences (16).	1	2	3	4	5	6

FAMILY ATMOSPHERE

The counselor recognizes the importance of identifying the family atmosphere (17).	1	2	3	4	5	6

PARENTS

The counselor integrates information about the parents in the data gathering process (18).	1	2	3	4	5	6

SIBLINGS
The counselor seeks attributes of siblings and is aware of the
implied relationships of each to the client (19).
                                                              1 2 3 4 5 6

EARLY RECOLLECTIONS
The counselor appropriately solicits early recollections (20).
                                                              1 2 3 4 5 6

DREAMS
The counselor appropriately solicits dreams or daydreams (21).
                                                              1 2 3 4 5 6

DIAGNOSIS
The counselor identifies maladaptive symptomatology as
consistent with the notions of social interest (22).
                                                              1 2 3 4 5 6

INTERP RETATION
The counselor assists the client in recognizing his/her mistaken
goals (23).
                                                              1 2 3 4 5 6

INITIATING REDIRECTION
The counselor explores with the client the alternatives to the
mistaken goal (24).
                                                              1 2 3 4 5 6

CONFRONTATION
The counselor is able to utilize the technique of confrontation
for purpose of:
keeping the client's attention on the problem being explored
(25), and
                                                              1 2 3 4 5 6

assisting the client in understanding the apparent contradiction
between statements and behaviors (26).
                                                              1 2 3 4 5 6

SUMMARY
The counselor assists the client in understanding his/her
subjective views, mistaken beliefs, private logic, or destructive
behavior (27).
                                                              1 2 3 4 5 6

The counselor summarizes the client's life style in a succinct
phrase or statement intelligible to the client (28).
                                                              1 2 3 4 5 6

Bibliography

"A Wife Adds Satisfaction to Man's Life." *USA Today*, 29 Feb. 1988, p. 10.

Adler, A. *Der Aggressionstrieb in A. Adler*. C. Furtmuller and E. Wexberg eds. Heilen and Bilden. 2nd ed. Munich: Bergmann, 1922, 18–25.

Adler, A. "Life-Lie and Responsibility in Neurosis and Psychosis." In *The Practice and Theory of Individual Psychology*, trans. P. Radin. Totowa, NJ: Littlefield, Adams and Company, 1937.

Adler, A. "Nochmals-die Einheit der Neurosen." *International Journal of Individual Psychology* 8(1930): 201–216.

Adler, A. "On the Interpretation of Dreams." *International Journal of Individual Psychology 2*, no.1 (1936): 3–16.

Adler, A. "Position in Family Constellation Influences Life Style." *International Journal of Individual Psychology* 3, no. 3 (1937): 211–227.

Adler, A. *Problems of Neurosis: A Book of Case Histories*. New York: Harper & Row, 1964.

Adler, A. *Social Interest: A Challenge to Mankind*. London: Faber & Faber, Ltd., 1938. Trans. Rolf Passer from *Der Sinn des Lebens*. Vienna: Leipzig.

Adler, A. *Superiority and Social Interest: A Collection of Later Writings*. H.L. and Rowena R. Ansbacher, eds. Evanston, IL: Northwestern University Press, 1964.

Adler, A. *The Individual Psychology of Alfred Adler*. H.L. Ansbacher and R. Ansbacher, eds. New York: Harper and Row, 1956.

Adler, A. *The Practice and Theory of Individual Psychology*. Paterson, NY: Littlefield, Adams, 1959.

Adler, A. *The Science of Living*. New York: Greenberg Publishers, Inc., 1929.

Adler, A. [1927]*Understanding Human Nature*. Greenwich, CT: Premier Books, 1954.

Adler, A., [1927], *Understanding Human Nature* (W.B. Wolf, Trans.) New York: Fawcett Premier, 1954.

Adler, A. *What Life Should Mean to You*. Boston: Little, Brown and Company, 1931.

Adler, A. *What Life Should Mean to You*. A. Porter, ed. New York: Capricorn Books, 1958.

Adler, A. [1931]. *What Life Should Mean to You*. New York: Perigree, 1980

Adler, A. *The Science of Living*. Garden City, NY: Greenberg, 1929.

Adler, A. [1964]"Superiority and Social Interest: A Collection of Later Writings." In *The Individual Psychology of Alfred Adler*, ed. H.L. Ansbacher and R.R. Ansbacher. New York: Norton, 1979.

Adler, A. [1933] *Social Interest: A Challenge to Mankind*. New York: Capricorn Books, 1964.

Adler, A. *The Individual Psychology of Alfred Adler*. H.L. Ansbacher and R. Ansbacher, ed. H.L. Ansbacher and R. Ansbacher. New York: Harper and Row, 1956.

Adler, K. "Techniques That Shorten Psychotherapy." *Individual Psychology* 45, no.1 (1989): 62–74.

Alfred, G. *On the Level with Self, Family, Society*. Provo, UT: Brigham Young University, 1974.

Allen, T. "Adlerian Interview Strategies for Behavior Change." *The Counseling Psychologist 3*, no. 1 (1971): 40–48.

Allen, T. "The Individual Psychology of Alfred Adler: An Item of History and a Promise of a Revolution." *Counseling Psychologist* 3, no. (1971): 3–24.

Allers, C., White, J., and Hornbuckle, D. "Early Recollections: Detecting Depression in the Elderly." *Individual Psychology* 46 (1990): 61–66.

Altman, K. "The Relationship between Social Interest Dimensions of Early Recollections and Selected Counselor Variables." Unpublished doctoral dissertation, University of South Carolina, 1973.

Altus, W. "Birth Order and Its Sequence." *International Journal of Psychiatry* 3 (1967): 23–31.

Ansbacher, H. "Adler's Place in the Psychology of Memory." *Journal of Personality* 3 (1947): 197–207.

Ansbacher, H. "Life Style: A Historical and Systematic Review." *Journal of Individual Psychology* 23 (1967): 191–212.

Ansbacher, H. "The Concept of Social Interest." *Individual Psychologist* 47, no.1 (1991): 30–44.

Ansbacher, H. "Adler's Interpretation of Early Recollections: Historical Account." *Journal of Individual Psychology* 29, no. 2 (1973): 135–145.

Ansbacher, H. "Humanistic Psychology." *Journal of Humanistic Psychology* 30, no. 4 (1990): 45–53.

Ansbacher, H. A. "The Sociologist's Conception of Lack of Social Interest." *Individual Psychologist* 47, no. 1 (1991): 22–29.

Ansbacher, H., and Ansbacher, R., ed. *The Individual Psychology of Alfred Adler*. New York: Harper & Row, 1964, 1967.

Argyle, M., and Furnham, A. "Sources of Satisfaction and Conflict in Longterm Relationships." *Journal of Marriage and the Family* 45 (1983): 481–493.

Arredondo-Dowd, P., and Gonsalves, J. "Preparing Culturally Effective Counselors." *The Personnel and Guidance Journal* 58 (1980): 657–661.

Auld, F., and Hyman, M. *Resolution of Inner Conflicts: An Introduction to Psychoanalytic Therapy*. Washington, D.C.: American Psychological Association, 1991.

Axelson, J. *Counseling and Development in a Multicultural Society*. Monterey, CA: Brooks/Cole Publishing, 1985.

Bach, Richard. *Illusions*. New York: Dell, 1977.

Bandura, A. *Social Foundation of Thought and Action: A Social Cognitive Theory*. Englewood Cliffs, NJ: Prenctice-Hall, 1986.

Bartlett, J. *Familiar Quotations*. Ed. C. Morely and L. Everett. 12th ed. Boston: Little, Brown, 1951.

Baruth, L., and Eckstein, D. *Life-style: Theory, Practice, and Research.* Dubuque, IA: Kendall-Hunt Publishing Company, 1981.

Baruth, L., and Eckstein, D. *Life-style: Theory, Practice, and Research.* 2nd ed. Dubuque, IA: Kendall-Hunt Publishing Company, 1981.

Baruth, L., and Manning, M. "God, Religion and the Life Tasks." *Individual Psychology* 43, no. 4 (1987): 429–435.

Baruth, L., and Manning, M. *Multicultural Counseling and Psychotherapy.* New York: MacMillan, 1991.

Baruth, L.G., and Huber, C.H. *Counseling and Psychotherapy.* Columbus, OH: Merrill, 1985.

Baum, L. F. *The Wizard of Oz.* New York: Schocken Books, 1900.

Beck, A. "Cognitive Therapy: Nature and Relation to Behavior Therapy." *Behavior Therapy* 1 (1970): 184-200.

Beck, A.T. *Cognitive Therapy and the Emotional Disorders.* New York: New American Library, 1976.

Beck, A.T. "Cognitive Approaches to Stress." In *Principles and Practice of Stress Management, ed. R.L. Woolfolk and P.M. Lehrer,* 225–305. New York: Guilford Press, 1984.

Beck, A.T., and Weishaar, M.E. "Cognitive Therapy." In *Current Psychotherapies,* ed. R.J. Corsini and D. Wedding, 229–261. 5th ed. Itasca, IL: Peacock, 1995.

Becvar, D.S., and Becvar, R.J. *Family Therapy: A Systematic Integration.* 2nd ed. Needham Heights, MA: Allyn & Bacon, 1993.

Belloc, N.B. "Relationship of Health Practices and Mortality." *Preventive Medicine* 2 (1973): 67–81.

Belloc, N.B., and Brewlow, L. "Relationship of Physical Health Status and Health Practices." *Preventive Medicine* 1 *(1972):* 409–421.

Benson, H. with Proctor, W. *Beyond the Relaxation Response.* New York: Times Books, 1979.

Berkman, L., and Syme, S.L. "Social Networks, Host Resistance, and Mortality: A Nine-year Study of Alameda County Residents." *American Journal of Epidemiology* 109 (1979): 186–204.

Berne, E. *What Do You Say After You Say Hello? The Psychology of Human Destiny.* New York: Grove Press, 1972.

Bitter, J. "The Narrative Study of Lives: Lifestyle Assessment as Qualitative Research." Program presented at NASAP Annual Converence, Minneapolis, MN. May 27, 1995.

Bottome, P. *Alfred Adler: A Portrait from Life.* New York: Vanguard Press, 1957.

Bradshaw, J. "An Evening with John Bradshaw: Living in the Growth Process." Phoenix, AZ. November 7, 1991.

Borysenko, J.Z. "Healing Motives: An Interview with David McClelland." *Advances* 2 (1987): 29–41.

Brummer, L.M., Shostrum, E.L., and Abrego, P.J. *Therapeutic Psychology: Fundamentals of Counseling and Psychotherapy.* 5th ed. Englewood Cliffs, NJ: Prentice Hall, 1989.

California Department of Mental Health, Office of Prevention.*In Pursuit of Wellness* (Vol. 1, No. 1). San Francisco: 2340 Irving Street, Suite 108, 1979. Copies are available from the California Department of Mental Health at the Irving Street address.

California State Department of Education. *Toward a State of Esteem.* Sacramento, CA: Bureau of Publications, 1990.

Carich, M. "The Basics of Hypnosis and Trancework." *Individual Psychology* 46, no. 4 (1990): 401–410.

Carich, M. "Utilizing Task Assignments within Adlerian Therapy." *Individual Psychology* 46, no. 2 (1990): 217–224.

Carich, M. "Variations of the 'As If' Technique." *IndividualPsychology 45, no. 4* (1989): 538–545.

Carkhuff, R. *Helping and Human Relations.* Vols. 1, 11. New York: Holt,Rinehart and Winston, Inc., 1969.

Carkhuff, R. *The Art of Helping.* 6th ed. Amherst, MA: Human Resource Development Press, 1987.

Carle, Eric. *The Mixed-Up Chameleon.* New York: Harper Trophy, 1984.

Carlson, J. "Health, Wellness, and Transpersonal Approaches toHelping." *Elementary School Guidance Counseling 14* (1979): 85–94.

Chandler, C. "Tapping Creative Personal Power." *Individual Psychology 47*, no. 2 (1991): 222–227.

Chandler, C., and Willingham, W. "The Relationship between Perceived Early Childhood Family Influence and the Established Life-Style."*Individual Psychologist* 42, no. 3 (1986): 388–395.

Chesney, S., Fakouri, M., and Hafner, J. "The Relationship between Early Recollections and Willingness/Unwillingness of Alcoholics to Continue Treatment." *Individual Psychologist 42*, no. 3 (1986): 395–403.

Chopra, Deepak. *Ageless Body, Timeless Mind.* New York: Harmony Books, 1993.

Cinnamon, K., and Matulef, N. *Assessment and Interviewing.* Kansas City, MO: Applied Skills Press, 1979.

Clark, A. "An Examination of the Technique of Interpretation in Counseling." *Journal of Counseling and Development* 73 (1995): 483–490.

Cohen, S. "Psychosocial Models of the Role of Social Support in the Etiology of Physical Disease." *Health Psychology* 7 (1988): 269–297.

Comas-Diaz, L., and Jacobsen, F. "Ethnocultural Identification in Psychotherapy." *Psychiatry* 50(1987): 232–241.

Cooper, K.B. *The Aerobics Program for Total Well-Being.* New York: Bantam, 1982.

Copeland, M. *The Depression Workbook*. Oakland, CA: New Harbinger Publications, Inc., 1992.

Cousins, N. *Anatomy of an Illness as Perceived by the Patient.*New York: Norton, 1979.

Covey, S. *The Seven Habits of Highly Effective People*. New York:Simon & Schuster, 1989.

Covey, S. R. *The Seven Habits of Highly Effective People: Restoring the Character Ethic*. New York: Simon & Schuster, 1989.

Davidson, A. *The Collected Works of Lydia Sicher: An Adlerian Perspective*. Ft. Bragg, CA: Q & D Press, 1991.

Dewey, E. *Basic Applications of Adlerian Psychology*. Coral Springs, FL: MTI Press, 1978.

Dickerson, H. Personal communication with author, Silver City, NM, July 17, 1995.

Dillon, K.M., Minchoff, B., and Baker, K.H. "Positive Emotional States and Enhancement of the Immune System." *International Journal of Psychiatry in Medicine 15* (1985)*:* 13–17.

Dinkmeyer, D., and Dinkmeyer, D. "Concise Counseling Assessment: The Children's Life Style." *Elementary School Guidance & Counseling* 12,no. 2 (1977): 117–124.

Dinkmeyer, D., Dinkmeyer, D., and Sperry, L. *Adlerian Counseling and Psychotherapy*. Columbus, OH: Merrill Publishing, 1987.

Dinkmeyer D., and Eckstein, D. *Leadership By Encouragement*. Delray, FL: St. Lucie Press, 1995.

Dinkmeyer, D., Pew, W., and Dinkmeyer, D. *Adlerian Consulting and Psychotherapy*. Monterey, CA: Brooks/Cole, 1979.

Dreikurs, R. *Psychodynamics, Psychotherapy and Counseling.* (rev. ed.). Chicago: Alfred Adler Institute, 1973.

Dreikurs, R. *Fundamentals of Adlerian Psychology*. Chicago: Alfred Adler Institute, 1953.

Dreikurs, R. *Social Equality: The Challenge of Today.* Chicago: Regnery, 1971.

Dreikurs, R., and Cassel, P. *Discipline without Tears*. New York: Hawthorn Books, Inc., 1974.

Dreikurs, R., Grunwald, E., and Pepper, F. *Maintaining Sanity in the Classroom*. New York: Harper Collins, 1982.

Dreikurs, R., and Soltz, V. *Children: The Challenge*. New York: Hawthorne, 1964.

Drescher, J. *The Birth Order Blues*. New York: Viking Press, N.Y./Penguin Books, 1993.

Driscoll, R., and Eckstein, D. "Empirical Studies on the Relationship between Birth Order and Personality." In *The 1981 Annual Handbook for Group Facilitators*, ed. J. Jones and J. Pfeiffer. San Diego, CA: University Associates, 1981.

Driscoll, R., and Eckstein, D. "Life-Style Questionnaire." In *The 1982 Annual Handbook For Group Facilitators*. San Diego, CA: University Associates, 1982, 100-107.

Dutton, W., and Newlon, B. "Early Recollections and Sexual Fantasies of Adolescent Sex Offenders." *Individual Psychologist 44*, no. 1 (1988):85–94.

Dyer, W. W. *Your Erroneous Zones*. New York: Funk and Wagnalls,1976.

Dyer, W.W., and Vriend, J. *Counseling Techniques That Work: Applications to Individual and Group Counseling.* Washington, DC: American Personnel & Guidance Association, 1975.

Eckstein, D. *The Encouragement Process in Life-Span Development.* Dubuque, IA: Kendall\Hunt, 1995.

Eckstein, D. "Adlerian Contributions to Correctional Counseling."In *Theory, Practice, and Research of Life-Style Assessment.* Dubuque, IA: Kendall/Hunt, 1981, 166–169.

Eckstein, D. "Changes in Early Recollections after Nine Months of Counseling: A Case Study." *Journal of Individual Psychology 32*, no. 2 (1976): 212–222.

Eckstein, D. "Early Recollection Changes after Counseling: A Case Study." *Journal of Individual Psychology 32* (1976): 212–223.

Eckstein, D. "Encouragement: Sending out Powerful Invitations." In *The 1983 Annual for Facilitators, Trainers, and Consultants.* San Diego, CA: University Associates, 1983.

Eckstein, D. "The Use of Literature as a Projective Technique." *Journal of Individual Psychology* 40, no. 2 (1984):157–161.

Eckstein, D. "The Use of Early Recollections in Group Counseling." *Journal of Specialists in Group Work* 5, no. 2 (1980): 87–92.

Eckstein, D., and Driscoll, R. "An Introduction to Life-Style Assessment." In *The 1982 Annual Handbook for Group Facilitators.* San Diego, CA: University Associates, 1983, 182-189.

Edgar, T. "The Creative Self in Adlerian Psychology." *Individual Psychologist* 41, no. 3 (1985): 336–341.

Egan, G. *The Skilled Helper: A Systematic Approach to Effective Helping.* 4th ed. Pacific Grove, CA: Brooks/Cole, 1994.

Einstein, A. [1954] "Ideas and Opinions." (selected excerpts). In *Quantum Questions: Mystical writings of the World's Great Physicists,* ed. K. Wilber. (pp. 100-104). Boston: New Science Library, 1984.

Ellis, A. *Overcoming Resistance: Rational-Emotive Therapy with Difficult Clients.* New York: Springer, 1985.

Ellis, A. *Reason and Emotion in Psychotherapy.* Secaucus, NJ: Lyle Stuart, 1962.

Ellis, A. "A Rational Approach to Interpretation." In *Use of Interpretation in Treatment: Technique and Art,* ed. E.F. Hammer, 232–239. New York: Grunc & Stratton, 1968.

Ellis, A. "Humanism, Values, Rationality." *Journal of Individual Psychology* 26 (1970): 37–38.

Ellis, A. *Humanistic Psychotherapy: The National Emotive Approach.* New York: Julian Press, 1973.

Ellis, A. "Rational Emotive Therapy." *The Counseling Psychologist* 7, no. 1 (1977): 2–42.

Ellis, A. "Rational Psychotherapy." *The Journal of General Psychology* 59 (1958): 33–49.

Ernst, C., and Angst, J. *Birth Order: Its Influence on Personality.*Berlin: Springer Verlag, 1983.

Fairfield, B. "Reorientation: The Use of Hypnosis for Life-Style Change." *Journal of Individual Psychology* 46, no. 4 (1990): 451–458.

Fakouri, M., and Hafner, J. "Early Recollections of First-Borns." *Journal of Clinical Psychology* 40 (1984): 209–213.

Fakouri, M., Hartung, J., and Hafner, J. "Early Recollections of Neurotic Depressive Patients." *Psychological Reports* 57 (1985): 783–786.

Flanagan, J. "A Research Approach to Improving Our Quality of Life." *American Psychologist* 33 (1978): 138–147.

Foley, V., and Everett, C. *Family Therapy Glossary.* Washington, D.C: American Association for Marriage and Family Therapy, 1982.

Forer, L. K. "Bibliography of Birth Order Literature in the 70's."*Journal of Individual Psychology* 33 (1977a): 122–141.

Forer, L. K. "Use of Birth Order Information in Psychotherapy."*Journal of Individual Psychology* 33 (1977a): 105–113.

Frank, J.D. *Persuasion and Healing: A Comparative Study of Psychotherapy.* (rev. ed.) Baltimore, MD: Johns Hopkins University Press, 1973.

Frankl, V. *The Doctor and the Soul.* New York: Bantam Books, 1971.

Frey, D., and Carlock, C.J. *Enhancing Self-Esteem.* 2nd ed. Muncie, IN: Accelerated Development, 1989.

Fry, W.F., and Salameh, W.A., eds. *Handbook of Humor and Psychotherapy.* Sarasota, FL: Professional Resource Exchange, 1987.

Galentier, E., Miller, G., and Pribram, K. *The Structure of Behavior.* New York: Holt, Rinehart and Winston, 1960.

Garduk, E.L., and Haggard, E.A. "Immediate Effects on Patients of Psychoanalytic Interpretations." *Psychological Issues* 7 *(1972):* 1–84.

Gelso, C.J., and Fretz, B.R. *Counseling Psychology.* New York: Harcourt Brace Jovanovich, 1992.

Gushurst, R. S. "The Technique, Utility, and Validity of Life Style Analysis." *Counseling Psychologist* 3, no.1 (1971): 30–39.

Haley, J. *Problem-Solving Therapy.* San Francisco: Jossey-Bass,1976.

Hall, M.H. "An Interview with 'Mr. Humanist', Rollo May." *Psychology Today,* (September, 1967): 25–29, 72–73.

Hargrove, R. "Getting Your Message Through" In *The 1996 Annual: Developing Human Resources.* San Diego: Pfeiffer & Co., 1996, 251–276.

Harman, W.W. *Global Mind Change: The Promise of the Last Years of the Twentieth Century.* Indianapolis, IN: Knowledge Systems, 1988.

Harvey, J.H., and Weary, G. *Perspective on Attributional Processes.* Dubuque, IA: Brown, 1981.

Hawkes, G., Burchinal, L., and Gardner, B. "Size of Family and Adjustment of Children." *Marriage and Family Living* 20 (1958): 65–68.

Hayes, R. F., and Bronzaft, A. L. "Birth Order and Related Variables in an Academically Elite Sample." *Journal of Individual Psychology* 35 (1979): 214–224.

Helmreich, R., Kuiken, D., and Collins, B. "Effects of Stress and Birth Order on Attitude Change." *Journal of Personality* 36 (1968): 466–473.

Heppner, P.P., and Krauskopf, C.J. "An Information Processing Approach to Personal Problem Solving." *The Counseling Psychologist* 15 (1987): 371–447.

Herr, E.L., and Cramer, S.H. *Career Guidance and Counseling Through the Lifespan.* 3rd ed. Boston: Little, Brown, 1988.

Hoffman, E. *The Right to Be Human: A Biography of Abraham Maslow.* Los Angeles, CA: J.P. Tarcher, 1988.

Houston, J. *The Search for the Beloved.* Los Angeles: Jeremy Tarcher, 1984.

Huber, J. "Psychotherapy: A Graceful Activity." *Individual Psychologist* 43, no. 4 (1987): 437–441.

Hyer, L., Woods, M., and Boudwyns, P. "Early Recollections of Vietnam Veterans with PTSD." *Individual Psychology* 45 (1989): 300–312.

Ivey, A.E. *Intentional Interviewing and Counseling: Facilitating Client Development in a Multicultural Society.* 3rd ed. Pacific Grove, CA: Brooks/Cole, 1994.

Ivey, A.E., Ivey, M.B., and Simek-Morgan, L. *Counseling and Psychotherapy: A Multicultural Perspective.* 3rd ed. Needham Heights, MA: Allyn & Bacon, 1993.

Ivey, M.B. and Simek-Downing, L. *Consulting and Psychotherapy: Integrating Skills, Theory and Practice* (2nd ed.) 1987, p. 104. Adapted by permission of Prentice-Hall, Inc., Englewood Cliffs, New Jersey.

Ivey, A. *Microcounseling: Innovations in Interviewing Techniques.*Springfield, IL: Charles C. Thomas, 1971.

Ivey, A. *Microcounseling: Innovations in Interviewing Training.*Springfield, IL: Charles C. Thomas, 1972.

Jones, J. "The Sensing Interview." In *The 1973 Annual Handbook for Group Facilitators.* San Diego, CA: University Associates, 1973, 213-224.

Julius, M. "The Effects of Chronic Anger on Women over 18 Years." Paper presented at the Gerontological Society of America meeting at the University of Michigan, 1990.

Kaplan, H. "A Guide for Explaining Social Interest Laypersons." *Individual Psychology* 47, no. 1 (1991): 820–85.

Kaplan, H. "A Method for the Interpretation of Early Recollection and Dreams." *Individual Psychologist* 41, no. 4 (1985): 525–533.

Kefir, N. "Impasse/Priority Therapy." In *Handbook for Innovative Psychotherapies,* ed. R. Corsini, 401-415. New York: Wiley, 1981.

Kefir, N., and Corsini, J. "Dispositional Sets: A Contribution to Typology." *Journal of Individual Psychology* 30 (1974): 163–187.

Kefir, N. "Priorities." Unpublished manuscript, 1972.

Kelly, G. *The Psychology of Personal Constructs.* Vol. 1, *A Theory of Personality;* Vol. 2, *Clinical Diagnosis and Psychotherapy.* New York: Norton, 1955.

Kern, et al. *A Case for Adlerian Counseling.* Chicago: Alfred Adler Institute, 1978.

Kern, R., and White, J. "Brief Therapy Using the Life-Style Scale." *Individual Psychologist* 45, no. 2 (1989): 186–190.

Kern, R.M. *Lifestyle Scale.* Coral Springs, FL: CMTI, 1986.

Kern, R.M., and White, J. "Brief Therapy Using the Life-Style Scale." *Individual Psychology* 22, no. 2 (1989): 163–165.

Kleinman, A. *Rethinking Psychiatry.* New York: Free Press, 1988.

Kobasa, S.C. "The Hardy Personality: Toward a Social Psychology of Stress and Health." In *Social Psychology of Health and Illness,* ed. G.S. Sanders and J. Suls. Hillsdale, NJ: Erlbaum, 1982.

Koch, H. "The Relation of Certain Family Constellation Characteristics and the Attitude of Children Toward Adults." *Child Development* 26 (1955): 37–40.

Kogod, S. "Managing Diversity in the Workplace." In *The 1992 Annual:Developing Human Resources.* San Diego, CA: Pfeiffer & Company, 1992.

Kopp, R., and Kivel, C. "Traps and Escapes." *Journal of Individual Psychology* 46, no. 2 (1990): 134–147.

Lasko, J. "Parent Behavior toward First and Second Children." *Genetic Psychology Monographs.* (1954): 96–137.

Lazarus, R.S., and Folkman, S. *Stress, Appraisal, and Coping.* New York: Springer, 1984.

Levy, L.H. P*sychological Interpretation.* New York: Holt, Rinehart and Winston, 1963.

Levy, S. *Principles of Interpretation.* New York: Aronson, 1984.

Lewin, K. "Quasi-Stationary Social Equilibria and the Problem of Permanent Changes." In *The Planning of Change,* ed. W.G. Beanes, K.D. Benne, and R. Chin. New York: Holt, Rinehart and Winston, 1989.

Lingg, M., and Kottman, T. "Changing Mistaken Beliefs Through Visualization of Early Recollections." *Journal of Individual Psychology* 47, no. 2 (1991): 255–260.

Lippitt, G., and Lippitt, R. *The Consulting Process in Action.* San Diego, CA: University Associates, 1978.

Locke, S., and Colligan, D. *The Healer Within: The New Medicine of Mind and Body.* New York: New American Library, 1986.

Locke, S.E., et al. "Life Change Stress, Psychiatric Symptoms, and Natural Killer Cell Activity." *Psychosomatic Medicine 46 (1984):* 441–453.

Lombardi, D. "Eight Avenues of Life Style Consistency." *Individual Psychologist* 10, no. 2 (1973): 5–9.

Looff, D. "Consulting to Children in Crisis." *Child Psychiatry and Human Development* 10, no. 1 (1979): 5–14.

Lovejoy, A. *Reflections on Human Nature.* Baltimore: Johns Hopkins University Press, 1961.

Lum, D. *Social Work Practice and People of Color.* Monterey, CA: Brooks/Cole, 1986.

Lynch, J.J. *The Broken Heart: The Medical Consequences of Loneliness.* New York: Basic Books, 1977.

MacIver, R. M. *The Ramparts We Guard.* New York: Macmillan, 1950.In *Outside Readings in Sociology,* ed. E.A. Schuler, et al. New York: Crowell, 1956, 782-788.

Manaster, G., and Corsini, R. *Individual Psychology: Theory and Practice.* New York: F. E. Peacock, 1982.

Manaster, G., and Perryman, T. "Early Recollections and Occupational Choice." *Journal of Individual Psychology* 30, no. 2 (1974): 232-237.

Manaster, G. J. "Birth Order - An Overview." *Journal of Individual Psychology* 33 (1977): 3-8.

Mansager, E., et al. "Interactive Discussion of Early Recollections: A Group Technique with Adolescent Substance Abusers." *Journal of Individual Psychology* 51, no. 4 (1995): 413-421.

Martin, J., and Stelmaczonek, K. "Participants' Identification and Recall of Important Events in Counseling." *Journal of Counseling Psychology 35 (1988):* 385-390.

Maslow, A. *Motivation and Personality.* New York: Harper & Row, 1970.

Maslow, A. "The Dynamics of Psychological Security-Insecurity."*Character and Personality* 10 (1942): 331-344.

Maslow, A.H. (ed.). (1959) *New Knowledge in Human Values* (Gateway edition published by Harper & Row, 1970.) Chicago: Henry Regnery Company.

Maslow, A.H. *Toward a Psychology of Being.* 2nd ed. New York: D. Van Nostrand, 1968.

Maslow, A.H. *Motivation and Personality.* 2nd ed. New York: Harper & Row, 1970.

Maslow, A.H. *Toward a Psychology of Being.* Princeton, NJ: Van Nostrand, 1982.

McClelland, D.C., Ross, G., and Patel, V. "The Effect of an Academic Examination on Salivary Norepinephrine and Immunoglobulin Levels." *Journal of Human Stress* 11 (1985): 52-59.

McKay, M., Davis, M., and Fanning. *Thoughts and Feelings: The Art of Cognitive Stress Intervention.* Oakland, CA: New Harbinger Publications, Inc., 1981.

Mischel, W. "A Cognitive-Social Learning Approach to Assessment." In *Cognitive Assessment,* ed. T.V. Merluzzi, C.R. Glass, and M. Genest, 479-502. New York: Guilford Press, 1981.

Montagu, A. *The Direction of Human Development: Biological and Social Bases.* New York: Harper, 1955.

Montagu, A. *Growing Young.* New York: McGraw-Hill, 1981.

Montaqu, A. "Social Interest and Agression as Potentialities."*Individual Psychologist* 47, no. 1 (1991): 47-50.

Moody, R.A. *Laugh After Laugh: The Healing Power of Humor.* Jacksonville, FL: Headwaters Press, 1978.

Mosak, H. "Adlerian Psychotherapy." In *Current Psychotherapies,* ed. Raymond Corsini. Itasca, 56-107. Itasca, IL: F. E. Peacock, 1984.

Mosak, H. "Early Recollections as a Projective Technique." *Journal of Projective Techniques* 22 (1958): 302–311.

Mosak, H. "Early Recollections: Evaluation of Some Recent Research." *Journal of Individual Psychology* 25, no. 1 (1969): 56–63.

Mosak, H. "Interrupting a Depression: The Pushbutton Technique."*Individual Psychologist* 41, no. 2 (1985): 210–214.

Mosak, H.H. *Ha, Ha and Aaha: The Role of Humor in Psychotherapy.* Muncie, IN: Accelerated Development, 1987.

Mosak, H.H., and Dreikurs, R. "The Life Tasks III, the Fifth Life Task." *Individual Psychology* 5, no. 1 (1967): 16–22.

Mosak, H.H. *On Purpose.* Chicago: Alfred Adler Institute, 1977.

Mosak, N. "Adlerian Psychotherapy." In *Current Psychotherapies,* ed. R. Corsini. Itasca, IL: F. E. Peacock, 1979.

Mozdzierz, G. J., Macchitelli, F. J., and Lisiecki, J. "The Paradox in Psychotherapy: An Adlerian Perspective." *Journal of Individual Psychology* 32 (1976): 232–242.

Mullis, F., Kern, R., and Curlette, W. "Life-Style Themes and Social Interest: A Further Factor Analytic Study." *Individual Psychologist* 43, no. 3 (1987): 339–352.

Murray, H. *Explorations in Personality.* New York: Oxford University Press, 1963.

Murphey, T. "Encouraging Client Responsibility." *Individual Psychologist* 40, no. 2 (1984): 122–132.

Myers, G., and Myers, M. *The Dynamics of Human Communication.* New York: McGraw-Hill, 1973.

Napier, R.W., and Gershenfeld, M.K. *Groups: Theory and Experience.* 4th ed. New York: Holt, Rinehart and Winston, 1988.

Nelsen, J., and Lott, L. *Positive Discipline for Teenagers.* Rocklin, CA: Prima Publishing, 1994.

Nelsen, J. Personal communication with author, Scottsdale, AZ, 7 Feb. 1996.

Newlon, B., and Arciniega, M. "Respecting Cultural Uniqueness: An Adlerian Approach." *Journal of Individual Psychology* 39, no. 2 (1983): 133–143.

Nikelly, A., ed. *Techniques for Behavior Change.* Springfield, IL: Charles C. Thomas, 1971.

Nikelly, A. "Social Interest: A Paradigm for Mental Health Education." *Individual Psychologist* 47, no. 1 (1991): 79–84.

Nikelly, A. "The Origins of Equality." *Individual Psychologist* 46, no. 1 (1990): 20–27.

Nystul, M. "The Use of Motivation Modification Techniques in Adlerian Psychotherapy." *Journal of Individual Psychology* 41, no. 4 (1985): 489–494.

O'Connell, W. *Action Therapy and Adlerian Theory.* Chicago: Alfred Adler Institute, 1975.

O'Connell, W. "Humanistic Identification: A New Translations from Gemeinschaftsgefuhl." *Individual Psychology* 47, no 1 (1991): 26–27.

O'Connell, W. "The Friends of Adler's Phenomenon." *Journal of Individual Psychology* 32, no. 1 (1976): 5–17.

O'Reilly, B., and Edgar, T. "Therapeutic Memoir Technique." *Journal of Individual Psychology* 43, no. 2 (1987): 148–159.

Ofuchowski. "Alfred Adler: Precursor of Humanisitic Psychology."*Individual Psychologist* 44, no. 3 (1988): 264–269.

Orgler, H. *Alfred Adler: The Man and His Work.* London: Sedgwick & Jackson, 1973.

Ornstein, R., and Sobel, D. *The Healing Brain.* New York: Simon & Schuster, 1987.

Pancner, K., and Pancner, R. "The Quest, Gurus, and the Yellow Brick Road." *Individual Psychology* 44, no. 2 (1988): 158–166.

Paulus, T. *Hope for the Flowers.* New York: Paulist Press, 1972.

Pelletier, K.R. *Longevity: Fulfilling Our Biological Potential.* New York: Delacorte Press/Seymour Lawrence, 1981.

Pennebaker, J.W. *Opening Up: The Healing Power of Confiding in Others.* New York: William Morrow, 1990.

Phinney, J. "A Three-stage Model of Ethnic Identity in Adolescence." In *Ethnic Identity,* 61-79. Albany, NY: SUNY Press, 1993.

Piaget, J. "Intellectual Evaluation from Adolescence to Adulthood." *Human Development* 15 (1972): 1–12.

Plewa, F. "The Meaning of Childhood Recollections." *International Journal of Individual Psychology* 1 (1935): 88–101.

Powers, R. "The President's Letter." American Society of Adlerian Psychology Newsletter 1, January, 1975.

Progoff, I. *At a Journal Wrkshop.* New York: Dialogue House, 1980.

Quick, J. "Emotional Isolation and Loneliness." *The 1992 Annual:Developing Human Resources.* San Diego, CA: Pfeiffer & Company, 1992.

Quinn, J. "Predicting Recidivism and Type of Crime from Early Recollections of Prison Inmates." Unpublished doctoral dissertation, University of South Carolina, 1973.

Rogers, C. "The Necessary and Sufficient Conditions of Therapeutic Personality Change." *Journal of Consulting Psychology* 21 (1957): 95–103.

Rogers, C.R. *Counseling and Psychotherapy: Newer Concepts in Practice.* Boston, MA: Houghton Mifflin, 1942.

Rogers, C.R. *Client-Centered Therapy.* Boston, MA: Houghton Mifflin, 1951.

Rossi, E.W. *The Psychobiology of Mind-Body Healing: New Concepts of Therapeutic Hypnosis.* New York: Norton, 1986.

Rotter, J. "Generalized Expectancies for Internal Versus External Control of Reinforcement." *Psychological Monographs* 80, no. 1 (1966): 1-28.

Rotter, J. *Social Learning and Clinical Psychology.* New York: Johnson, 1980/1973/1954.

Rubin, R. *Using Bibliotherapy: A Guide to Theory and Practice.*Phoenix, AZ: Oryx Press, 1978.

Rule, W. "The Relationship between Early Recollections and Selected Counselor and Life-Style Characteristics." Unpublished doctoral dissertation, University of South Carolina, 1972.

Savill, G., and Eckstein, D. "Changes in Early Recollections as a Function of Mental Status." *Individual Psychologist* 43, no. 1 (1987): 3–17.

Schaefer, C., Coyne, J.C., and Lazarus, R.S. "The Health-Related Functions of Social Support." *Journal of Behavioral Medicine* 4 (1982): 381–406.

Schottky, A. "Life-Style and Psychotherapy." Translated by A. Ehlers and G. Linden Goals. *Journal of Individual Psychology* 43, no. 1 (1987): 59–70.

Seuss, Dr. *On Beyond Zebra.* New York: Random House, 1971.

Shulman, B. *A Comparison of Allport's and the Adlerian Concept of Life-Style.* Chicago: Alfred Adler Institute, 1973.

Shulman, B., and Mosak, H. *Manual for Life-Style Assessment.* Muncie, IN: Accelerated Development, Inc., 1988.

Shulman, B., and Mosak, H. "Birth Order and Ordinal Position: Two Adlerian Views." *Journal of Individual Psychology* 33 (1977): 114–121.

Sicher, L. "Education for Freedom." *American Journal of Individual Psychology* 11 (1955): 97–103.

Siegel, B.S. *Love, Medicine and Miracles.* New York: Harper & Row, 1986.

Sime, W.E. "Psychological Benefits of Exercise." *Advances I, no. 4* (1984): 15–29.

Skinner, B. F. *Contingencies of Reinforcement.* New York: Appleton-Century-Crofts, 1969.

Slavik, S. "Presenting Social Interest to Different Life-Styles." *Individual Psychology* 51, no. 2 (1995): 166–177.

Slavik, S., and Croake, J. *Psychological Tolerance and Mood Disorders.* Port Coquitlam, B.C.: Canadian Counseling Institute, 1995.

Spiegel, S.B., and Hill, C.E. "Guidelines for Research on Therapist Interpretation: Toward Greater Methodological Rigor and Relevance to Practice." *Journal of Counseling Psychology* 36 (1989): 121–129.

Sonstegard, M., Hogerman, H., and Bitter, J. "Motivation Modification: An Adlerian Approach." *Individual Psychologist* 12 (1975): 17–22.

Sperry, L. "Incorporating Hypnotherapeutic Methods into Ongoing Psychotherapy." *Journal of Individual Psychology* 46, no. 4 (1990): 443–450.

Stein, H. "Twelve Stages of Creative Adlerian Psychotherapy." *Individual Psychology* 44, no. 2 (1988): 138–144.

Stewart, T. *TA Today: A New Introduction to Transactional Analysis.* Chapel Hill, NC: Lifespace, 1987.

Stone, A.A., et al. "Evidence That IgA Antibody Is Associated with Daily Mood." *Journal of Personality and Social Psychology* 52 *(1987)*: 988–993.

Strickland, B.R. "Internal-External Expectancies and Health-Related Behaviors." *Journal of Counseling and Clinical Psychology* 46 (1978): 1192–1211.

Strong, S.R., and Claiborn, C.D. *Change through Interaction: Social Psychological Processes of Counseling and Psychotherapy.* New York: Wiley, 1982.

Swanson, B. "Ordinal Position, Family Size, and Personal Adjustment." *The Journal of Psychology* 81 (1972): 53–58.

Sweeney, T.J. *Adlerian Counseling.* 3rd ed. Muncie, IN: Accelerated Development, 1979, 1989.

Thorne, F. "The Life-Style Analysis." *Journal of Clinical Psychology* 31 (1975): 236–240.

Thorne, F., and Pishkin, V. "A Factorial Study of Needs in Relation to Life-Styles." *Journal of Clinical Psychology* 31 (1975): 240–248.

Tiger, L. *Optimism: The Biology of Hope.* New York: Simon & Schuster, 1979.

Toman, W. *Family Constellation: Its Effects on Personality and Social Behavior.* New York: Springer Publishing Company, Inc., 1969.

Torrance, E.P. *The Search for Satori & Creativity.* Buffalo, NY: Creativity Education Foundation, 1979.

Troemel-Ploetz, S. "I'd Come to You for Therapy": Interpretation, Redefinition, and Paradox in Rogerian Therapy." *Psychotherapy: Theory, Research and Practice* 17 *(1980):* 246–257.

U.S. Department of Health and Human Services, Public Health Service. *Healthy People 2000: National Health Promotion and Disease Prevention Objectives.* Washington, DC: Superintendent of Documents, Government Printing Office, 1990.

U.S. Public Health Service. *Smoking and Health: A Report of the Surgeon General.* (DHEW Publication No. (PHS) 79-5006). Washington, DC: U.S. Government Printing Office, 1979.

Vaillant, G.E. *Adaptation to Life.* Boston: Little, Brown, 1977.

Walker, M., and Belove, P. "The Loyalty Dilemma." *Journal of Individual Psychology* 38 (1982): 161–172.

Walton, F. "Group Workshop with Adolescents." *Individual Psychologist* 12, no. 1 (1975): 26–28.

Walton, F. *Winning Teenagers Over.* West Columbia, SC: Lexcom Productions, 1990.

Ward, B. "Can the West Regain the Initiative?" *Atlantic Monthly* 201, no. 2 (1958): 33–37.

Wasserman, Dale. "Man of La Mancha." (a play) New York: Tams-Witmark Music Library, 1966.

Watkins, C. "A Decade of Research in Support of Adlerian Psychological Theory." *Journal of Individual Psychology* 38, no. 1 (1982):90–99.

Watkins, C. "Research Bibliography on Adlerian Psychological Theory." *Individual Psychologist* 42, no. 1 (1986): 123–132.

Watkins, C. "Some Characteristics of Research on Adlerian Psychological Theory, 1970-1981." *Individual Psychologist* 34, no. 1 (1983): 99–110.

Watzlawick, P., Weakland, J., and Fisch, R. *Change Principles of Problem Formulation and Problem Resolution.* New York: W. W. Norton, 1974.

Watzlawick, P., Weakland, J., and Fisch, R. *Change.* New York: W.W. Norton & Company, 1974.

Weber, M. *Essays in Sociology.* Translated and edited by H. H. Gerth and C. W. Mills. New York: Oxford University Press, 1946.

Weiner, I.B. *Principles of Psychotherapy.* New York: Wiley, 1975.

Wheeler, M., Kern, R., and Curlette, W. "Life-Style Can Be Measured." *Individual Psychologist* 47, no. 2 (1991): 229–240.

Wheeler, M., Kern, R., and Curlette, W. "Factor Analytic Scales Designed to Measure Adlerian Life-Style Themes." *Individual Psychologist* 42, no. 1 (1986): 1–16.

Wherly, B. *Pathways to Multicultural Counseling Competence: A Developmental Model.* Monterey, CA: Brooks/Cole, 1995.

White, T.H. *The Once and Future King.* New York: G.P. Putnam's Sons, 1965.

Williams, E., and Manaster, G. "Restricter Anorexia, Bulimic Anorexia, and Bulimic Women's Early Recollection and Thematic Apperception Test Response." *Individual Psychology* 46, no. 1 (1990): 93–107.

Williams, R. "Hostility as a Risk Factor for Early Death." Paper presented at the American Heart Society Meeting at Duke University Medical Center, 1990.

Witmer, J.M., et al. "Psychosocial Characteristics Mediating the Stress Response: An Exploratory Study." *The Personnel and Guidance Journal* 62 (1983): 73–77.

Witmer, J.M., and Sweeney, T. "A Holistic Model for Wellness and Prevention over the Life Span." *Journal of Counseling and Development* 71 (1992): 140–147.

Wurtman, J. *Managing Your Mind and Mood through Food.* New York: Rawson, 1986.

Young, M.E., and Witmer, J.M. "Values: Our Internal Guidance System." In *Pathways to Personal Growth,* J. M. Wittmer (co-author), 275-291. Muncie, IN: Accelerated Development, 1985.

Zarski, J. "The Early Recollections Rating Scale: Development and Applicability in Research." In *Life-Style: Theory, Practice & Research,* ed. L. Baruth and D. Eckstein. Dubuque, IA: Kendall-Hunt Publishing Company, 1981.

Zarski, J., Sweeney, T., and Barcikowski, R. "Counseling Effectiveness as a Function of Counselor Social Interest." *Journal of Counseling Psychology* 24 (1977): 1–5.